A REVIEW

OF THE

PRINCIPAL QUESTIONS

IN

MORALS

A REVIEW

OF THE

PRINCIPAL QUESTIONS

IN

MORALS

By

RICHARD PRICE

Edited by

D. D. RAPHAEL

Professor of Philosophy in the
University of London

CLARENDON PRESS

OXFORD

1974

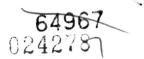

Oxford University Press, Ely House, London W. 1

GLASGOW NEW YORK TORONTO MELBOURNE WELLINGTON
CAPE TOWN IBADAN NAIROBI DAR ES SALAAM LUSAKA ADDIS ABABA
DELHI BOMBAY CALCUTTA MADRAS KARACHI LAHORE DACCA
KUALA LUMPUR SINGAPORE HONG KONG TOKYO

ISBN 0 19 824518 1

FIRST PUBLISHED 1948
REPRINTED WITH CORRECTIONS 1974

Printed in Great Britain by
Billing & Sons Limited, Guildford and London

PREFACE TO THE 1974 IMPRESSION

SEVERAL STUDIES of Richard Price's moral philosophy have appeared since 1948, when this edition of the *Review of Morals* was published. Some of them were no doubt stimulated in part by the availability of the text. They include three books, a number of articles, and some unpublished theses. Of the books, *Reason and Right* by W. D. Hudson shows the fullest understanding of Price's position and of criticisms that may fairly be brought against it.

The renewed interest in Price has not been confined to his ethics. Carl B. Cone has written *Torchbearer of Freedom*, a lively biography with a wide perspective. Henri Laboucheix, in his admirable study, *Richard Price*, has brought out the manifold yet connected character of Price's thought and public activities. Both these books have an important bearing on Price's ethics. So have two papers by D. O. Thomas, which relate Price's political theory and action to his moral outlook. There have been other recent publications dealing simply with aspects of his contribution to economics, politics, or mathematics. M. Laboucheix's book includes a comprehensive bibliography of works by and about Richard Price. The bibliographical note on pp. xi–xiii below is confined to the text of the *Review*, to substantial interpretation and discussion of the ethical theory contained in it, and to relevant biography. Several of the entries are not in Laboucheix's bibliography.

In reproducing the text, the opportunity has been taken to correct a few printing errors, of the 1948 edition or of the original Third Edition of 1787. Two or three details in the editor's introduction have been modified.

If I were to write now a new introduction to Price's moral philosophy, I should keep my eye more on history and less on the philosophy of our own time. In this and in one or two other respects I should follow the advice of Professor J. A. Passmore when reviewing the book in *Mind*, lviii (1949), pp. 263–4. I do not, however, accept his statement, there and in *Ralph Cudworth*, pp. 103–5, that Price simply took his epistemology from Cudworth, with inadequate acknowledgement. As I indicated in my introduction (§1), Price derived his epistemological views from Cudworth, Plato's *Theaetetus*, and Locke. He did indeed owe much to Cudworth, but having been led by Cudworth to Plato, he was enough of a classical scholar to read and interpret Plato for himself; his version of Platonism is not Cudworth's. Apart from that, his approach to epistemology was obviously affected by the general framework of Locke's theory, despite his criticism of it. As for acknowledgement of his debt to Cudworth (and others), Price is vastly more explicit than was customary in his time. His comparative scrupulousness in this regard is a mark of his modesty and candour alike, qualities that he possessed to a fault.

One, though not the only or the main, objection to interpreting a classical thinker in the light of current thought is that the discussion soon becomes dated. Ethical theory has moved on since 1948, and I should now express less sympathy for Price's intuitionism. The strength of this type of ethical theory, however, lies less in its intuitionism than in its account of duty and conscientious action. Price's intuitionism is historically important, but the enduring interest that his ethical theory commands depends more, I think, on the vigour and clarity with which he espouses a deontological position. I do not want to retract much of what I wrote about that in my introduction, but since the final remarks in particular could do with elaboration, I should perhaps say that this can be found in my *Moral Judgement* (London, 1955).

I wish to thank Dr. D. O. Thomas for help with the bibliographical note.

D.D.R.

IMPERIAL COLLEGE, LONDON
1973

EDITOR'S PREFACE

RICHARD PRICE'S *Review of Morals* deserves to be made more easily accessible to students of philosophy. Rashdall recorded in 1907 his opinion that the book was 'the best work published on Ethics till quite recent times'[1] (I think he meant, till Sidgwick wrote *The Methods of Ethics*). More recently, Professor Barnes has urged the renewed study of Price as an unjustly 'neglected moralist'.[2] Professor Broad has written: 'Until Ross published his book *The Right and the Good* in 1930 there existed, so far as I know, no statement and defence of what may be called the "rationalistic" type of ethical theory comparable in merit to Price's.'[3] And Mr. Carritt, in *Ethical and Political Thinking*,[4] has said that, apart from the well-known classics on the subject, he owes most to Price's *Review* and to Rashdall.

The text which I have adopted reproduces the Third Edition of 1787 with no substantial alteration. I have corrected what seem clearly to be misprints, and I have given Greek quotations their due measure of accents and breathings. Inconsistencies of spelling and, generally speaking, of typography have been left unaltered.

I have reinstated the Preface to the First Edition, which Price included in the Second, but omitted from the Third—perhaps because he had by that time realized that his obligations to Butler were not so central as he had formerly supposed. I think that the remarks in this Preface about the cardinal importance of the epistemological material in Chapter I should remain on record. Although Price is less clear on some questions of epistemology and metaphysics than on

[1] *The Theory of Good and Evil*, vol. i, p. 81, footnote.
[2] *Philosophy*, 1942.
[3] *Proceedings of the Aristotelian Society*, 1944–5.
[4] Preface.

ethics, his criticism of the empiricist theory of knowledge is, I believe, well worth considering in its own right, and to this extent the *Review* deserves to be noticed in relation to the British Empiricists as well as to the British Moralists. Rationalism, like deontology, was not confined to the Continent of Europe.

The history of the *Dissertation on the Nature and Attributes of the Deity*, which forms part of the Appendix added to the Third Edition, is curious. The Preface to the Second Edition of the *Review* (not included in the Third or the present edition) says:

'*In note p.* 54 *there is a reference to a* DISSERTATION *on the Being* and Attributes of GOD *at the end of this work, which the Reader will not find there. This dissertation I have long had by me, and always intended to publish as a supplement to this work. But upon revising it with this view, after the note I have mentioned was printed, I was led to think that it contained a thread of argument which, tho' in my opinion important, so few would enter into or approve, that it would only swell this work too much without recommending it. This has engaged me to drop my intention, and to resolve to keep the dissertation for the present, and perhaps for ever, in obscurity.*'

The reader may compare the second paragraph of the 'Advertisement', which forms the Preface to the Third Edition. I have felt a little doubtful whether the content of the *Dissertation* is sufficiently germane to the *Review* itself to justify its inclusion in the present edition; it seems to me less relevant than (indeed I think the argument is inconsistent with) the remarks on God, in relation to morality, that are contained in Chapters V and X of the *Review*. However, since Price himself eventually decided that the *Dissertation* should be printed with the *Review*, and tells us that it was always intended to be so included, I have felt that his judgement should determine the issue.

Price's footnotes are shown, as in the original, with asterisks and daggers. Editorial footnotes are shown with numerals and are enclosed in square brackets: almost all of these merely indicate such changes of wording from earlier editions as seemed to me worthy of mention; they constitute only a small, and necessarily arbitrary, selection of Price's amendments.

I am indebted to the Senate of the University of New Zealand for providing a research grant to cover the cost of microfilms and typing, and to my former pupil, Mr. Thomas McPherson, who has repeated the somewhat tedious task of collating the typescript with the original Third Edition and of reading the proofs. I wish to express also my gratitude to the Delegates of the Clarendon Press for undertaking the publication of a new edition of Price, and to the officers of the Press for their unfailing helpfulness.

D. D. R.

DUNEDIN

1947

CONTENTS

BIBLIOGRAPHICAL NOTE

THE TEXT

A Review of the Principal Questions and Difficulties in Morals; ed. 1, London, 1758.

Ed. 2, corrected, London, 1769.

A Review of the Principal Questions in Morals; ed. 3, corrected and enlarged, London, 1787.

The present edition reproduces the whole of ed. 3, together with the preface to ed. 1 and with notes of some of the variant readings of eds. 1 and 2.

Substantial extracts from ed. 3 are reprinted in L. A. Selby-Bigge, *British Moralists*, Oxford, 1897, and in D. D. Raphael, *British Moralists 1650–1800*, Oxford, 1969.

A considerable part of Chapter I is reproduced, to exemplify ethical intuitionism, in Frank A. Tillman, Bernard Berofsky, and John O'Connor, *Introductory Philosophy*, ed. 2, New York, 1971. The extracts are incorrectly said to be reprinted from D. D. Raphael, *British Moralists 1650– 1800*. They are in fact taken from the 1948 printing of the present edition of the *Review* as a whole.

Much of Chapter I and a short extract from Chapter VI are reproduced, from ed. 3, in D. H. Monro, *A Guide to the British Moralists*, London, 1972.

DISCUSSION

Sir James Mackintosh, *Dissertation on the Progress of Ethical Philosophy, chiefly during the Seventeenth and Eighteenth Centuries*, Edinburgh, 1830; then prefixed to ed. 7 of *Encyclopaedia Britannica*, 1842; sect. 6.

Sir Leslie Stephen, *History of English Thought in the Eighteenth Century*, London, 1876; ed. 3, 1902; ch. 9.

James Martineau, *Types of Ethical Theory*, Oxford, 1885; ed. 3, 1901; Part I, Book II, branch ii, ch. 3.

Henry Sidgwick, *Outlines of the History of Ethics*, London, 1886; ed. 6, 1931; ch. 4, §11.

BIBLIOGRAPHICAL NOTE

E. C. Lavers, *The Moral Philosophy of Richard Price*, privately printed, Easton, Pennsylvania, 1909.

E. S. Price, 'A dissertation comprising a critical commentary and analysis of the system of intuitional ethics expounded by Richard Price', M.A. thesis, University of Bristol, 1930.

W. H. F. Barnes, 'Richard Price: A Neglected Eighteenth Century Moralist', *Philosophy*, xvii (April 1942).

C. D. Broad, 'Some Reflections on Moral Sense Theories in Ethics', *Proceedings of the Aristotelian Society*, xlv (1944–5).

A. N. Prior, 'Eighteenth Century Writers on Twentieth Century Subjects', *Australasian Journal of Psychology and Philosophy*, xxiv (1946).

D. D. Raphael, *The Moral Sense*, London, 1947; ch. 4.

A. N. Prior, *Logic and the Basis of Ethics*, Oxford, 1949; chs. 6, 9.

A. N. Prior, 'The Virtue of the Act and the Virtue of the Agent', *Philosophy*, xxvi (April 1951).

J. A. Passmore, *Ralph Cudworth: An Interpretation*, Cambridge, 1951; ch. 8.

E. M. Edwards, 'The Moral and Religious Philosophy of Richard Price', Ph.D. thesis, University of London, 1953.

Bernard Peach, 'The Indefinability and Simplicity of Rightness in Richard Price's *Review of Morals*', *Philosophy and Phenomenological Research*, xiv (March 1954).

Henry D. Aiken, 'The Ultimacy of Rightness in Richard Price's Ethics: A Reply to Mr. Peach', *Philosophy and Phenomenological Research*, xiv (March 1954).

Bernard Peach, 'History of Philosophy as Justifiable Interpretation: A Reply to Henry Aiken', *Philosophy and Phenomenological Research*, xvi (September 1955).

D. O. Thomas, 'The Political Philosophy of Richard Price', Ph.D. thesis, University of London, 1956.

Samuel E. Gluck, 'Richard Price, G. E. Moore, and the Analysis of Moral Obligation', *Philosophical Quarterly*, Calcutta, xxxi (October 1958).

BIBLIOGRAPHICAL NOTE

D. O. Thomas, 'Richard Price and Edmund Burke', *Philosophy*, xxxiv (October 1959).

Lennart Åqvist, *The Moral Philosophy of Richard Price*, Lund and Copenhagen, 1960.

A. S. Cua, 'Some Reflections on Richard Price's Theory of Obligation', *Ohio University Review*, iii (1961).

Giorgio Tonelli, 'Deux sources britanniques oubliées de la morale kantienne', in *Mélanges Alexandre Koyré*, vol. ii, *L'Aventure de l'esprit*, Paris, 1964.

A. S. Cua, *Reason and Virtue: A Study in the Ethics of Richard Price*, Athens, Ohio, 1966.

W. D. Hudson, *Ethical Intuitionism*, London, 1967; ch. 4.

Charles Vereker, *Eighteenth-Century Optimism*, Liverpool, 1967; ch. 2.

W. D. Hudson, *Reason and Right: A Critical Examination of Richard Price's Moral Philosophy*, London, 1970.

BIOGRAPHY

William Morgan, *Memoirs of the Life of the Rev. Richard Price*, London, 1815.

Roland Thomas, *Richard Price, Philosopher and Apostle of Liberty*, London, 1924.

Carl B. Cone, *Torchbearer of Freedom: The Influence of Richard Price on Eighteenth Century Thought*, Lexington, Kentucky, 1952.

Henri Laboucheix, *Richard Price: théoricien de la révolution américaine, le philosophe et le sociologue, le pamphlétaire et l'orateur*, Paris, 1970.

D. O. Thomas, 'Richard Price, 1723–91', *Transactions of the Honourable Society of Cymmrodorion*, 1971–2.

EDITOR'S INTRODUCTION

1. *Historical*

RICHARD PRICE was born in 1723 at Tynton, Glamorganshire, and died in 1791 at Hackney. A book of *Memoirs* of his life was written by his nephew, William Morgan, in 1815, and there is a good modern biography by Roland Thomas (*Richard Price*, Clarendon Press, 1924).

The *Review of Morals* was first published in 1758, when Price was thirty-five years of age. A corrected Second Edition appeared in 1769, and a Third Edition, with further corrections and an Appendix containing additional notes and a Dissertation on the Deity, in 1787. No complete edition has been printed since that time, but extracts from the book were included in Sir L. A. Selby-Bigge's *British Moralists* (Clarendon Press, 1897). The present edition reproduces that of 1787 including its Appendix. The First and Second Editions were entitled *A Review of the Principal Questions and Difficulties in Morals*. The title of the Third Edition omitted the words 'and Difficulties'.

Price's views on ethical questions seem to have changed very little. Alterations in the Second and Third Editions of the *Review* show changes in his opinions on epistemology and metaphysics, but not on ethics; amendments here seem to be almost wholly on grounds of style. The system of ethics which is to be found in the present edition was fully worked out when Price was thirty-five. The typically 'deontological' or 'Kantian' approach, the insistence that duty often conflicts with private interest and sometimes with public; the distinction between 'absolute' and 'practical' virtue, the realization that what is imputable to a man is his obligation to do what he thinks right; and the perception that obligations may conflict: all these distinctions, which have recently been set out in the revised Kantian ethics of Professor Prichard, Sir David Ross, and Mr. Carritt, were seen fairly clearly by the youthful Price. So far as I know, he was an innovator in these doctrines. His epistemology and metaphysics he had learned from Cudworth, Locke, and Clarke; his arguments for rationalism are Platonic; his test of the fault in definition that Professor Moore rediscovered under the name of the 'naturalistic fallacy' is to be found, in embryo, in earlier moralists.[1] But his account of the objective content of the moral consciousness, which is so like Kant and even more like the system of Sir David Ross, is, I think, original. It owes practically nothing to Clarke's vague talk of 'relations' and 'the reason of things'. In his Introduction[2] Price claims that he has considered many of the questions relating to morality and virtue 'in a manner different from that in which they have been hitherto treated'. This claim has more justification than Sir Leslie Stephen's view that Price's 'book on morality is the fullest exposition of the theory which it advocates; but the theory was already antiquated'.[3]

But the impressiveness of the objective side of Price's theory should not blind us to the importance of the epistemological side. As Professor Barnes has said, 'what is most characteristic in his work is that in its general approach it is neither metaphysical nor psychological, but epistemological'.[4] Price is aware that the problem of universals lies at the heart of epistemology. Like others, he is puzzled or misled by the word 'ideas', and has not clearly distinguished questions

[1] This has been shown by Mr. A. N. Prior in a paper published in the *Australasian Journal of Psychology and Philosophy* for December 1946.

[2] p. 11.

[3] *History of English Thought in the Eighteenth Century*, ch. ix, § 3. In general, Stephen's account of Price's moral philosophy is strangely lacking in understanding and sympathy. For example, in § 12 he accuses Price of systematically confusing the questions of the criterion and the motive, a charge that is particularly absurd in the light of Price's admirable distinctions at the beginning of chap. x of the *Review*.

[4] *Philosophy*, 1942.

proper to the psychology of perception and thought from questions proper to ontology. 'Ideas' for him mean both conceptions and real universals. He criticizes the empiricist theory of knowledge with Platonic arguments, mainly drawn from the *Theaetetus*. But his metaphysics seems to have been at first that of Locke. Expressions in the First Edition suggest that he held a theory of representative perception in regard to primary qualities. This was later modified, I think owing to the influence of Reid.[1] Price does not seem to have cleared his mind altogether on these questions, and his perplexity is illustrated in Notes A, B, C, and E in the Appendix.

It is obvious to a reader of the *Review* that Price was something of a mathematician, and no doubt this flair helped him considerably in his actuarial economics. I imagine too that, as with Plato and Descartes, it is connected with his tendency to excessive rationalism in epistemology. If Hume had been a mathematician, and Price an historian, their philosophies would present a very different picture. At any rate, when Price talks of probability, it is always mathematical probability, which seems to have had a special fascination for him. For example, he ends the main body of the *Review* with an account of natural religion, as we might expect from a clerical moralist, and (for once) rises to exalted language in commending the good life: '*Beauty* and *wit* will die, *learning* will vanish away, and all the *arts of life* be soon forgot; but *virtue* will remain for ever.' The sublime is followed by the ridiculous. Price cannot forbear a concluding chapter giving a gambler's argument for moral living and religious belief.

---

[1] Cf. editor's footnote to p. 29. Reid's *Enquiry into the Human Mind* appeared in 1764; the Second Edition of the *Review* in 1769; Reid's *Essays on the Intellectual Powers of Man* in 1785; and the Third Edition of the *Review* in 1787. Notes A, C, and D in the Appendix to the Third Edition are instructive for the influence of Reid on Price. In Note D he looks forward to Reid's promised *Essays on the Active Powers of Man*, which in fact appeared in the following year, 1788. It would be interesting to know whether this book induced Price to modify any of his views on ethical questions, e.g. on the question whether prudence is a duty.

In the First Edition the chapter struck an even more ludicrous note, with elaborate fractions of the mathematical chances involved. This preoccupation with mathematical probability prevents Price from seeing the force of Hume's observations on probable reasoning. He was able to put his finger on Hume's mistakes, but Hume's greatness escaped him.

2. *Epistemology*

Since Price's object is, as he says in the Introduction, 'to trace the obligations of virtue up to the truth and the nature of things' (i.e. to show that moral judgements are objective, and that the facts denoted by them are necessarily true), he must first refute the view of contemporary empiricists, notably Hutcheson and Hume, that moral judgements refer simply to human feelings. Price is aware that the ethical theories of Hutcheson and Hume arise from their empiricist theory of knowledge: they hold that all ideas are derived from the impressions of sense and feeling, and they *therefore* bring moral ideas within this general scheme; their subjective view of ethics does not arise from an independent examination of moral judgement. Consequently, any criticism that examined moral judgement alone would fail to convince. 'For', an empiricist might say, 'granted that examination of moral ideas seems to show that they come from reason, this apparent conclusion must be false since it conflicts with the ultimate doctrines of the new philosophy. The position is the same as, for example, that of the idea of necessity in causation. Examination of our conception of causation alone discloses an idea of necessary connexion, which is not observed by sense, and which therefore seems to come from reason; but in fact we know that all ideas must come from sense, and we may therefore affirm that, despite appearances to the contrary, the idea of necessity (and likewise moral ideas) can only be derived from impressions of sense or feeling.' Price must, therefore, refute the primary principles of empiricism, and he accordingly gives us a critique of empiricist epistemology as such. It comes, rightly, at the beginning of the book, in the second section of the first chapter, while the remainder of that chapter deals with the particular epistemology of morals. There is no doubt that Price himself realized the fundamental importance of epistemology for moral philosophy. In the Preface to the First Edition he says: 'There is nothing in this *Treatise*, which I wish more I could engage the reader's attention to, or which, I think, will require it more, than the first Chapter, and particularly the second Section of it. If I have failed here, I have failed in my chief design.' Naturally the treatment of epistemology, in a book whose subject is ethics, must be brief, but for all its brevity this section of the *Review* is a serious contribution to the dispute between empiricism and rationalism in the general theory of knowledge. It is not altogether free from objection; it assumes, for example, that the principles of Newtonian physics are self-evident, a view which would not command acceptance to-day. But some of its arguments show convincingly the need at least to broaden Hume's conception of empiricism before that can be an adequate tool for philosophical inquiry.

Price points out that Locke's initial statement of empiricism is extremely vague. Locke cannot mean that all ideas are in fact immediately given to us by sensation or introspection ('reflection', Locke calls it), for obviously we have many ideas of things which we have not met in experience. He must mean that ideas are either immediately given by sense or introspection, or are compounded out of those so given, in which event sensation and introspection are not strictly the 'sources' of these compound ideas. However, Locke clearly holds that all *simple* ideas come immediately from sense or introspection, and it is this doctrine, the last stronghold of empiricism, that Price says he is going to attack. The understanding, he holds, is also a source of simple ideas. He is careful to add that, of the two acts of the understanding, he is talking of the Cartesian intuition or immediate discernment, and not of deduction; and he rightly notes that contemporary empiricists, in criticizing rationalist theories of morals, have confined their attention to deduction and have neglected intuition. We must add that some of their opponents were equally at fault. Moralists like Clarke (and Locke himself) had written as if moral judgement was a matter of deduction. Price was the first to apply the word 'intuition' to moral judgement, but he does not mean by it some mystical faculty. He is simply saying that the Cartesian intuition of self-evident truths is to be found in our awareness of moral principles, and that morals is in *this* respect (and not in respect of any deduction) like mathematics and (according to Descartes and Price) physics. In fact we may say that Price's contribution to epistemology is to reaffirm the Cartesian view against empiricism and to show (or allege) that Cartesian intuition has its place in the epistemology of morals. But Price himself reaches his opposition to empiricism from a study, not of Descartes, but of Plato's *Theaetetus*, to which he was evidently led by Cudworth's *Treatise concerning Eternal and Immutable Morality*. Cudworth's book, though nominally about ethics, is chiefly devoted to the theory of universals, and this no doubt was what caused Price to see that ethical theory should be grounded in epistemology.

Arguing against empiricism, he points out that sense does not give us general ideas (the awareness of universals), or ideas applicable to the objects of more than one sense (e.g. equality, resemblance, difference). In discussing universals, Price gives sound reasons for rejecting nominalism, but is not therefore prepared to embrace a theory of innate ideas such as Cudworth's. 'This, no doubt, many will very freely condemn as whimsical and extravagant. I have, I own, a different opinion of it; but yet, I should not care to be obliged to defend it.'[1] It is not clear just what view Price himself took. His final thoughts on the subject are given in Note C in the Appendix, and he there refers to his theology, but I do not see how his theology would account for universals of contingent things.

As to ideas common to different senses, Price has an interesting note[2] on Locke's problem of whether a man born blind and then enabled to see could correlate the new percepts of vision with the familiar percepts of touch before exercising both at the same time. Locke, it will be remembered, wrote of placing before the man a cube and a sphere. Price's argument for taking the rationalist's answer to this problem is ingenious. He suggests that if we were to present the man first with a square and an oblong rectangle (they would of course have to be the surfaces of solid objects), the subject would be able to infer which was which by reflecting on the equality of all sides in the first and the inequality between the two pairs of sides in the second. To put the point in another way, a highly intelligent subject might well be able to perform the correlation by reflecting on the symmetry of the visual *Gestalt* of the square, as contrasted with the visual *Gestalt* of the oblong, and comparing their difference in this respect with the difference between the remembered tactual *Gestalten*.

'General ideas', then, and such ideas as equality, resemblance, and difference, require the understanding. Of course a sensible empiricist could admit this. Empiricism does not necessarily involve a nominalist view of universals, and most versions of it attribute the discernment of relations to the understanding. Price fairly enough points out that Locke's view of relations conflicts with the very wide statement of his initial empiricism.

'It [the understanding] has, indeed, been always considered, as the source of *knowledge*: But it should have been more attended to,

[1] pp. 30–1, footnote. [2] pp. 35–6.

that as the source of knowledge, it is likewise the source of new ideas, and that it cannot be one of these without being the other. The various kinds of *agreement* and *disagreement* between our ideas, which Mr. Locke says, it is its office to discover and trace, are so many new simple ideas, obtained by its discernment.'[1]

But this is simply a dispute about words, or an illustration of the vagueness of the word 'ideas'. Empiricists do agree that the awareness of relations, such as constitutes mathematical thinking, is the business of the understanding. Perhaps empiricism should be interpreted as the view that simple *qualities* are all sense-given.

But Price does not confine himself to the function of abstracting and the awareness of relations. He gives us also a list of notions used in physics, which, he holds, cannot come from sense: solidity (impenetrability), inactivity, substance, duration, space, infinity, necessity, contingency (possibility), power (causation). The trouble with this list is that few (empiricists might say none) of these notions are *simple*. Price's real point here (though he does not see it very clearly) is that the key notions of physics are bound up with propositions asserting necessity and universality. His main contention about solidity, for example, is that we know it to be *impossible* for one piece of matter to penetrate another, and such a necessary proposition is of course not reached from experience. So too with the rest. The point comes out most clearly in the case of power or causation. 'It should be observed, that I have not said that we have no idea of power, except from the understanding.'[2] We may receive the idea of power from introspection of our own activity. It is the understanding, however, that acquaints us with 'our certainty that every new event requires some cause'.[3] He is concerned with the causal *maxim*, not with the *idea* of cause or power. In short, Price is really groping towards the problem of the synthetic *a priori* proposition. This question is, needless

[1] p. 36.   [2] p. 26.   [3] Ibid.

to say, of key importance for the dispute between rationalism and empiricism. But I do not see that it bears on the question Price is supposed to be discussing, namely whether any new *simple* ideas (other than relations) are given by the understanding. When setting out the thesis which he wished to prove ('the power, I assert, that *understands* . . . is a spring of new ideas'), Price asked us to note 'that by *ideas*, I mean here almost constantly *simple ideas*, or original and uncompounded perceptions of the mind'.[1] But his list of physical notions strays far from this original intention.

Price was justified in pointing out that the empiricists' treatment of relations was slipshod, and perhaps the conclusion we should reach on simple ideas is that qualities are given by sense, relations not. If this conclusion is correct, however, it will follow that ethical ideas, if simple, cannot be qualities. Goodness cannot be, as Professor Moore has held,[2] a 'simple quality' analogous to yellow; and rightness cannot be a 'simple quality' of actions. I do not think that Price need be committed to either of these views. At any rate his arguments against empiricism should lead him to the view that moral ideas, if analogous to the simple ideas in his list, are relations, and if analogous to the other ideas in his list, are not simple. We find a hint of this sounder line of argument at the end of his list of ideas of reason.

' 'Tis obvious, that the ideas now meant presuppose certain subjects of contemplation, of whose natures, connexions, and qualities they are perceptions. And, therefore, the division of all our simple ideas into *original* and *subsequent* ones may not, perhaps, be improper. The former are conveyed to us immediately by our organs of sense, and our reflexion upon ourselves. The latter presuppose other ideas, and arise from the perception of their natures and relations.'[3]

Unfortunately Price does not follow up this suggestion, but

---

[1] p. 18, footnote.   [2] Notably in *Principia Ethica*.
[3] p. 38.

turns aside to set out in greater detail a different classification, which I cannot think particularly clear or helpful. His discussion of the notions of physics really shows that some ideas 'arise from' and 'presuppose' simple ideas of sense or introspection and of relations, that is, they are entailed by 'original ideas'. These entailed ideas Price calls 'subsequent ones'. His distinction here is the same as that drawn in our own day by Sir David Ross between 'constitutive' and 'consequential' ideas.[1] And if we wish to draw an analogy between ethics on the one hand, and physics and mathematics on the other, this is, I suggest, the line we should follow.

Price's treatment of epistemology in Chapter I is a criticism of empiricism. In Chapter V we find a reply to scepticism and a brief outline of his view of the sources of knowledge.

The reply to scepticism is helpful. Here Price is not a Cartesian, but takes the shorter road that Descartes should have taken. To suppose that our faculties always deceive us involves, as he points out, a self-contradiction. For this supposition itself comes from the suspected faculties, and if it be true that all the deliverances of our faculties are false, then this deliverance also will be false. Thus the truth of the supposition entails its own falsity. Again, doubt itself rests on grounds: 'Doubting supposes evidence; and there cannot, therefore, be any such thing as doubting, whether evidence itself is to be regarded. A man who doubts of the veracity of his faculties, must do it on their own authority; that is, *at the very time, and in the very act of suspecting them*, he must *trust* them.'[2]

Price sees the distinction between, to use modern terminology, 'psychological doubt' and 'logical doubt'. Thus he says that the mental state of doubting can only come from evidence, and if the evidence available is in favour of belief, and not of doubt, we are bound to believe. Sceptics merely

---

[1] *The Right and the Good*, p. 121.   [2] p. 92.

show us that some other state of affairs is *possible*; they do not psychologically doubt what they say is dubitable. But even so, Price points out, their argument for dubitability merely takes in one part of the evidence, a part which shows that the proposition believed is possibly false (e.g. the fact that I have been deceived before is evidence that I might be deceived now), and neglects evidence on the other side which shows that the belief is possibly, and often probably, true.

All the same, Price is not very clear about probability in relation to induction (he knows a good deal about mathematical probability, as may be seen from some of his notes), and has failed to appreciate the force of Hume's arguments on this question. Thus his positive exposition of epistemology is faulty. He finds three sources of knowledge, introspection of sense contents and of feelings, intuition, and argumentation. The last of these he calls 'argumentation or deduction', but it is plain that he includes induction in it, and regards the distinction between probable and demonstrative argument as one of degree only. Argumentation 'supplies us with all the degrees of evidence, from that producing full certainty, to the lowest probability'.[1] Likewise he regards intuition as admitting of degrees, and here he seems, like some other philosophers, to confuse the intuition of necessary propositions with the taking for granted of propositions that have been rendered probable by past experience of which we are not explicitly aware at the time of making the present judgement.

Because of his confusion between demonstrative and probable argument, intuition and taking for granted, Price's account of our knowledge of the material world is defective. He assumes too readily that acceptance of Berkeley's arguments about matter involves the acceptance of Hume's about mind. 'The same principles on which the existence of *matter* is opposed, lead us equally to deny the existence of *spiritual* beings. And those who reject the one, while they believe the

[1] p. 99.

other, should tell us, "on what grounds they believe there exist any beings whatsoever besides themselves."[1] A Berkeleian could do so easily enough. Like Price, he would hold that we have direct knowledge of ourselves by introspection, and would add that this knowledge enables us to infer by analogy to the existence of other such selves, while a similar inference for matter would be illegitimate since we have no direct awareness of any material substance. Price is vaguely aware that his account of matter is unsatisfactory, as we see from Notes E (to which he here refers us) and B in the Appendix.

3. *Epistemology of Morals*

Price does not realize that in his critique of empiricism he has departed from his original intention of showing that the understanding perceives simple ideas; and so, when he turns to the epistemology of morals, he thinks that he must first show that moral ideas are simple in order to proceed to a proof that they are given by the understanding. If my comments on his critique of empiricism are sound, he would do better to show that moral ideas are either (*a*) relations, or (*b*) 'consequential' or 'subsequent' ideas. I think that rightness, obligation, and desert fall under (*a*), while goodness (where not used naturalistically) falls under (*b*).

Price's argument to show that right and wrong are simple ideas consists in pointing out that some suggested definitions do not have the same connotation as the word to be defined. If 'right' were properly defined as, for example, 'what God commands' or 'what produces happiness', then 'the propositions, *obeying a command is right*, or *producing happiness is right*, would be most trifling, as expressing no more than that obeying a command, is obeying a command, or producing happiness, is producing happiness'.[2] In other words, Price

[1] p. 102. [2] pp. 16–17.

requires a definition to be tautologous with its definiendum. At the same time he would not accept as a definition a mere 'synonymous expression'.[1] One is tempted to ask, could there be any definition that was the one and not the other?[2] I suppose the answer is that an analysis of a concept into its constituent parts could be tautologous with the concept, but would not be a synonym, a mere alternative name, since it *is* an analysis into parts. But there will be tautology, the same connotation, only if the analysis is relatively simple.[3] Sir David Ross says that a definition must express *explicitly* what we have in mind *implicitly*;[4] but then it will not be connotatively tautologous with the definiendum. Let us assume that 'the shortest distance between two points' is a correct definition or analysis of 'a straight line'. It may well be sensible, and not absurd, to ask: 'Is the shortest distance between two points a straight line?' For the question may mean, for example, 'When you (or most people using the English language) speak of "a straight line", do you (or they) have in mind "the shortest distance between two points"?' And the answer may be: 'When I speak of "a straight line", I do not normally have in mind "the shortest distance between two points" but a certain sort of *Gestalt*. And I suspect this is true of most people using the English language. But when, in considering certain parts of Euclidean geometry, I speak of "a straight line", I do have in mind "the shortest

[1] p. 41.

[2] Compare recent discussions in *The Philosophy of G. E. Moore*, and subsequently in *Mind* (nos. 211, 213, 215, 216), arising from Professor Moore's similar argument for the view that 'good' is indefinable.

[3] Professor Moore's example of an adequate definition (*The Philosophy of G. E. Moore*, p. 664) is 'A brother is a male sibling'. Here the analysis is into two constituents, and it is reasonable to say that the proposition is a tautology. But if we take a more complex concept, e.g. 'material thing', 'man', 'the State', our initial thought is vague and indefinite as compared with any analysis. Consequently the analysis has a fuller (or at least a more precise) connotation.

In *The Moral Sense* (pp. 111–13) I argued that Price's and Professor Moore's test of a definition is sound. I now think this view needs qualification.

[4] *Foundations of Ethics*, p. 259 (my italics).

distance between two points". I agree that the concept which I have in mind in common usage of "a straight line" does in fact refer to the same things as "the shortest distance between two points", but I cannot say that I think of the latter when I say the former.'

Further, if we consider a 'consequential' or 'subsequent' characteristic, which is entailed by 'constitutive' characteristics, we may say that a description of the constitutive characteristics is, in one sense, a partial 'analysis' of the consequential characteristic. It would, of course, not be a complete analysis. Thus we may say that Hume's account of the observed facts in instances of causation is a partial and incomplete analysis of the concept of causation. We could use Price's argument to show that the analysis is inadequate or incomplete: we can significantly ask, 'Does an event which invariably precedes another *cause* that other?' and thus show that the suggested analysis is inadequate, but we should not thereby show that the concept of cause is *simple*. I suggest that this is the position of the concept of good, when used non-naturalistically, and that if good, thus used, is a 'consequential' characteristic, it is misleading to add that it is simple. Of course it is still true that a consequential characteristic, i.e. one which only comes into existence if entailed by other characteristics, must be discerned by the understanding, for it is the understanding that discerns entailments. The discussion of simplicity, then, is irrelevant to the question whether a characteristic is given by the understanding or sense. If we can show that the characteristic is a relation, its character as a relation, and not its simplicity (should it happen to be a simple relation), is the criterion for calling it an idea of reason. And if we can show that it is a 'consequential' or entailed characteristic, its character of being entailed, and not the invalid assumption of simplicity, is the criterion.

In the final event Price does appeal to entailment. His

arguments about right, as about the list of physical concepts previously discussed, aim to show that we know certain types of action to be *necessarily* right. While this conclusion, if justified, would show that moral principles are *a priori* (whatever account we give of *a priori* principles), it does not show that the *concept* of right is *a priori*. For we may know necessary propositions about empirical concepts; for example, Price himself has admitted that we are acquainted in introspection with the idea of power or activity, while going on to hold that we know *a priori* the principle that every occurrence must have been produced by activity. Likewise we could hold that we gain the idea of rightness from the introspection of feeling or from a moral sense, but know *a priori* such principles as that it is always prima facie right to help the needy, to reward conscientiousness, to be grateful to benefactors, and so on.

Thus Price has not, in fact, shown that moral concepts are *a priori*. His actual arguments are as follows. (1) It is possible that they are, since a full-blown empiricism is false. This argument of course does not prove, but simply clears the way for proof. (2) Ordinary speech and thought take it for granted that they are objective. But he agrees that this is also the case, and in his opinion delusively, for secondary qualities. (3) But we can show, he thinks, that ordinary thought about secondary qualities conflicts with self-evidence, while this is not so in regard to moral attributes. Few people would accept Price's argument about secondary qualities here. He does not rely on the empirical evidence of illusions, &c., for he has learned from Berkeley that this applies equally to primary qualities. He holds that a body cannot have the attribute of being coloured, because the colour is a sensation in the mind, just as a regular form cannot have the attribute of being pleasant—the pleasure is a sensation caused in the mind by the form. But if these two examples were properly analogous, ordinary language would not speak differently about them. Colour presents itself as an attribute of material objects, pleasure does not. And it is only because of the empirical evidence of illusions, hallucinations, and the rest, that we come to doubt the objectivity of colour. We do not know *a priori*, either that colour is subjective, or that pleasure is. Experience presents pleasure as such, and presents colour as objective; later experience suggests that colour may not be objective. There is no question of *a priori* knowledge in either case. (4) Objective actions must have some character, and if right and wrong are subjective, all actions would have to be indifferent; for there is no other objective characteristic for them to have. This argument is fallacious. A subjective theory of morals would hold that the attribute 'morally indifferent' is equally subjective with 'right' and 'wrong'. This would not leave actions with no objective characteristics, for they would all still have non-moral characteristics such as being willed and being directed to such-and-such an end.

After dealing with the ideas of right and wrong, Price proceeds to beautiful and ugly, and good and bad. Beauty and ugliness he holds to be subjective. They are strictly the pleasure and displeasure we feel when contemplating certain objects, but are caused by objective characteristics which, he says, are 'naturally adapted' to please or displease. The perception of 'moral beauty', that is, the pleasure we feel for virtuous persons and actions, is caused by the contemplation of virtue. The perception of natural beauty, that is, the pleasure we feel for regular forms, is caused by the contemplation of uniformity amidst variety. He suggests that the reasons why uniformity or regularity amidst variety pleases us are: first, it facilitates comprehension and memory; second, it is useful in the sense of stabilizing the object or organism possessing it; and third, it is evidence of design. Good and evil, as contrasted with beauty and ugliness, he holds to be objective characteristics of the things to which they are attributed. His argument for this distinction lies merely in an appeal to reflection on what we mean by the words. An empiricist might say that reflection leads him to regard 'good' and 'evil', like 'beautiful' and 'ugly', as names for the pleasure and pain caused in us by the contemplation of certain objects. Price realizes that mány thinkers take a similar view of beauty and goodness, Hutcheson and Hume regarding them both as subjective, Balguy as objective; but this does not lead him to seek further arguments in support of his differentiation. The argument which he used earlier against naturalistic definitions of 'right' will not help him here, for we must all agree that the plain man's usage of 'beautiful' attributes a quality of beauty to the object thus described, so that Price's account of beauty cannot state the meaning (i.e. connotation) of the word in ordinary speech.

But I think that we can derive from another section of the *Review* an argument to show that moral goodness at least (and this is what Price has chiefly in mind when speaking of goodness) must be an idea of reason, in that it is, or includes, a 'consequential' or entailed characteristic. Hume would say that when we call an agent morally good we are referring to the feeling of approval caused in us by the contemplation of conscientious action. This view would deny that there is any 'consequential' characteristic of the agent entailed by his having acted as he thought right. But such an account is inadequate. For, as Price points out in Chapter IV, when we speak of the moral worth of a conscientious agent, we mean 'his virtue considered as implying the fitness, that good should be communicated to him'.[1] The idea of moral goodness includes the idea of merit, of deserving happiness. Desert is a moral notion, and may, Price suggests, be analysed in terms of 'right' or 'ought'. Moral goodness, then, is not fully analysable into naturalistic terms, it is a 'consequential' characteristic containing as one of its elements a moral

[1] p. 81.

characteristic entailed by another element in the situation (or perhaps it would be better to describe the entailed element, merit, as the consequential characteristic). As with causation, it does not follow that the idea of moral goodness is simple; on the contrary, it must be complex if it contains at least two elements, one of them being entailed by the other.

4. *Psychology of Morals*

Price does not have a great deal to say on psychological questions. His refutation of psychological hedonism is derived from Butler. While sound enough in general, it carries too far the criticism that psychological hedonism places the cart before the horse in making desire dependent on pleasure. Though it is true that pleasure is usually the result of satisfied desire, not the stimulus to desire, it is false to say, as Price does, that thought of pleasure is never the stimulus to desire. And pleasure may in some instances arise without either causing or being caused by desire; as when I am assailed by an agreeable scent on a walk in the country.

Price's criticism of egoistic hedonism generally, however, goes farther than Butler's. He recognizes clearly the falsity of the view that duty and interest, even if they are not identical, at least coincide. Shaftesbury, of course, had held that they do; Butler, demurring a little, had agreed that they coincide in this world 'for the most part'. Price pays lip-service to Butler's view, but he does not really believe it. An eighteenth-century peer, chiefly interested in the pursuit of culture, and doubtless ruling his own estate with justice and benevolence, may perhaps, like the Psalmist, have never seen a righteous man forsaken or his children begging for bread. A cleric could not be quite so complacent, though perhaps the fashionable Rolls Chapel and the Bishop's Palace disclosed little of unrewarded virtue. But the minister of Newington Green must have found plenty of it. 'All things considered, this world appears fitted more to be a school for the *education* of virtue, than a station of honour to it.'[1] 'The most worthy characters are so far, in the present state of things, from *always* enjoying the highest happiness, that they are *sometimes* the greatest sufferers; and the *most* vicious the *least* unhappy.'[2] Although Price is weak on introspective psychology, he has his eyes wide open, where others are blind, in observational psychology. He sees that, though virtue may be its own reward, it can lead to discomfort too, for the highly virtuous man feels remorse at peccadilloes, while hardened vice is callous to the stings of conscience. 'It can scarcely be denied with respect to wickedness, that it would very frequently be much better for a man, (I mean, more for his own present ease) to be *thoroughly* wicked than *partially* so.'[3] Price does not agree with Plato that the most vicious soul is the most tormented. No, it is the average decent person who wants to do what is right but backslides at times, 'such a person must doubtless be very miserable. He possesses neither virtue nor vice enough to give him any quiet. He is the seat of a constant intestine war, always full of vexation with himself'.[4] The vicious man feels this only when he is on the way to reform. But 'the *most* wicked endure the *least* uneasiness from the checks of conscience'.[5] Here is an honest moralist, who follows his own precept of avoiding self-deception. Plato and Butler would hardly have dared to say this if they had seen it. They might have felt that, if this be true, what hope is there of persuading men to virtue? But Price no doubt knew from experience that the rational persuasion of the moralist and preacher can have some effect on the average, decent but weak, individual; for the hardened criminal it is, by itself, useless. At any rate Price's psychology is the more true, and I suspect that, in consequence, he achieved more genuine improvement among the moderately

[1] p. 257. [2] p. 258. [3] p. 259.
[4] p. 259. [5] p. 260.

lecent parishioners of Newington Green than did Butler among the fashionable congregation of the Rolls Chapel.

Price draws a useful distinction between 'affections' on the one hand and 'passions' or 'appetites' on the other. Affections are desires which involve reason; passions or appetites are instinctive', that is, 'implanted' in our 'arbitrary constitution'. Price's polemic against regarding self-love, benevolence, and certain other desires as 'instinctive' or 'implanted' seems at first sight needlessly artificial. He holds that we desire the happiness of ourselves and of others because the 'nature of happiness' necessarily excites desire; happiness being what it is, we must desire it. One might think it is purely a verbal question whether we say that the desire of every person for his own happiness arises from the nature of happiness or from the nature of man. Again, is there more than verbal difference between saying that this desire is 'implanted in us' by God, and saying that it is necessary? No doubt God *could* have made us differently, so that the implanted desire would be 'arbitrary' in that sense; but in fact we know, Price would himself say, that God will have chosen the best constitution possible, and we know too that he is not going to change his mind to-morrow and make future human beings differently, so that the 'arbitrary' constitution he has given us is quite as stable and reliable as any arising from 'the nature of things'. Price would not, however, agree that the difference is verbal. He bifurcates the world into what necessarily exists ('the truth and nature of things') and what is contingent. Anything that involves reason is, for him, a part of necessary truth. Thus his distinction between affections and passions implies that the former are necessary and would be possessed by any rational being, while the latter are contingent. This consequence of his metaphysical position affects his ethics in the following way. We learn later that necessary existence *is* God, while contingent existence is the product of God. Thus if morality, and all the elements of our human psychology that pertain to it, are part of necessary truth, it follows that they are part of God, and in this way Price will have 'traced the obligations of virtue up to the truth and nature of things, and thus to the Deity'.

It is, however, a pity that Price did not rely on empirical considerations (as Butler, and later Reid, did) to show that self-love and benevolence involve rational thought. He attempts to prove his view by deductive argument. In the case of the agent's own happiness Price aims at a deductive demonstration by equating 'desiring' with 'liking', and points out that to speak of 'liking what is unpleasant' is self-contradictory since it means 'being pleased with what is unpleasant'. This might appear plausible for private happiness (though the argument confuses the state of desiring with the state of satisfaction that supervenes on the fulfilment of desire, a distinction which Price himself took pains to stress in his refutation of psychological hedonism), but is hardly so for public happiness; Price could not suggest that the desire of misery for others is self-contradictory, for it obviously occurs. And so his argument in respect of public happiness runs as follows. An intelligent being will see, by the former argument, that his own happiness is an essential object of desire to every agent: hence he must conclude 'that the happiness of others is to them as important as his is to him; and that it is in itself equally valuable and desirable, whoever possesses it'.[1] This argument seems to come dangerously near the fallacy of deducing 'desirable' from 'desired'. We cannot reach a moral proposition (e.g. that happiness as such is desirable or valuable, or that we ought to pursue the happiness of others) from a non-moral proposition (that each of us desires his own happiness) even if the latter be a necessary proposition. Price may try to show us that right and wrong, good and bad, are part of necessary truth, but even if that be so, we cannot conclude from a premiss asserting

[1] p. 71.

ecessity to a conclusion asserting goodness or rightness
hough the converse would hold.

5. *The Moral System*

Rightness, we have seen, is for Price a simple, indefinable
idea. Obligation he regards as a synonym for the same
characteristic. To say that an action is right is the same as
saying that we are obliged to do it. He thus concludes, in
Kantian language, that rectitude is a law binding all rational
creatures. His view further enables him to state that the
question, what obliges us to do right, is meaningless, since
rectitude is its own obligation; if it were not obligatory, it
would not be right. To those who say that obligation is a
mental state, the feeling or excitement impelling us to act
when we perceive the proposed action to be right, Price
replies that, while our use of the word sometimes suggests
that obligation is a mental state, the two must in fact be
distinguished since otherwise we could not speak of a man's
judgement concerning obligation'; the obligation, what he
ought to do, must be an objective characteristic that can
become the object of a judgement. When I judge that I
ought to act, I am not judging that I feel impelled so to act.

Price then considers a more difficult objection. If duty and
right are coincident, and indeed synonymous, what are we
to say of 'works of supererogation'? There are many actions,
particularly in the field of benevolence, which we do not
regard as incumbent upon a man, but which nevertheless, if
done, we consider right or virtuous; indeed we regard them
as more praiseworthy than the mere performance of strict
duty. Price's view on this question of 'works of supererogation' deserves careful consideration. First, he says, his position
could be amended so as to make the sphere of obligation
coincident, not with the whole of what is right, but with
those right actions whose non-performance would be wrong.

This is an attractive suggestion, but Price thinks that he need not modify his original position even to this extent. He believes he can still maintain that the right and the obligatory coincide. 'Duties of supererogation', according to him, really are duties, but they are so in general terms only, the particular occasions for fulfilment being left to the judgement of the agent. Thus it is a strict duty to do positive good to others, but the duty is confined to this general principle; whether we fulfil it by doing good to John Smith to-day or to Tom Brown to-morrow, by donating to charity or speaking comfortable words to the sick, this, the particular application of the duty, is left to our own judgement. Thus we cannot say that I am obliged to help John Smith to-day, for if I decide instead to help Tom Brown to-morrow that is equally a fulfilment of my obligation. The same applies, Price points out, to our duty of worshipping God; it is a strict duty, but the particular occasions of its fulfilment are left to our own decision; we do not neglect it if we choose to worship at our bedside rather than at morning chapel. This being so, Price can still hold that duty and right coincide. If I donate to charity, I have done what is right and have fulfilled my duty, but if you do not, you have not neglected your duty, provided that you fulfil the same duty (the duty of general beneficence) in some other way. As to the suggestion that acts of supererogation are more praiseworthy than acts strictly obligatory, Price answers that praise is given to the acting from a regard to right. Thus, if I donate to a charity, thinking it right to do so (i.e. applying my duty of beneficence to this instance), I deserve praise, not for going beyond duty (for I have not done that), but for acting from a regard to duty. The greater praise which we seem to give to some such actions arises when the agent, realizing that in these matters of general duty no hard and fast line can be drawn, takes care to err on the generous side; this is often true of beneficent actions, and we give the greater praise because the motive is a greater regard to virtue than is (or can be) shown in actions that are obligatory in themselves as particular actions.

Other expressions which have been used by rationalists, e.g. 'fitness', 'conformity to truth', 'conformity to the natures of things', Price holds are likewise mere synonyms for 'right'. But whereas 'obligation' is a useful synonym, these terms of art are apt to be misleading. Their only use is to show that right is a species of necessary truth, but they cannot be definitions or criteria, since necessary truth is the genus and of wider application than right. As used by philosophers they in fact presuppose the idea of rightness, but lead readers to think that rightness can be deduced from more abstract notions.

Since Price considers 'right', 'obligatory', and 'fit' to be synonyms, it is worth considering whether this throws any light on the category to which the characteristic so named belongs. I have suggested that an idea of reason, if simple, must be a relation and not a quality. Price certainly says that right is a simple idea. Does he also think it is a relation? Obligation, one would think, is certainly a relation between a person and an action (and, usually, another person to whom the agent has the obligation); and Sir David Ross, in describing the ultimate moral characteristic as the fitness or suitability of an action to a situation, has said that his view, in which fitness is a relation, is essentially that of Samuel Clarke and Richard Price.[1] Let us inquire, then, whether moral fitness is for Price a relation. His clearest statement about moral fitness comes at the beginning of Chapter VI, where he distinguishes the moral and a non-moral sense of the word 'fitness'. The non-moral sense, which is synonymous with 'being a successful means', is clearly relational. Price speaks here of the 'congruity' or 'aptitude of any means to accomplish an end', of objects having 'a fitness to one another', or of being 'fit to answer certain purposes'. While

[1] *Foundations of Ethics*, pp. 52, 54.

he holds that this non-moral notion and the moral notion of fitness are alike in 'signifying a simple perception of the understanding', his examples of moral fitness differ from those of non-moral fitness in being, apparently, non-relational.[1] They are: 'reverencing the Deity is fit' and 'beneficence is fit to be practised'. This does not look like Sir David Ross's 'fitness to the situation'. Later, however, in the same chapter, when considering the expressions used by his rationalist predecessors, he seems to allow that such phrases as 'suitability to the natures of things'[2] or 'the agreement of fitness between actions and relations'[3] are, while apt to mislead, legitimate synonyms for the fitness of which he has previously written. Again, he writes of misery being 'unsuited to' innocence.[4] But I think we must say that the discussion here represents Price's defence of his predecessors, and not his own view, although he appears (wrongly) to think that the two views are compatible. Elsewhere, when he is not discussing his predecessors, Price does not write of fitness as being suitability *to* anything. Even with the example of merit, where it does seem natural to speak of rewards being appropriate or suitable to virtue, and misery to vice, Price does not use this language in his own discussion of merit in Chapter IV. The word 'fitness' is introduced there only in the absolute sense. Merit, he says, implies fitness *that* good should be done to the agent.[5] I doubt if it is reasonable to conclude that Price therefore considers fitness or rightness to be a quality (though it looks as if he would have to say that, if pressed; and in Chapter VIII[6] he says that 'abstract virtue', i.e. objective rightness, 'is, most properly, a quality of the external action or event'). But I think it is clear that he did not regard moral fitness as a relation.

Merit, Price holds, is to be analysed in terms of 'right' or

---

[1] In ed. 1 he calls the non-moral sense relative, and the moral absolute. See editor's footnote to p. 104. 　　[2] pp. 125 ff. 　　[3] p. 128.
[4] p. 129. 　　　　　　　[5] p. 81. 　　　　　　[6] p. 177.

'ought'. To say that a man deserves happiness is to say that it is right or fit he should be made happy, or that he ought to be made happy. This particular species of rightness is entailed by virtue, and correspondingly demerit, the rightness of being made unhappy, is entailed by vice. Price's later distinction between 'absolute' and 'practical virtue' shows that merit is entailed by the latter. The doing of what he thinks right entails that an agent deserves happiness; the doing of what he thinks wrong entails that he deserves unhappiness. Being an entailment, the relation between virtue and merit, vice and demerit, is perceived immediately by the understanding to follow of necessity. It is not the result of a calculation of the utility of making the virtuous happy and the vicious miserable. For the production, without regard to distributive justice, of an equal amount of happiness in the total result would not be equally right. Again, the justification of punishment involves a reference to the desert of guilt and is not solely determined by useful consequences. In these arguments against a utilitarian account of merit, Price is clearly in accord with the deliverances of the moral consciousness.

Price renews his attack on utilitarianism in Chapter VII, where he shows in greater detail that conduciveness to general happiness cannot be the sole criterion of right. In many instances, e.g. in questions of merit, truth-telling, promises, duty to God, the rights of property, we do not think of utility in deciding what is right; and situations can be imagined where we should regard the most useful action possible as not the right one because it would conflict with a stronger obligation arising from one of the other principles mentioned. Price's criticism here is thoroughly sound in showing that utilitarianism conflicts with the moral consciousness of ordinary life. Still, it may be argued that our regard to justice, veracity, and the rest have *arisen* from the experience of our ancestors in finding those types of action to be generally useful, although we have now forgotten that this is what produced their obligation. This line of argument would by-pass the evidence of the developed moral consciousness. It of course implies an hypothesis of historical development, and to confirm or invalidate it we should have to undertake an inquiry into the moral beliefs of primitive peoples and (as shown in their records) of past civilizations. Price of course was in no position to do this. But there is another line of inquiry, and Price does refer to this. Evidence for a theory of the genesis of concepts is to be found in children as well as in primitive peoples. Price points out that children often do not refer to utility in their judgements of right. A child, he says, knows that truth-telling is right without reference to utility. We should of course have to add that the child knows this also without having been told so by its elders. Price's example of truth-telling may appear dubious if we add this qualification, but it is a matter of common observation that children have a strong sense of fairness, irrespective of (and often contrary to) what their elders tell them is right, and without reference to utility. Price's actual example is not as good as it might be, but the line of argument is sound enough to refute the genetic form of utilitarianism.

Price does not, then, think that considerations of general happiness alone constitute the criteria of right. He gives us a list of six 'heads of virtue'. It would seem that he does not regard his list as necessarily complete. He says that these are 'the main and leading branches of Virtue. It may not be possible properly to comprehend all the particular instances of it under any number of heads.'[1] However, the six main branches are: (1) Duty to God (and superiors generally); (2) Duty to self, or prudence; (3) Beneficence; (4) Gratitude; (5) Veracity; (6) Justice.

(1) *Duty to God.* From some of Price's statements it would seem that our duty to God is one of gratitude for benefac-

[1] p. 164.

tions, and one might wonder whether this duty is not, then, merely a species of (4). But there is included another element besides gratitude, namely reverence for a superior being. A like duty we have, though of course in an incomparably lower degree, to men who are superior to us and have benefited us. By 'superior' I suppose Price means, ultimately, morally superior. If so, one might say that the duty to render reverence to superiors might be comprised under distributive justice (6 *b*). But Price would reply, I think, that distributive justice requires us to give *happiness* to the virtuous, and we cannot make God happier than he is. The duty to God required of us is to show him proper reverence, not to make him happy.

(2) *Duty to self.* Price regards prudence as a duty. This may be doubted, on the ground that we think imprudence folly but not vice; we pity, and may despise, but do not blame it, unless it also involves neglect of responsibilities to others. Price refers to his earlier argument that the nature of happiness necessitates desire, so that aversion to happiness would be self-contradictory; and he adds here that the same self-contradiction would be involved in supposing that we do not approve of the pursuit of happiness. But, while we may agree that desire of happiness is factually (not logically) necessary, this does not imply, nor does experience show, that we are bound to approve, or think right, what we necessarily desire. Price goes on to argue that if it is right to consult the happiness of others, the same must be true of our own happiness, assuming that the obligation in the former case arises from the nature of happiness alone. I think the assumption is a mistake, one which led the Utilitarians astray. The obligation to produce happiness for others is an obligation to *them*, and arises from our relation to them as personalities; the fact that it is happiness, and not something else, which we are obliged to produce for them, does arise from the fact that the desire of happiness is fundamental to personality; this deter-

mines the character of the obligation, but its existence is determined by the inter-personal relationship, which is lacking in the case of prudence.

(3) *Beneficence*. Price agrees so far with utilitarianism as to say that this is 'the most general and leading consideration' in our calculation of right, and that the production of considerable public interest commonly outweighs conflicting particular obligations of justice and the like. This is a sound observation (though there are certain aspects of justice that refuse to be outweighed by public utility), and accounts, I think, for the Utilitarians' concentration on this obligation.

(4) *Gratitude*. Price here observes that the obligation of gratitude, like many of the obligations of justice, is to *particular* persons, and so different in kind from that of beneficence, which is general in scope and not strictly defined in its particular applications.

(5) *Veracity*. Price evidently founds the duty of veracity on the intrinsic superiority of knowledge over ignorance. He apparently agrees with Plato that the badness of false belief is, in principle, the same as the badness of lying. Again, I should say that, as in his comparison of prudence with beneficence, he neglects the fact that the inter-personal relation involved in lying (as in beneficence) plays a fundamental part in determining its moral character. For the same reasons Price includes the obligation of promises in that of veracity. With promise-breaking at least, he agrees with Wollaston that the wrongness consists in denying truth. A promise, he says, is the statement of a future fact the production of which is within our own power, and therefore promise-breaking is like making a statement known to be false about present or past facts. Here again, it seems to me, the inter-personal relationship involved in promises is insufficiently stressed. If Price's view were correct, the breaking of New Year resolutions (i.e. statements to ourselves about our future actions) would be equally culpable with promise-breaking.

(6) *Justice*, meaning (*a*) the right to property, and (*b*) equity. In his discussion of justice as one of the 'heads of virtue' Price confines himself to questions about property. But at the end of his discussion he refers us to his earlier treatment of distributive justice or equity. (*a*) Price sees that the claims to property cannot all be brought under the principle of public utility, and he therefore posits a separate principle for them. But he is not very clear about the varied nature of these claims. He seems to rely on an intuition of what is right in each type of case. But, whatever we think about the possibility of bringing the different 'heads of virtue' under a single principle, it can be shown[1] that the various just claims in regard to property are simply instances of the claims arising from the principles or 'heads' of morality (e.g. that the property has been earned, contracted for, or gifted). We do not need to specify a separate 'head', still less a series of unrelated intuitions, for property. (*b*) In his treatment of equity Price deals only with distribution according to merit, and evidently does not recognize any basic claim to equality of consideration in the absence of questions of merit. Nor does he take account, as he should, of the claim of need (which may be regarded as a special application of the claim to equality) as an element in distributive justice.

Does this list mean that obligations constitute 'an unrelated heap'? Price protests against the utilitarian and egoistic attempts to over-simplify the moral consciousness, looking for one general principle to which all others are to be reduced. 'Why must there be in the human mind approbation only of one sort of actions? . . . How unreasonable is that love of uniformity and simplicity which inclines men thus to seek them where it is so difficult to find them? It is this that, on other subjects, has often led men astray.'[2] At the same time he evidently feels, as we all do, that somehow the moral

[1] See Carritt, *Ethical and Political Thinking*, chap. xv, § iii.
[2] pp. 137–8.

system constitutes a unity. 'However different from one another the heads which have been enumerated are, yet, from the very notion of them, as *heads of virtue*, it is plain, that they all run up to one general idea, and should be considered as only different modifications and views of one original, all-governing law. . . . Virtue thus considered, is necessarily *one* thing.'[1] But his cautious attitude on this point leads him to discern, as none of his contemporaries did, that obligations may conflict in particular instances. He agrees with Butler that duty and interest, and likewise the other heads of virtue, coincide for the most part, but he sees very plainly that there are instances where they conflict, and here, as he puts it, a greater degree of one obligation 'cancels' the other. Price further points out that disputes about moral questions are usually about the relative strength of conflicting obligations. The general principles, he holds, are self-evident, like the axioms of geometry, and acknowledged by all. But in the application of them to particular instances, and particularly in weighing up their relative force when they conflict, we lack knowledge and must rely on doubtful opinion. Here again, there is an analogy with natural science. But, we must add, the analogy with geometry and its application is not complete. For, while we cannot know that our applications of Euclidean geometry to the material world are exact, we do not have to deal with a conflict of axioms, of weighing them up against one another. The process of weighing conflicting obligations looks like a function of empirical reasoning and this suggests that the axioms of morality are postulates derived from experience, and that their force or strength likewise depends somehow on the evidence of experience.

On this question of the conflict of obligations Price anticipates modern discussion.[2] It is followed by a further such anticipation. In Chapter VIII Price distinguishes between

---

[1] p. 165.

[2] Cf. especially Ross, *The Right and the Good*, chap. ii.

'abstract virtue' and 'practical virtue'. 'Abstract virtue' is what is objectively right, what we would judge to be obligatory if we knew all the relevant facts of the situation, a position we are rarely, if ever, in. 'Practical virtue' is what is obligatory in relation to our opinion of the facts. This we can usually know. Price adds that although objective duty is often unknowable, it is, in a different sense, objectively our duty to do the 'practically virtuous' act. The fulfilment or omission of practical virtue is what gives rise to praise or blame. The difficult questions involved here have been closely discussed by Professor Prichard,[1] Sir David Ross,[2] and Mr. Carritt.[3] Mr. Carritt notes that Price was perhaps the first to see the distinction (Price compares[4] it with a different, traditional, distinction drawn between actions that are 'materially good' and those that are 'formally good'). Sir David Ross has pointed out that yet a third species of right must be added, the obligatoriness of the action that we (fallibly) judge to be right in the light of our opinion of the facts.

This distinction leads Price to discuss moral freedom, which of course applies only to practical virtue, for we are not free to do that of which we are ignorant. Price's brief discussion of freedom is interesting. 'The *liberty* I here mean is the same with the power of *acting* and *determining*.'[5] An efficient cause proper is necessarily free in this sense, that is, it determines and is not determined. When a man *acts*, properly speaking, it is *he*, not some part of his empirical self, that does the determining. The chief difficulty brought against moral freedom arises from thinking of an action as caused by the motive. But the motive is what the man has regard to in deciding to act. It is incorrect to speak of the

[1] *Duty and Ignorance of Fact* (Hertz Lecture, British Academy, 1932).
[2] *Foundations of Ethics*, chap. vii.
[3] *Ethical and Political Thinking*, chap. ii.
[4] p. 177.
[5] p. 181.

motive as therefore *determining* him, as being an efficient cause. It is the occasion of the act, Price holds, not the cause. We may not like the introduction of the notion of 'occasion' with its particular Cartesian associations, but the main point is that the causation dealt with in physical science (and, we may add, empirical psychology) is not causation proper in the sense of efficient agency. Of course there is still the question whether human actions conform to scientific causation, i.e. happen in accordance with causal laws, and, if so, whether this is compatible with the view that they are freely caused in the sense of efficient causation. Price does not offer any view on this question, but he sees it is there and suggests (doubtless from his knowledge of Hume's view) that what the advocates of necessity mean may not be inconsistent with the idea of agency.[1] And again in Chapter X[2] he points out that a free action is compatible with 'the utmost certainty of event', that is, with the highest possible probability derived from regular sequences.

A second requisite for practical virtue, Price adds, is intelligence. We must be able to judge that actions are right or wrong, before we can be morally imputable for them. He holds that a judgement of right can be a motive to action, and appeals to common experience and thought. Thus, like Kant, he considers that reason can be practical. However, it seems that he agrees with those who hold that, to be moved by thought of duty, we must also have a desire to do what is right. Price accepts this view, provided we agree with him that some desires (those which he calls 'affections') are rational and not 'instinctive'. 'An affection or inclination to rectitude cannot be separated from the view of it.'[3] Thus he evidently would agree that the 'inclining' or 'exciting' motive is affection, and different from the judgement of right, but he would say that the first necessarily accompanies the second.

[1] p. 183. [2] p. 244 ff. [3] p. 187.

Price now proceeds to the view (and again he reminds us of Kant) that an action is virtuous only in so far as it is done from the thought of its rightness. He distinguishes between the 'virtue of the action' (i.e. its abstract rightness) and the 'virtue of the agent' (i.e. 'practical virtue' or moral goodness), and points out that an objectively right act may be done by an agent who is, because of his motive, morally neutral or even vicious. If a right action be done from instinctive benevolence (rational benevolence Price holds to involve thought of obligation), it is not virtuous. 'We may, it is true, love the person, as we commonly do the inferior creatures when they discover mildness and tractableness of disposition; but no regard to him as a *virtuous* agent will arise within us.'[1] Likewise an action is vicious or blameable only in so far as the agent acts contrary to thought of right. If the evil effects we may unwittingly produce are due to previous neglect, we are blameworthy for that but not for the present action.

It follows that degree of virtue is proportionate to the degree of regard to what is right. While ability to overcome temptation is a sign of a strong virtuous principle, and the presence of severe temptation mitigates the vice of failing to do what we think right, this does not mean that the temptation of passion is essential for virtue, or that such temptation is not, of itself, a sign of earlier vice. The presence of obstacles (internal or external) to the practice of virtue affords a sign of the strength of virtue, but the virtue may be just as strong without having obstacles to face, i.e. it *would* be able to overcome the obstacles if they were present. Indeed, the highly virtuous man is faced with less impediment to virtue from passion simply because he has succeeded in controlling passion in the past; and God and angels are perfectly virtuous without such impediments to test their virtue. Similarly, the presence of strong passion, though it may mitigate blame for

[1] p. 191.

weakness now, is evidence of vice in the past when the growth of the passion could have been more easily checked.

Since he makes the degree of virtue depend on the strength of conscientiousness, Price opposes Hutcheson's utilitarian calculus for ascertaining degree of virtue. But such a calculus relates to the 'virtue of the action' or 'abstract virtue' (i.e. objective rightness), and must we not agree that this too admits of degrees? It is true that the amount of happiness or good to be produced cannot be the whole of the criterion, since rightness may depend on other 'heads of virtue' than utility; and again, while the millionaire's endowments undoubtedly do more good than the widow's mite, we should not say that his action was more virtuous or had more rightness in it, if the widow had made an at least equal sacrifice. But we do judge the objective rightness or obligation of actions to be greater and less when opposing alternatives face the *same* agent; his duty is to do the action which is the most obligatory of those facing him. Price says that the strongest obligation 'cancels' the force of the others, but it must in the first place have a greater, and they a smaller, degree of rightness for the 'cancellation' of their obligation to take place.

6. *Morals and Theology*

Price must consider the relation of ethics to theology, if only because of the objection that his theory of morals makes right and wrong independent of the will of God, and thus would appear to limit God's omnipotence. Price points out that, whether or no we agree with him that morality is a part of necessary truth, we must certainly say that necessary truth is independent of the will of God. Further, the objection, if pressed to its conclusion, would imply that all God's other attributes are dependent on his will. There is no reason to give will this supreme position among his attributes. On the contrary, we must say that his will is determined by his understanding, for he surely wills because he understands that what he intends to do is right. Still, the objection remains that all this seems to limit God's power. Price's answer to this objection is that necessary truth (including morality) is a part of God's nature. So that when we say it is independent of his will, this does not mean that it is wholly independent of him. And when Price says that God's will is determined by necessary truth (including morality), that is only another way of saying that his will is determined by another part of his nature, namely, his understanding. It appears, then, that necessary truth *is* God's understanding. 'He is intelligent, not by the *apprehension* of truth, but by *being* truth.'[1] This seems inconsistent with Price's earlier statement[2] that mind implies truth or knowables, and God's infinite mind implies infinite truth or knowables, which suggests that God's mind and infinite truth are different, the first knowing the second. But doubtless Price would say, with the idealists, that in the case of God (though not of man, for our minds know a separate object, which is part of God) mind and its objects are the same; God is the infinite mind that knows itself as infinite truth.

If what is right be a branch of necessary truth, and if we know it to be right that virtue should be rewarded, it follows that virtue must in fact be rewarded. But we see it is often not so in this world, and thus we have a proof of the retribution being completed after death. This moral argument for survival, Price points out, does not prove eternal immortality, for the working out of retributive justice need require no long period of time; still less does it assure us of eternal bliss, for which of us deserves this? Natural religion takes us a certain way, but must then be supplemented by revelation.

Price's answer to the problem of undeserved evil in this world strikes me as better than that usually given. He does not say simply, as some apologists do, that it is the price we

---

[1] p. 290. [2] p. 86.

must pay for freedom of choice. He adds that adversity is usually necessary for the training of virtue. If God's purpose for men be that they become virtuous, then they will often need the trials of adversity for the training and growth of virtue. But our intuitions of what is right and fit assure us that the purpose is uncompleted in this world, and must go on in the next.

In his view of the nature of God Price follows an argument of Samuel Clarke (perhaps derived, as Price finds reason to suggest, from Newton). We know intuitively, he holds, that some existences are contingent; if A can be conceived without the conception of B, then B's existence is not necessary but contingent. If anything exists necessarily, the conception of it must be required for the conception of the existence of anything else. Thus Clarke (and, it would seem, Newton) holds that space and time exist necessarily. Now whatever exists contingently must have a necessary ground, and therefore there is a first cause existing necessarily. But that which exists necessarily must be a unity, as Clarke argues, for necessity implies self-sufficiency, i.e. the possibility of the non-existence of everything else, and what can be conceived to be possibly non-existent is not necessarily existent. Thus all that is necessarily existent is part of the one necessary existence. Hence God is infinite space and time (the conception of which is necessary for the conception of the existence of anything), and (this is Price's contribution to the argument) all necessary truth, including morality, which is a part or branch of necessary truth. I do not think that Price's conclusion can be squared with the assumption of Clarke's argument; for it is possible to conceive space and time without conceiving of morality, and therefore morality, according to Clarke's argument, would not be a necessary existent. The root of the trouble is that Price assumes that necessary truth is, or implies, necessary existence; he does not allow for hypothetical necessity, for a system of propositions internally coherent (i.e. entailing each other) but resting on postulated axioms which may not have existential reference. The systems of Newtonian mechanics and of Euclidean geometry may be regarded in this way, in that alternative deductive systems can be constructed, equally coherent internally but resting on different postulates. And it is possible that the same is true of moral systems. Which of the sets of alternative deductive systems is to be selected for application to the facts of the material world (in the case of physics) or of human society (in the case of morals), cannot be settled *a priori*, but must be determined in some other way. However, Price's theology, as it stands, is not even internally coherent, for the argument used to prove the unity of necessary existence would deny necessary existence to that part of necessary truth which Price is most anxious to regard as part of God's nature.

I have suggested[1] that Price's analogy between ethics and physics should have rested on the fact that their central concepts are of 'consequential characteristics', concerning which we are able to assert necessary and universal principles. The question arises, however, whether this line of argument would trace the moral system 'up to the truth and nature of things'. Price of course holds that mathematics and the laws of Newtonian physics do state 'the nature of things', but it is not so easy to hold that nowadays when faced with alternative systems of geometry and alternative frameworks for physics. Price says[2] that he is willing for morality and abstract truth to stand or fall together. Of course he does not conceive it possible that Newtonian physics and Euclidean geometry should not state 'the nature of things', but I think a rationalist in ethics would be wise to seek no more objectivity for the moral system than for physics. Whatever view we take of the status of physics and other sciences, it is still the case that a system of scientific knowledge has a stability and relative permanence not possessed by the whims and fancies of a

[1] pp. xxi–xxiii. [2] p. 85.

particular person's taste or feeling. By 'the truth and nature of things' Price means, not all objective fact, but necessary truths as opposed to contingent facts. He holds that the principles of the moral system are like those of mathematics and physics. In this he is right. Moral propositions entail, and are entailed by, each other. It may be held, in opposition to Price, that the ultimate presuppositions, both of mathematics and physics, and likewise of morals, are postulates, and some may add that these postulates are set up as the result of experience. Such a suggestion, combining rationalism and empiricism (and clearly there is some truth in each), will perhaps take us farther than Price's account but does not seriously invalidate his account so far as it goes.

A

R E V I E W

OF THE

PRINCIPAL QUESTIONS

IN

M O R A L S.

PARTICULARLY

Those respecting the ORIGIN of our IDEAS of VIR-
TUE, its NATURE, RELATION to the DEITY,
OBLIGATION, SUBJECT-MATTER, and SANCTIONS.

THE THIRD EDITION CORRECTED,

AND ENLARGED BY AN APPENDIX,

CONTAINING ADDITIONAL NOTES,

AND A DISSERTATION

On the BEING and ATTRIBUTES of the DEITY.

By RICHARD PRICE, D.D. F. R.S.

Οὐ γὰρ ἔχω ἔγωγε οὐδὲν οὕτω μοι ἐναργὲς ὄν, ὡς τοῦτο; τὸ ΕΙΝΑΙ ὡς
οἷόν τε μάλιστα ΚΑΛΟΝ τε καὶ ΑΓΑΘΟΝ.   PLAT. in Phædone.

In Homine autem summa omnis animi est; in animo, rationis; ex qua
VIRTUS *est, Quæ rationis absolutio definitur. Quam etiam atque*
etiam *explicandam putant.*   CICERO, *De finibus*, lib. v. 14.

L O N D O N:

PRINTED FOR T. CADELL IN THE STRAND.

M DCC LXXXVII.

The title-page of the third edition

PREFACE TO THE FIRST EDITION

[Not included in the original Third Edition]

I Am very sensible, that the following work offers itself to the publick under many disadvantages, and at a time when it is not to be expected that it can gain much of the attention of men. So important, however, are the questions discussed in it, that if, amidst many imperfections, it has any merit, it cannot be unseasonable, but will probably find some, who will give it a candid and careful perusal. The Notes which will be found in it, were occasioned chiefly by its having lain by the Author for some years, and received in that time several revisals.— There is no writer to whom I have near so much reason to acknowledge myself indebted, as Dr. Butler, *the late Bishop of* Durham. *But whenever I have been conscious of writing after him, I have almost always either mentioned him, or quoted his words; and the same I have also scrupulously done with respect to other writers.*

There is nothing in this Treatise, *which I wish more I could engage the reader's attention to, or which, I think, will require it more, than the first Chapter, and particularly the second Section of it. If I have failed here, I have failed in my chief design. But I should be sorry that any one should fix this as his judgment, without going through the whole treatise, and comparing the different parts of it, which will be found to have a considerable dependence on one another. The point which I have endeavoured to prove in the last section of the chapter I have mentioned, must appear so plain to those who have not much studied the question about the foundation of* Morals, *or*

3

who have not before viewed it in the light in which I have placed it, that, I fear, it will be difficult for them not to think that I have trifled in bestowing so much pains upon it. And indeed my own conviction is so strong on this point, that I cannot help considering it as some reproach to human reason, that, by the late controversies, and the doubts of some of the wisest men, it should be rendered necessary to use many arguments to shew, that right *and* wrong, *or* moral good *and* evil, *signify somewhat* really true *of actions, and not merely* sensations.

ADVERTISEMENT.

THE following Work was first published thirty years ago. It was then the Author's first production; and contained the result of some of his earliest thoughts. A careful revisal has now made it the result of his latest and maturest thoughts. The Notes in the Appendix contain an account of all the alterations which, since that time, have taken place in the Author's views and sentiments on the subjects discussed in it.

The Dissertation on the being and attributes of the Deity which follows these notes, has been always intended for this Treatise; but was omitted in the former editions on account of the difficulty there is in giving a just explanation of the subject of it. This consideration has now less weight with the Author; and therefore, after endeavouring to make the reasoning in it as concise and perspicuous as possible, he has determined to give it a place in this edition.

Several corrections have been made in the style and composition; but, in this respect, the following Treatise is still very deficient, and will require much indulgence and candour.

Hackney, June 21st, 1787.

CONTENTS.

CONTENTS

CHAP. IX.

CHAP. X.

APPENDIX.

8

INTRODUCTION.

THE liberty which all readers take to pronounce concerning the merit of books, 'tis fit they should enjoy; nor is he sufficiently qualified for the province of writing, who finds himself at all disposed to be out of humour with it, or who is not prepared for all its consequences. It is however much to be wished, that readers would, before they pronounce, take more time to consider and examine, than they generally do. There are hardly any subjects so plain, as not to require care and attention to form a competent judgment of them. What then must we think of those whom we continually see readily delivering their sentiments concerning points they have never considered; and deciding peremptorily, without thought or study, on the most difficult questions? If such are ever right, it can be only by chance. They speak and think entirely at random, and therefore deserve no regard. But it is melancholy to see many, even of those who take some pains to examine, almost as little entitled to regard, and as incompetent judges, as the most careless and unthinking; determined in their judgments by arguments the most trifling, and under the influence of passions the most unfavourable to the discovery of truth.

These are considerations which afford a discouraging prospect to writers in general, especially to those who write on any abstruse and controverted subjects. So great is the inattention of most persons, their carelessness and haste in thinking and yet forwardness to determine, and so much do they like or dislike according to their pre-conceived notions and prejudices, and not according to reason or upon any close and impartial consideration, that an author who should entertain any sanguine hopes of success, whatever he might think of his cause or his arguments, would, in all probability, be greatly mortified. It might be added, that we are, in general, no less inclined to attach ourselves immoderately to our opinions; than we are to embrace them before due examination, and to decide prematurely and capriciously.

I have, for my own part, such a notion of the truth of these observations, that there are not perhaps many who less expect to be ever able to convince one person of a single error. The more we know of men, the more we find that they are governed, in forming and maintaining their opinions, by their tempers, by interest, by humour and passion, and a thousand nameless causes and particular turns and casts of mind, which cannot but produce the greatest diversity of sentiments among them, and render it impossible for them not to err. There are in truth none who are possessed of that cool and dispassionate temper, that freedom from all wrong byasses, that habit of attention and patience of thought, and, also, that penetration and sagacity of mind, which are the proper securities against error. How much then do modesty and diffidence become us? how open ought we to be to conviction, and how candid to those of different sentiments? Indeed the consideration of the various ways, in which error may insinuate itself into our minds; the many latent prejudices, by which we are liable to be influenced; the innumerable circumstances in our own dispositions, and in the appearances of things which may insensibly draw us astray, and the unavoidable darkness and infirmities of the best and ablest men, shewing themselves frequently in mistakes of the strangest kind: such reflections are enough to dispose a considerate man to distrust almost all his opinions.

But yet, to indulge such a disposition, would be unreasonable. Notwithstanding these difficulties and discouragements, truth is still discoverable, and the honest and diligent may expect (at least in some measure, and on the most important points) to succeed in their enquiries after it. These reflections afford the strongest arguments for caution and care in enquiring, but none for despair or a desultory levity and fickleness of sentiment. They ought not to make us *sceptical*, though they demonstrate the folly of being *dogmatical*.

In the following treatise, most of the questions that are of any importance relating to morality and virtue will be considered; and many of them in a manner different from that in which they have been hitherto treated. The author offers it to the public with real diffidence, sensible that it has many defects; and conscious of his own liableness to the causes of blindness and error which he has mentioned.—His principal view has been to trace the obligations of virtue up to the truth and the nature of things, and these to the Deity. The considerations he has offered on this important point have, in a great degree, satisfied his own mind; and this has led him to hope they may be of some use in assisting the enquiries of others.

A

TREATISE

OF

Moral GOOD and EVIL.

CHAP. I.

Of the Origin of our Ideas of Right and Wrong.

IN considering the actions of moral agents, we shall find in ourselves three different perceptions concerning them, which are necessary to be carefully distinguished.

The *first*, is our perception of right and wrong.

The *second*, is our perception of beauty and deformity.

The *third* we express, when we say, that actions are of *good* or *ill* desert.

Each of these perceptions I propose separately to examine, but particularly the *first*, with which I shall begin.

It is proper the reader should carefully attend to the state of the question here to be considered; which, as clearly as I can, I shall lay before him.

SECT. I.

The Question stated concerning the Foundation of Morals.

SOME actions we all feel ourselves irresistibly determined to approve, and others to disapprove. Some actions we cannot but think *right*, and others *wrong*, and of all actions we are led to form some opinion, as either *fit* to be performed or *unfit*; or neither fit nor unfit to be performed; that is, *indifferent*. What the power within us is, which thus determines, is the question to be considered.

A late very distinguished writer, Dr. *Hutcheson*, deduces our moral ideas from a *moral sense*; meaning by this *sense*, a power within us, different from reason, which renders certain actions pleasing and others displeasing to us. As we are so made, that certain impressions on our bodily organs shall excite certain ideas in our minds, and that certain outward forms, when presented to us, shall be the necessary occasions of pleasure or pain. In like manner, according to Dr. *Hutcheson*, we are so made, that certain affections and actions of moral agents shall be the necessary occasions of agreeable or disagreeable sensations in us, and procure our love or dislike of them. He has indeed well shewn, that we have a faculty determining us *immediately* to approve or disapprove actions, abstracted from all views of private advantage; and that the highest pleasures of life depend upon this faculty. Had he proceeded no farther, and intended nothing more by the *moral sense*, than our *moral faculty* in general, little room would have been left for any objections: But then he would have meant by it nothing *new*, and he could not have been considered as the *discoverer* of it.* From the term *sense*, which he applies to it, from his rejection of all the arguments that have been used to prove it to be an intellectual power, and from the whole of his language on this subject; it is evident, he considered it as the effect of a *positive constitution* of our minds, or as an *implanted* and *arbitrary* principle by which a *relish* is given us for certain moral objects and forms and aversion to others, similar to the relishes and aversions created by any of our other senses. In other words; our ideas of morality, if this account is right, have the same origin with our ideas of the sensible qualities of bodies, the harmony of sounds,† or the beauties of painting

---

* In the Preface to his *Treatise on the Passions,* he tells us; (after taking notice of some gentlemen, who, by what he had writ, had been convinced of a *moral sense;*) that they had made him a *compliment which he did not think belonged to him, as if the world were indebted to him for the discovery of it.*

† If any person wants to be convinced, that this is a just representation of Dr. *Hutcheson*'s sentiments, he need only read his *Illustrations on the Moral Sense,* and particularly the 4th section at the conclusion. See also a *Note* at the end of the first of Mr. *Hume*'s *Philosophical Essays.*

or sculpture; that is, the mere good pleasure of our Maker adapting the mind and its organs in a particular manner to certain objects. Virtue (as those who embrace this scheme say) is an affair of taste. Moral right and wrong, signify nothing *in the objects themselves* to which they are applied, any more than agreeable and harsh; sweet and bitter; pleasant and painful; but only *certain effects in us*. Our perception of *right*, or moral good, in actions, is that agreeable *emotion*, or feeling, which certain actions produce in us; and of *wrong*, or moral evil, the contrary. They are particular modifications of our minds, or impressions which they are made to receive from the contemplation of certain actions, which the contrary actions *might* have occasioned, had the Author of nature so pleased; and which to suppose to belong to these actions themselves, is as absurd as to ascribe the pleasure or uneasiness, which the observation of a particular form gives us, to the form itself. 'Tis therefore, by this account, improper to say of an action, that it *is right*, in much the same sense that it is improper to say [1]of an object of taste, that it is *sweet*; or of *pain*, that it is *in* fire.[1]

The present enquiry therefore is; whether this be a true account of virtue or not; whether it *has* or has *not* a foundation in the *nature* of its object; whether *right* and *wrong* are real characters of *actions*, or only qualities of our *minds*; whether, in short, they denote what actions *are*, or only *sensations* derived from the particular frame and structure of our natures.

I am persuaded, all attentive persons, who have not before considered this question, will wonder that it should be a subject of dispute, and think I am going to undertake a very needless work. I have given the naked and just state of it. And it is worth our attention, as we go along, that it is the *only* question about the foundation of morals, which can

[[1] Ed. 1 reads: 'of an object of sight, that it is *coloured*, or of an object of taste, that it is *sweet*.' Cf. p. 102.]

rationally and properly be made a subject of debate. For, granting that we have perceptions of *moral right* and *wrong*, they must denote, either what the actions, to which we apply them, *are*, or only our *feelings*; and the *power* of perceiving them must be, either that power whose object is truth, or some *implanted power* or *sense*. If the former is true, then is *morality* equally unchangeable with *all truth*: If, on the contrary, the latter is true, then is it that only which, according to the different constitutions of the *senses* of beings, it *appears* to be to them.

As to the schemes which found morality on self-love, on positive laws and compacts, or the Divine will; they must either mean, that moral good and evil are only other words for *advantageous* and *disadvantageous*, *willed* and *forbidden*. Or they relate to a very different question; that is, not to the question, what is the nature and true *account* of virtue; but, what is the *subject-matter* of it.*

As far as the former may be the intention of the schemes I have mentioned, they afford little room for controversy. Right and wrong when applied to actions which are commanded or forbidden by the will of God, or that produce good or harm, do not signify merely, that such actions are commanded or forbidden, or that they are useful or hurtful, but a *sentiment*[1] concerning them and our consequent approbation or disapprobation of the performance of them. Were not this true, it would be palpably absurd in any case to ask, whether it is *right* to obey a command, or *wrong* to disobey it; and the propositions, *obeying a command is right*, or *producing happiness is right*, would be most trifling,[2] as expressing no

---

* It should be considered, that the phrase *foundation* of virtue has the different significations of an account or origin of virtue; of a consideration or principle inferring and proving it in particular cases; and of a motive to the practice of it: and that it is here used in the first of these senses only.—See the beginning of the last Chapter in the Second Part [pp. 233 ff.].

[1 Price uses the word 'sentiment' to mean opinion, not feeling.]

[2 Ed. 1 reads 'most triflingly identical'.]

more than that obeying a command, is obeying a command, or producing happiness, is producing happiness. Besides; on the supposition, that right and wrong denote only the relations of actions to will and law, or to happiness and misery, there could be no dispute about the faculty that perceives right and wrong, since it must be owned by all, that these relations are objects of the investigations of *reason*.

Happiness requires something in its own nature, or in ours, to give it influence, and to determine our desire of it and approbation of pursuing it. In like manner; all laws, will, and compacts suppose *antecedent right* to give them effect; and, instead of being the *constituents* of right, they owe their whole force and obligation to it.

Having premised these observations; the question now returns—What is the power within us that perceives the distinctions of *right* and *wrong*?

My answer is. The UNDERSTANDING.

In order to prove this, it is necessary to enter into a particular enquiry into the origin of our ideas in general, and the distinct provinces of the *understanding* and of *sense*.

SECT. II.

Of the Origin of our Ideas in general.

SENSATION and REFLECTION have been commonly reckoned the sources of all our ideas: and Mr. *Locke* has taken no small pains to prove this. How much soever, on the whole, I admire his excellent *Essay*, I cannot think him sufficiently clear or explicit on this subject. It is hard to determine exactly what he meant by *sensation* and *reflection*. If by the former we understand, the effects arising from the impressions made on our minds by external objects; and by the latter, the notice the mind takes of its own operations; it will be impossible to derive some of the most important of our ideas from them. This is the explanation Mr. *Locke* gives of them in the beginning of his *Essay*. But it seems probable that what he chiefly meant, was, that all our ideas are either derived *immediately* from these two sources, or ultimately *grounded* upon ideas so derived; or, in other words, that they furnish us with all the subjects, materials, and occasions of knowledge, comparison, and internal perception. This, however, by no means renders them in any proper sense, the sources of all our ideas: Nor indeed does it appear, notwithstanding all he has said of the operations of the mind about its ideas, that he thought we had any faculty different from sensation and reflection which could give rise to any *simple ideas*; or that was capable of more than compounding, dividing, abstracting, or enlarging ideas previously in the mind. But be this as it may, what I am going to observe, will, I believe, be found true.

The power, I assert, that *understands*; or the faculty within us that discerns *truth*, and that compares all the objects of thought, and *judges* of them, is a spring of new ideas.*

As, perhaps, this has not been enough attended to, and as the question to be discussed, is; whether our *moral ideas* are derived from the *understanding* or from a *sense*; it will be necessary to state distinctly the different natures and provinces of sense and reason.

---

* The reader is desired to remember, that by *ideas*, I mean here almost constantly *simple ideas*, or original and uncompounded perceptions of the mind. That our ideas of right and wrong are of this sort, will be particularly observed hereafter. It may also be right to take notice, that I all along speak of the understanding, in the most confined and proper sense of it. What gives occasion for observing this, is the division which has been made by some writers, of all the powers of the soul into understanding and will; the former comprehending under it, all the powers of external and internal sensation, as well as those of judging and reasoning; and the latter, all the affections of the mind, as well as the power of acting and determining.

There may be further some occasion for observing, that the two acts of the understanding, being intuition and deduction, I have in view the former. 'Tis plain, on the contrary, that those writers, who argue against referring our moral ideas to reason, have generally the latter only in view.

To this purpose we may observe, first, that the power which judges of the perceptions of the senses, and contradicts their decisions; which discovers the nature of the sensible qualities of objects, enquires into their causes, and distinguishes between what is real and what is not real in them, must be a power within us which is superior to sense.

Again, it is plain that one sense cannot judge of the objects of another; the eye, for instance, of harmony, or the ear of colours. The faculty therefore which views and compares the objects of *all* the senses, cannot be sense. When, for instance, we consider sound and colour together, we observe in them *essence, number, identity, diversity,* &c. and determine their reality to consist, not in being properties of *external substances*, but in being modifications of *our souls*. The power which takes cognizance of all this, and gives rise to these notions, must be a power capable of subjecting all things alike to its inspection, and of acquainting itself with necessary truth and existence.

Sense consists in the obtruding of certain impressions upon us, independently of our wills; but it cannot perceive what they are, or whence they are derived. It lies prostrate under its object, and is only a capacity in the soul of having its own state altered by the influence of particular causes. It must therefore remain a stranger to the objects and causes affecting it.

Were not *sense* and *knowledge* entirely different, we should rest satisfied with sensible impressions, such as light, colours, and sounds, and enquire no farther about them, at least when the impressions are strong and vigorous: Whereas, on the contrary, we necessarily desire some farther acquaintance with them, and can never be satisfied till we have subjected them to the survey of reason.—Sense presents *particular* forms to the mind; but cannot rise to any *general* ideas. It is the intellect that examines and compares the presented forms, that rises above individuals to universal and abstract ideas;

and thus looks downward upon objects, takes in at one view an infinity of particulars, and is capable of discovering general truths.—Sense sees only the *outside* of things, reason acquaints itself with their *natures*.—Sensation is only a mode of feeling in the mind; but knowledge implies an active and vital energy of the mind. Feeling pain, for example, is the effect of sense; but the understanding is employed when pain itself is made an object of the mind's reflexion, or held up before it, in order to discover its nature and causes. Mere sense can perceive nothing in the most exquisite work of art; suppose a plant, or the body of an animal; but what is painted in the eye, or what might be described on paper. It is the intellect that must perceive in it order and proportion; variety and regularity; design, connection, art, and power; aptitudes, dependencies, correspondencies, and adjustment of parts so as to subserve an end, and compose one perfect whole;* things which can never be represented on a sensible organ, and the

* See Dr. *Cudworth's* Treatise *of eternal and immutable Morality*, Book IV. Chap. 2. where he observes, that the mind perceives, by occasion of outward objects, as much more than is represented to it by sense, as a learned man perceives in the best written book, more than an illiterate person or brute. To the eyes of both the same characters will appear; but the learned man in those characters (to use Dr. *Cudworth's* words) will 'see heaven, earth, sun, and stars; read profound theorems of philosophy or geometry; learn a great deal of knowledge from them, and admire the wisdom of the composer: While to the other nothing appears but black strokes drawn upon white paper. The reason of which is, that the mind of the one is furnished with certain previous inward anticipations, ideas, and instruction, that the other wants.—In the room of this book of *human* composition, let us now (adds he) substitute the book of nature, written all over with the characters and impressions of *divine* wisdom and goodness, but legible only to an intellectual eye; for the sense both of man and brute, there appears nothing else in it, but as in the other, so many inky scrawls; *i.e.* nothing but figures and colours: But to the mind, which hath a participation of the divine wisdom that made it, and being printed all over with the same archetypal seal, upon occasion of those sensible delineations, and taking notice of whatsoever is cognate to it, exerting its own inward activity from thence, will have not only a wonderful scene, and large prospects of other thoughts laid open before it, and variety of knowledge, logical, mathematical, and moral displayed; but also clearly read the divine wisdom and goodness in every page of this great volume, as it were written in large and legible characters.'

ideas of which cannot be passively communicated, or stamped on the mind by the operation of external objects.—Sense cannot perceive any of the modes of thinking beings; these can be discovered only by the mind's survey of itself.

In a word, it appears that *sense* and *understanding* are faculties of the soul totally different: The one being conversant only about *particulars*; the other about *universals*: The one not *discerning*, but *suffering*; the other not *suffering*, but *discerning*; and signifying the soul's *Power* of surveying and examining all things, in order to judge of them; which *Power*, perhaps, can hardly be better defined, than by calling it, in *Plato*'s language, the power in the soul to which belongs κατάληψις τοῦ ὄντος, or the apprehension of TRUTH.*

But, in order farther to shew how little a way mere sense (and let me add *imagination*, a faculty nearly allied to *sense*) can go, and how far we are dependent on our higher reasonable powers for many of our fundamental ideas; I would instance in the following particulars.

The idea of *solidity* has been generally reckoned among the ideas we owe to sense; and yet perhaps it would be difficult to prove, that we ever had actual experience of that *impenetrability* which we include in it, and consider as essential to all bodies. In order to this, we must be sure, that we have, some time or other, made two bodies really touch, and found that they would not penetrate one another: but it is not impossible to account for all the facts we observe, without supposing, in any case, *absolute contact* between bodies. And though we could make the experiment, yet one experiment, or even a million, could not be a sufficient foundation for the[1] absolute assurance we have that no bodies *can* penetrate one another. Not to add, that all that would appear to the senses in such experi-

---

* Most of these observations concerning the difference between sense and knowledge, may be found in *Plato*'s *Theaetetus*; and in the Treatise quoted in the last note.

[1 Ed. 1 adds 'universal and'.]

ments, would be the *conjunction* of two events, not their *necessary connexion*. Are we then to affirm, that there is no idea of *impenetrability*; that two atoms of matter, continuing distinct and without the annihilation of either, *may* occupy the same place; and all the atoms of matter be crowded into the room and bulk of one; and these, for the same reason, into room less and less to infinity, without in the mean while making any diminution of the quantity of matter in the universe? This, indeed, might be the consequence, were it certain that all our ideas, ·on this subject, are derived from *sensation*; and did nothing further than it acquaints us with, appear to *reason*. There are many instances in which two material substances apparently run into one another. It is reason, that, from its own perceptions, determines such to be fallacious appearances, and assures us of the universal and strict necessity of the contrary. The same power that perceives two particles to be *different*, perceives them to be *impenetrable*; for they are as necessarily the one as the other; it being self-evident, that they cannot occupy the same place without losing all difference.

Again, what is meant by the *vis inertiae*, or *inactivity* of matter, is rather a perception of reason, than an idea conveyed to the mind by sense. This property of matter is the foundation of all our reasoning about it: And those who reject it, or who will allow no other source of our knowledge of matter and motion, than *experience*, or the information conveyed to the mind through the senses, would do well to consider, whether the three axioms (or laws of motion) on which Sir *Isaac Newton* founds his philosophy, are not entirely without evidence and meaning.—What is it acquaints us, that every body will for ever continue in the state of rest or motion it is in, unless something produces an alteration of that state; that every alteration of its motion must be proportional to the force impressed, and in the same line of direction; and that its action upon another body, and the action of that other upon it, are always equal and contrary? In other words; what furnishes us with our ideas of resistance and inactivity?—Not *experience*: for never did any man yet see any portion of matter that was void of *gravity*, and many other active powers; or that would not immediately quit its state of rest, and begin to move; and also *lose* or *acquire* motion after the impressing of new force upon it, without any *visible* or *discoverable* cause. Ideas so contradictory to sense cannot be derived from it. They must therefore be ascribed to a higher origin.

But though we should suppose them the objects of constant *experience*, as well as the perceptions of *reason*, yet, as discovered by the former, they must be very different from what they are, as apprehended by the latter. Though, for instance, *experience* and observation taught us always, that the alteration of motion in a body is proportional to the impressed force, and made in the line of direction in which this force acts; yet they can teach us this but very imperfectly: they cannot inform us of it with precision and exactness. They can only shew us, that it is so *nearly*; which, strictly speaking, is the same with not being so at all. The eye of sense is blunt. The conceptions of the imagination are rude and gross, falling *infinitely* short of that certainty, accuracy, universality, and clearness, which belong to *intellectual discernment*.

The idea of *substance*, likewise, is an idea to which our minds are necessarily carried, beyond what mere sensation suggests to us; which can shew us nothing but accidents, sensible qualities, and the outsides of things. 'Tis the understanding that discovers the general distinction between substance and accident; nor can any perception be more unavoidable, than that motion implies *something* that moves; *extension* something *extended*; and, in general, *modes* something *modified*.

The idea of *Duration* is an idea accompanying all our ideas, and included in every notion we can frame of reality and existence. What the observation of the train of thoughts following one another in our minds, or the constant flux of external objects, suggests, is *succession*; an idea which, in common with all others, presupposes that of *duration*; but is as different from it as the idea of motion, or figure. It would, I think, have been much properer to have said, that the reflection on the succession of ideas in our minds is that by which we estimate the *quantity* of duration intervening between two events; than, that we owe to it the idea of duration.

Observations to the same purpose might be made concerning *Space*. This, as well as duration, is included in every reflection we can make on our own existence, or that of other things; it being self-evidently the same with *denying* the existence of a thing, to say, that it exists *no where*. We, and all things, exist in *time* and *place*; and therefore, as self-conscious and intelligent beings, we must have ideas of them.

What may be farther worth observing concerning space and duration, is, that we perceive intuitively their *necessary existence*. The very notion of annihilation[1] being the removal of a thing from space and duration; to suppose these themselves annihilated, would be to suppose their separation from themselves. In the same intuitive manner we perceive they can have no *bounds*, and thus acquire the idea of *Infinity*. The very notion of *bounds* implies them, and therefore cannot be applicable to them, unless they could be bounded by themselves.* These perceptions are plainly the notice the understanding takes of necessary truth; and the same account is to be given of the manner in which we come by our ideas of *infinity* and *necessity* in *time* and *space* (and I may add in abstract truth and power) as, of the manner in which we come by our ideas of any other self-evident reality; of the

* It is also in the same manner we perceive the parts of space to be immoveable and inseparable. *Ut partium temporis ordo est immutabilis, sic etiam ordo partium spatii. Moveantur hae de locis suis, & movebuntur (ut ita dicam) a seipsis.* Newt. Princip.

[1 Eds. 1 and 2 add 'or non-existence'.]

equality, for instance, between the opposite angles of two lines crossing one another, or of the *identity* of any particular object while it continues to exist.

There are other objects which the same faculty, with equal evidence, perceives to be *contingent*; or whose actual existence it sees to be not *necessary*, but only *possible*.

Thus, the Understanding, by employing its attention about different objects, and observing what is or is not *true* of them, acquires the different ideas of necessity, infinity, contingency, possibility, and impossibility.

The next ideas I shall instance in are those of *Power* and *Causation*. Some of the ideas already mentioned imply them; but they require our particular notice and attention. Nothing may, at first sight, seem more obvious, than that one way in which they are conveyed to the mind, is, by observing the various changes that happen about us, and our constant experience of the events arising upon such and such applications of external objects to one another: And yet I am well persuaded, that this experience is alone quite incapable of furnishing us with these ideas.

What we observe by our external senses, is properly no more than that one thing *follows* another,* or the *constant conjunction* of certain events; as of the melting of wax, with placing it in the flame of a candle; and, in general, of such and such alterations in the qualities of bodies, with such and such circumstances of their situation. That one thing is the *cause* of another, or *produces* it, we never see: Nor is it indeed true, in numberless instances where men commonly think they observe it: And were it in no one instance true; I mean, were there no object that contributed, by its own proper

---

* Several observations to this purpose are made by *Malebranche*, who ('tis well known) has maintained, that nothing in nature is ever the proper *cause* or *efficient* of another, but only the *occasion*; the Deity, according to him, being the sole agent in all effects and events. But Mr. *Hume* has more particularly insisted on the observation here made, with a very different view. See his *Phil. Essays*.

force, to the production of any new event; were the *apparent* causes of things universally only their *occasions* or *concomitants*; (which is nearly the real case, according to some philosophical principles;) yet still we should have the same ideas of cause, and effect, and power. Our certainty that every new event requires some cause, depends no more on experience than our certainty of any other the most obvious subject of intuition. In the idea of every *change* is included that of its being an *effect*.

The necessity of a cause of whatever events arise is an essential principle, a primary perception of the understanding; [1]nothing being more palpably absurd than the notion of a change which has been *derived* from nothing,[1] and of which there is no reason to be given; of an existence which has *begun*, but never was *produced*; of a body, for instance, that has *ceased* to move, but has not been *stopped*; or that has *begun* to move, without being *moved*. Nothing can be done to convince a person, who professes to deny this, besides referring him to common sense. If he cannot find there the perception I have mentioned, he is not farther to be argued with, for the subject will not admit of argument; there being nothing clearer than the point itself disputed to be brought to confirm it. And he who will acknowledge that we have such a perception, but will at the same time say that it is to be ascribed to a different power from the understanding, should inform us why the same should not be asserted of all self-evident truth.

It should be observed, that I have not said that we have no idea of power, except from the understanding. Activity and self-determination are as essential to spirit, as the contrary are to matter; and therefore inward consciousness gives us the idea of that particular sort of power which they imply. But the universal source of the idea of power, as we conceive it necessary to the production of all that happens, and of our notions of influence, connexion, aptitude, and dependence in

[1 Ed. 1 reads 'nothing being more palpably absurd and contradictory, than the notion of a change without a *changer*'.]

general, must be the understanding. Some active or passive powers, some *capacity* or *possibility* of *receiving* changes and *producing* them, make an essential part of our ideas of all objects: And these powers differ according to the different natures of the objects, and their different relations to one another. What can *do* nothing; what is fitted to answer no purpose, and has no kind of dependence, aptitude, or power belonging to it, can be nothing real or substantial. Were all things wholly unconnected and loose; and did no one event or object, in any circumstances, imply any thing beyond itself; all the foundations of knowledge would be destroyed. It is, on all hands, confessed, that things appear otherwise to us, and that in numberless instances we are under a necessity of considering them as connected, and of inferring one thing from another. Why should not this be accounted for by a *real* connection between the things themselves? Is it possible, for example, any one should think, that there is no sort of real connection perceiveable by reason, between probity of mind and just actions, or between certain impulses of bodies on one another and an alteration of their motions?

Indeed, the whole meaning of *accounting* for a fact, implies something in the nature of objects and events that includes a connexion between them, or a fitness in certain ways to influence one another. 'Till we can discover this, we are always conscious of somewhat farther to be known. While we only see one thing constantly attending or following another, without perceiving the real dependence and connexion; (as in the case of gravitation, and the sensations attending certain impressions on our bodily organs) we are necessarily dissatisfied, and feel a state of mind very different from that entire acquiescence, which we experience upon considering Sir *Isaac Newton*'s laws of motion, or any other instances and facts, in which we see the necessary connexion and truth.

In conformity to these observations we always find, that

when we have adequate ideas of the natures and properties of any beings or objects, we at the same time perceive their *powers*, and can foretel, independently of experience, what they will produce in given circumstances, and what will follow upon such and such applications of them to one another. Were we thoroughly acquainted with the heart of a man, the turn of his temper, and the make of his mind, we should never want experience to inform us, what he will do, or how far he is to be trusted. In like manner, did we know that inward fabric and constitution of the bodies surrounding us on which all their properties and powers depend, we should know before-hand what would be the result of any experiments we could make with them: Just as from having a complete idea of the real essence of a circle, we can deduce the several properties of it depending on that essence, and determine what will be the proportion of lines and angles drawn, after a certain manner, in it. And, had we a perfect insight into the constitution of nature, the laws that govern it, and the motions, texture, and relations of the several bodies that compose it; the whole chain of future events in it would be laid open to us. *Experience* and observation are only of use, when we are ignorant of the nature of the object, and cannot, in a more perfect, short, and certain way, determine what will be the event in particular cases, and what are the uses of particular objects.* *Instinct* is a still lower and

* The conviction produced by experience is built on the same principle with that which assures us, that there must be a cause of every event, and some account of whatever happens. The frequent repetition of a particular event, as of the falling of a heavy body to the earth, produces an expectation of its happening again in future trials: Because we see intuitively, that there being some reason or cause of this *constancy of event*, it must be derived from a cause regularly and constantly operating in given circumstances. In the very same manner, and upon the same principle, we should conclude, upon observing a particular number on a die thrown very often without one failure, that it would be thrown also in any succeeding trial: And the more frequently and uninterruptedly we knew this had happened, the stronger would be our expectation of its happening again, because the more evident would it be, that either all the sides of the die were marked with the same number, or that some art was used more imperfect means of supplying the same defect of knowledge.

With respect to all the ideas now mentioned, particularly the last, it is worth observing, that were it as difficult to find out their true origin, as it is to deduce them from the common sources explained by writers on these subjects, it would surely be very unreasonable to conclude, that we have no such ideas. And yet this is the very conclusion some have drawn.* If then we indeed have such ideas; and if, besides, they have a foundation in truth, ¹and are ideas of somewhat¹ really existing correspondent to them, what difficulty can there be in granting they may be apprehended by that faculty whose object is truth? But if we have no such ideas, ¹or if they denote nothing real¹ besides the qualities of our own minds; I need not say into what an abyss of scepticism we are plunged.

Let me add, in the last place, that our *abstract ideas* seem most properly to belong to the understanding. They are, undoubtedly, essential to all its operations; every act of judgment implying some abstract or universal idea. Were they formed by the mind in the manner generally represented, it seems unavoidable to conceive that it *has* them at the very

---

in throwing it, or that there was something in the constitution of it that disposed it to turn up that particular side, rather than any other.—However strange it may appear, it is probably true, that what occasions the doubts and difficulties which are raised about this, and some other points of the clearest nature, is their being self-evident; and that what is meant by saying, that it is not reason that informs us there must be some account of whatever comes to pass, and some *established* causes of constant and uniform events, or that order and regularity can proceed only from design, must be, that they are not subjects of *deduction*; that is, that they are so plain, that there is nothing plainer from which they can be *inferred*.

* See Mr. *Hume's Philosophical Essays*, p. 104, &c.

[¹ Eds. 1 and 2 read 'and represent somewhat . . . or if they represent nothing real'. There are other passages, too, in the early editions which suggest that Price at first held a representative theory of perception and knowledge for primary qualities; he evidently abandoned this view later, presumably influenced by Reid. Cf. pp. 38, 53, 94.]

time that it is supposed to be employed in *forming* them. Thus; from any *particular* idea of a triangle, it is said we can frame the *general* one; but does not the very reflexion said to be necessary to this, on a greater or lesser triangle, imply, that the general idea is already in the mind? How else should it know how to go to work, or what to reflect on?—That the universality consists in the *idea*; and not merely in the *name* as used to signify a number of particulars *resembling* that which is the immediate object of reflexion, is plain; because, was the idea to which the name answers and which it recalls into the mind, only a particular one, we could not know to what other ideas to apply it, or what particular objects had the resemblance necessary to bring them within the meaning of the name. A person, in reading over a mathematical demonstration, certainly is conscious that it relates to somewhat else, than just that precise figure presented to him in the diagram. But if he knows not *what* else, of what use can the demonstration be to him? How is his knowledge enlarged by it? Or how shall he know afterwards to what to apply it?— All that can be pictured in the imagination, as well as all that we take notice of by our senses, is indeed particular. And whenever any general notions are present in the mind, the imagination, at the same time, is commonly engaged in representing to itself some of the particulars comprehended under them. But it would be a very strange inference from hence, that we have none but particular ideas. As well almost might we conclude, that we have no other notion of any thing than of its name, because they are so associated in our minds that we cannot separate them; or of the sun, than as a white, bright circle, such as we see in the heavens, because this image is apt to accompany all our thoughts of it.*

* According to Dr. *Cudworth*, abstract ideas are implied in the *cognoscitive power of the mind*; which, he says, *contains in itself virtually (as the future plant or tree is contained in the seed) general notions of all things, which are exerted by it, or unfold and discover themselves as occasions invite and proper circumstances occur.* This, no doubt, many will very freely condemn as whimsical and extravagant. I have, I own,

of our Ideas in general

It is a capital error, into which those persons run who confound the understanding with the imagination, and deny

a different opinion of it; but yet, I should not care to be obliged to defend it. It is what he thought, *Plato* meant by making all *knowledge* to be *Reminiscence*; and in this, as well as other respects, he makes the human mind to resemble the Divine; to which the ideas and comprehension of all things are essential, and not to be derived from any foreign source.

It may at least be said, that thought, knowledge, and understanding, being the originals and causes of all particular *sensibles*, and therefore *before* them and *above* them, cannot be derived from them, or dependent upon them; and that what is thus true of *mind* in general, and particularly of that first and all-disposing mind from which all inferior minds sprung and of which they participate, 'tis reasonable to think true, in a lower degree also of these inferior minds, and of their ideas and knowledge.

The opinion that universal ideas are formed out of particular ones, by separating common from individuating circumstances, this learned writer rejects as very absurd, and founded on a mistake of *Aristotle*'s sense. And the other opinion, that they are only *singular* ideas annexed to a *common* term; or, in other words, names without any meaning; (held formerly by those, who were therefore called *Nominalists*, and of late revived) *he pronounces to be so ridiculously false, as to deserve no confutation.* Vid. Eternal and immutable morality.

'Do we allow it possible for God to signify his will to men; or for men to signify their wants to God?—In both these cases there must be an *identity of ideas.*—Whence then do these COMMON IDENTIC IDEAS come?—Those of men it seems come all from *sensation.* And whence come *God's Ideas?* Not surely from *sensation* too: For this we can hardly venture to affirm without giving to *body* that *notable precedence of being prior to the intellection of even God himself.*—Let them then be *original*; let them be *connate* and essential to the Divine mind.—If this be true, is it not a fortunate event, that Ideas of corporeal rise, and others of mental (things derived from subjects so totally distinct) should so happily coincide in the same wonderful identity?—Had we not better reason thus on so abstruse a subject?—Either all MINDS have their ideas *derived*; or all have them *original*; or *some have them original, and some derived.* If all minds have them *derived*, they must be derived from something *which is itself not mind*, and thus we fall insensibly into a kind of Atheism. If all have them *original, then are all minds Divine*; an hypothesis by far more plausible than the former. But if this be not admitted, then must *one* mind (at least) have *original* ideas, and the rest have them *derived.* Now supposing this last, whence are those minds whose ideas are derived most likely to derive them?—From MIND or from BODY?— From MIND, such as (from the hypothesis) has *original ideas*, or from body which we cannot discover to have any ideas at all?—It is thus we shall be enabled with more assurance to decide, whether we are to admit the doctrine of the Epicurean poet,

CORPOREA NATURA *animum constare,*
Animamque;

reality and possibility to every thing the latter cannot conceive, however clear and certain to the former. The powers of the imagination are very narrow; and were the understanding confined to the same limits, nothing could be known, and the very faculty itself would be annihilated.—Nothing is plainer, than that one of these often perceives where the other is blind; is surrounded with light where the other finds all darkness; and, in numberless instances, knows things to exist of which the other can frame no idea. What is more impossible, than for the imagination to represent to itself matter without colour; but thus is it perceived by the understanding, which pronounces, without doubt or hesitation, that colour is not a property of matter. Points, lines, and surfaces, also, as mathematicians consider them, are entirely intellectual objects, no notice whereof ever entered the mind by the senses, and which are utterly inconceivable to the imagination. Does it follow from hence, that there are no such things? Are we to believe that there can exist no particles of matter smaller than we can imagine to ourselves, or that there is no other kind or degree of equality, than can be

Or trust the *Mantuan Bard* when he sings in Divine numbers.

> *Igneus est ollis vigor, et* CAELESTIS ORIGO
> *Seminibus*—'

See HERMES, or a *Philosophical Inquiry concerning Universal Grammar.* By JAMES HARRIS, Esq; Page 399, &c. second Edition.

'Those Philosophers, (says the same learned writer,) whose ideas of *being* and *knowledge* are derived from *body* and *sensation,* have a short method to explain the nature of TRUTH. 'Tis a *factitious* thing, made by every man for himself, which comes and goes, just as it is remembered or forgot; which in the order of things makes its appearance the last of any, being not only subsequent to *sensible* objects, but even to our *sensations* of them, &c. But there are other reasoners, who must surely have had very different notions; those I mean who represent TRUTH not as the *last,* but the *first* of beings, who call it *immutable, eternal, omnipresent*; attributes that all indicate something more than human, &c. For my own part, when I read the detail about *sensation* and *reflection,* and am taught the process at large how my ideas are all generated, I seem to view the human soul in the light of a crucible, where truths are produced by a kind of logical chemistry.' Ib. p. 403.

judged of by the eye? This has been maintained; and on the same principles we must go on to say, that the mind itself and its operations are just what they appear to every one's reflexion, and that it is not possible for us to mistake in thinking of what we have formerly done or thought, or what we shall hereafter do or think. But surely, that philosophy cannot be very inviting, which thus explodes all independent truth and reality, resolves knowledge into particular modifications of sense and imagination, and makes these the measures of all things.*

The foregoing observations will receive farther light, from attending the following example of the stock of knowledge and new ideas, which the understanding may derive from *one* object of contemplation.

Let us suppose a being to have presented to his observation any particular portion, (a cubic inch, for instance) of matter. If all intelligence is wanting, he will stick for ever in the individual sensible object, and proceed to nothing beyond what it immediately presents to him. But add *intelligence*, and then let us observe what follows.

First, there will appear the ideas of *entity, possibility,* and *actual existence.* Every perception being the perception of something, implies some kind of *reality* distinct from and independent of itself; nothing being more grossly absurd, than to suppose the perception, or apprehension of a thing, to be the same with the thing itself. It would be as good sense to suppose examination, the same with the subject examined; the eye, the same with visible objects; memory, the same with the fact remembered; or desire, the same with the object desired. And yet this absurdity seems to be the

* Man the measure of all things, (πάντων χρημάτων μέτρον ἄνθρωπον— μέτρον ἕκαστον ἡμῶν εἶναι τῶν τε ὄντων καὶ μή.—τὰ φαινόμενα ἑκάστῳ, ταῦτα καὶ εἶναι. *Plat. Theaet.*) was a favourite maxim with *Protagoras*; by which he meant, that every thing *was* that, and no other, which to every one it *seemed* to be; and that there could be nothing true, nothing real, except from the mind's own fancies or perceptions.

foundation of a system of scepticism which has been lately taught the world.

But not to dwell on this. In every idea also is implied the *possibility* of the *actual existence* of its object; nothing being clearer, than that there can be no idea of an *impossibility*, or conception of what *cannot* exist. These are evident intuitions of the intellectual faculty; to which it is unavoidably led by every object of its contemplation.*

We may, next, observe that the *possibility* of the existence of matter, implies the *actual* existence of *space*, without presupposing which, it could not be *possible*, nor could there be any idea of it. And the discernment we have of this *possibility*, as necessary and inseparable from the idea of matter, is nothing else than the discernment of the *necessary actual* existence of space. The idea of space once obtained, we perceive the *Infinity* of it, as before represented.—From the idea of matter, we are in the same manner informed of the *necessary existence* of *Duration*.

Again; by farther examining the above-supposed portion of matter we shall find that we can conceive, without a contradiction, of one part of it as in one place, and another in another, and that consequently it is *divisible*. For the same reason it will appear, that this division may be carried on; and that an intelligent mind can penetrate so far beyond all the boundaries of imagination, as to perceive certainly, that no end can be put to this division, or that matter is *infinitely* divisible.†

From the same source it may farther gain the ideas of *cause*, and *effect*, and *connexion*. For let it conceive of two of the divided parts as moving in a direct line towards one another, and then consider what would follow. As it cannot conceive them to pass through one another, it would unavoidably determine, that *contact* and *impulse* will follow; and, as *neces-*

* See note A in the Appendix.
† See Note B in the Appendix.

sarily connected with these, some *alteration* in the motions of the conflicting bodies.—By what criterion can that person judge of what is true or false; and why will he refuse his assent to any absurdity that can be proposed to him, who finds no difficulty in conceiving, that two bodies may *penetrate* one another; or move towards one another, without meeting and impelling; or impel one another, without any *effect*, or any new modification of motion?

But not only would the mind thus perceive *causation* and *necessary connexion*, but, from any supposed direction and *momentum* of the moving bodies before impulse, it might foretel the precise change of direction and *momentum* that would be produced by it; and go on to determine *a priori*, and without the possibility of error, all the laws and effects of the collision of bodies, of the division and composition of motions, and of the resistance of fluids and centripetal forces, as they have been investigated by natural philosophers.

Nothing need be said to shew, that, from the same foundation laid, the mind would gain the ideas of *number* and *proportion*, and *lines* and *figures*; and might proceed to *arithmetic*, *geometry*, and all the different branches of *mathematics*.—It might, in short, from this single subject of enquiry, learn not only the elements and principles, but the main part of the whole body of science.—Such is the fecundity of reason, and so great is the injury done to it, by confining it within the narrow limits of *sense, fancy,* or *experience.**

* And so false is that maxim of the schools; *Nil est in intellectu quod non prius fuit in sensu.*—One instance of what is here observed, not directly to the purpose, but worth notice by the way, is the case mentioned by Mr. Locke of the man supposed to be born blind, restored to his sight, and required to distinguish between a globe and cube set before him, without feeling them. Mr. Locke has, in my opinion, certainly decided wrong in this instance. That such a person would not be able readily or immediately to say, which was one, or which the other, I acknowledge; but it seems certain, that he might, with the help of a little reflexion. For, instead of the globe or cube, let the objects proposed to him be a *square* and a *rectangular parallelogram* of unequal sides. To both senses the sides of the one would appear equal, and of the other unequal: Where there-

Of the Origin

When I consider these things, I cannot help wondering, that, in enquiring into the origin of our ideas, the understanding, which, though not first in time, is the most important source of our ideas, should have been overlooked. It has, indeed, been always considered, as the source of *knowledge*: But it should have been more attended to, that as the source of knowledge, it is likewise the source of new ideas, and that it cannot be one of these without being the other. The various kinds of *agreement* and *disagreement* between our ideas, which Mr. Locke says, it is its office to discover and trace, are so many new simple ideas, obtained by its discernment. Thus; when it considers the two angles made by a right line, standing in any direction on another, and perceives the *agreement* between them and two right angles; what is this *agreement* besides their *equality*? And is not the idea of this *equality* a new simple idea, acquired by the understanding, wholly different from that of the two angles compared, and denoting self-evident truth?—In much the same manner in other cases, knowledge and intuition suppose somewhat perceived in their objects, denoting simple ideas to which themselves gave rise. —This is true of our ideas of *proportion*; of our ideas of *identity*

fore could be the difficulty of his determining, that what he saw with *equal* sides was the square, and with *unequal* the oblong? Could he possibly suspect, that seeing was so fallacious a sense as to represent as equal, the most unequal things, or as *one*, the greatest *number* of things; and *vice versa*? In the same manner, he might distinguish between a square and a circle, and therefore between a globe and a cube, and, in various other instances, determine how what he *saw*, would *feel*, antecedently to experience.—He might also be enabled to distinguish between the globe and cube; and, in general, between one angle and figure, and another, by considering the different alterations of direction which a body must receive in moving along their *peripherys*, as they appeared to his sight, and comparing this with what he beforehand knew by feeling. Thus might judgment, in such instances, supply the want of experience and sensation; as in numberless other instances, it *corrects* sensation, and is substituted for it.

At the time of the first publication of this work, I did not know that Mr. *Locke*'s decision in this case had been ever questioned. But I have since found that it had been long before particularly confuted by Dr. Smith in his Treatise on *Opticks*.

and *diversity, existence, connexion, cause* and *effect, power, possibility* and *impossibility*; and let me add, though prematurely, of our ideas of moral *right* and *wrong*. The first concerns *quantity*; the last *actions*; the rest *all things*. They comprehend the most considerable part of what we can desire to *know* of things, and are the objects of almost all reasonings and disquisitions.*

* We find *Socrates*, to the like effect, in *Theaetet.* (after observing, that it cannot be any of the powers of sense that compares the perceptions of all the senses, and apprehends the general affections of things, and particularly *identity, number, similitude, dissimilitude, equality, inequality*, to which he adds, καλὸν καὶ αἰσχρόν,) asserting, that this power is *reason*, or the soul acting by itself separately from matter, and independently of any corporeal impressions or passions; and that, consequently, in opposition to *Protagoras, knowledge* is not to be sought for in *sense*, but in this superior part of the soul. Μοι δοκεῖ— οὐδ' εἶναι τοιοῦτον οὐδὲν τούτοις ὄργανον ἴδιον, ἀλλ' αὐτὴ δι' αὑτῆς ἡ ψυχὴ τὰ κοινά μοι φαίνεται περὶ πάντων ἐπισκοπεῖν—ὅμως δὲ τοσοῦτόν γε προβεβήκαμεν, ὥστε μὴ ζητεῖν αὐτὴν (ἐπιστήμην) ἐν αἰσθήσει τὸ παράπαν. ἀλλ' ἐν ἐκείνῳ τῷ ὀνόματι ὅτι ποτ' ἔχει ἡ ψυχὴ ὅταν αὐτὴ καθ' αὑτὴν πραγματεύηται περὶ TA ONTA. 'It seems to me, that for the perception of these things, a different organ or faculty is not appointed; but that the soul itself, and in virtue of its own power, observes these general affections of all things.—So far we have advanced, as to find, that *knowledge* is by no means to be sought in *sense*; but in that power of the soul which it employs when within itself it contemplates and searches out TRUTH.'

'Mark,' says Mr. *Harris*, 'the order of things according to the account of our later metaphysicians. First, comes that huge body, the *sensible world*. Then this and its attributes beget *sensible Ideas*. Then out of sensible Ideas by a kind of lopping and pruning are made ideas *intelligible, whether specific or general*. Thus, should they admit that MIND was coeval with the BODY, yet till the BODY gave it ideas and awakened its dormant powers, it could at best have been nothing more than a *sort of dead capacity*; for INNATE IDEAS it could not possibly have any.—At another time we hear of bodies so exceedingly fine, that their very *exility* makes them susceptible of *sensation* and knowledge, as if they shrunk into intellect by their exquisite subtlety, which rendered them too delicate to be bodies any longer, &c.'

'But the *intellectual* scheme, which never forgets Deity, postpones every thing *corporeal* to the *primary mental Cause*. 'Tis here it looks for the origin of *intelligible* ideas, even of those which exist in human capacities. For though *sensible* objects may be the destined medium to awaken the dormant energies of man's understanding, yet are those energies themselves no more contained in *sense*, than the explosion of a cannon in the spark which gave it fire.' Vid. *Hermes*, Page 392, &c. Second Edition.

In short. As bodily sight discovers to us *visible* objects; so does the understanding, (the eye of the mind, and infinitely more penetrating) discover to us *intelligible* objects; and thus, in a like sense with bodily vision, becomes the inlet of new ideas.—

'Tis obvious, that the ideas now meant presuppose certain subjects of contemplation, [1]of whose natures, connexions, and qualities they are perceptions.[1] And, therefore, the division of all our simple ideas into *original* and *subsequent* ones may not, perhaps, be improper. The former are conveyed to us immediately by our organs of sense, and our reflexion upon ourselves. The latter presuppose other ideas, and arise from the perception of their natures and relations.—But I prefer, on several accounts, the division of our ideas.

First, Into those implying nothing real *without* the mind; that is, nothing real besides its own affections and sensations. And,

Secondly, Into those which denote something distinct from sensation; and imply real and independent existence and truth.

Each of these classes may be again subdivided: The *First*, Into those that denote the immediate effects of impressions on the bodily senses without supposing any previous ideas, as all tastes, smells, colours, &c. and those that arise upon occasion only of other ideas; as the effects in us of considering order, happiness, and the beauties of poetry, sculpture, painting, &c.

The *Second* class may be subdivided into such as denote the real properties of external objects, and the actions and passions of the mind: And those, which I have described as derived immediately from intelligence. By the notices conveyed to the mind through the organs of the body, or its observation of the necessary attendants and concomitants of certain sensations and impressions, it perceives the figure,

[[1] Ed. 1 reads 'whose natures, connexions, and qualities they represent'.]

extension, motion, and other primary qualities of *material* substances. By contemplating itself, it perceives the properties of *spiritual* substances, volition, consciousness, memory, &c. To all these ideas, it is essential that they have invariable archetypes actually existing, to which they are referred and supposed to be conformable.*

After the mind, from whatever possible causes, has been furnished with ideas of any objects, they become themselves objects to our intellective faculty; from whence arises a new set of ideas, which are the perceptions of this faculty. Previously to this, whatever ideas we may be furnished with, nothing is *understood*.† Whatever subjects of knowledge there may be in the mind, nothing is *known*.

* It is a very just observation of Dr. *Hutcheson*'s, that extension, figure, motion, and rest, are more properly ideas *accompanying* the sensations of sight and touch, than sensations of either of these senses. See *Treatise on the Passions*, Sect. 1.

† It would, I believe, be best never to give the name of *ideas* to sensations themselves any more than to actual volitions or desires; but to confine this word to the mind's *conception* or *notice* of any object. An idea would thus always imply something distinct from itself which is its object; and the proper division of our ideas would be, according to their different objects, into those whose objects are matter and spirit and their qualities, the general affections of all things, and necessary truth.

It should be observed that I have all along endeavoured to avoid speaking of an idea as an *image* in the mind of the object we think of. It is difficult not to fall sometimes into language of this kind; but it may be misunderstood. A writer of deep reflexion has charged it with laying the foundation of all modern scepticism. Vid. *An inquiry into the human mind on the principles of common sense*, by Dr. *Reid*.

In short. There are three senses in which the word *idea* has been used, and which it is necessary to distinguish.—It has been used to signify sensation itself. Thus tastes, sounds and colours are often called ideas. But this is using the word very unwarrantably.—It is also used to signify the mind's conception or apprehension of any object. This, I think, is its most just and proper sense.—It is further used to signify the *immediate* object of the mind in thinking. This sense of an idea is derived from the notion that when we think of any object, there is something *immediately* present to the mind which it perceives and contemplates. But what is this?—Shall we call it a *representation* or *image* of the object? This, I think, is improper language.—Must we then deny the existence of an *immediate* object of the mind in thinking? When an abstract truth is contemplated, is not the very object itself present to the mind? When millions of

Of the Origin of our Ideas

Of all the different kinds of ideas now mentioned, brutes seem possess'd chiefly, if not solely, of those derived from the external senses. They think, and will, and remember; but are not capable of making these the objects of a reflex act, so as to obtain ideas of them. They may hear all the sounds in music, and see all the lines and colours in a picture; but they perceive not harmony, or beauty. All the ideas, therefore, founded on inward reflexion, on a previous assemblage and comparison of ideas, and on *intelligence*, seem, in a great measure, peculiar to ourselves.

It is an observation very necessary to be made, before we leave what we are now upon, that the source of ideas on which I have insisted, is different from the power of *reasoning*, and ought, by no means, to be confounded with it. This consists in investigating certain relations between objects, ideas of which must have been previously in the mind: that is; it supposes us already to have the ideas we want to trace; and therefore cannot give rise to new ideas. No mind can be engaged in investigating it knows not what; or in endeavouring to find out any thing concerning an object, of which it has no conception. When, from the view of objects to which they belong self-evidently, we have gained ideas of proportion, identity, connexion, &c. we employ deduction, or reasoning, to trace these amongst other objects, and in other instances, where they cannot be perceived immediately.

Sect. III.

Of the Origin of our Ideas of moral Right and Wrong.

LET us now return to our first enquiry, and apply the foregoing observations to our ideas of *right* and *wrong* in particular.

intellects contemplate the equality of every angle in a semicircle to a right angle, have they not all the same object in view? Is this object *nothing*? See more on this subject in note C in the Appendix.

of Moral Right and Wrong

'Tis a very necessary previous observation, that our ideas of *right* and *wrong* are simple ideas, and must therefore be ascribed to some power of *immediate* perception in the human mind. He that doubts this, need only try to give definitions of them, which shall amount to more than synonymous expressions. Most of the confusion in which the question concerning the foundation of morals has been involved has proceeded from inattention to this remark. There are, undoubtedly, some actions that are *ultimately* approved, and for justifying which no reason can be assigned; as there are some ends, which are *ultimately* desired, and for chusing which no reason can be given. Were not this true; there would be an infinite progression of reasons and ends, and therefore nothing could be at all approved or desired.

Supposing then, that we have a power *immediately* perceiving right and wrong: the point I am now to endeavour to prove, is, that this power is the *Understanding*, agreeably to the assertion at the end of the *first* section. I cannot but flatter myself, that the main obstacle to the acknowledgment of this, has been already removed, by the observations made in the preceding section, to shew that the understanding is a power of immediate perception, which gives rise to new original ideas; nor do I think it possible that there should have been many disputes on this subject had this been properly considered.

But, in order more explicitly and distinctly to evince what I have asserted (in the only way the nature of the question seems capable of) let me,

First, Observe, that it implies no absurdity, but evidently *may* be true. It is undeniable, that many of our ideas are derived from our INTUITION of truth, or the discernment of the natures of things by the understanding. This therefore *may* be the source of our moral ideas. It is at least *possible*, that *right* and *wrong* may denote what we *understand* and *know* concerning certain objects, in like manner with proportion

and disproportion, connexion and repugnancy, contingency
and necessity, and the other ideas before-mentioned.—I will
add, that nothing has been offered which has any tendency
to prove the contrary. All that can appear, from the objections and reasonings of the Author[1] of the *Enquiry into the
original of our ideas of beauty and virtue*, is only, what has been
already observed, and what does not in the least affect the
point in debate: Namely, that the words *right* and *wrong, fit*
and *unfit*, express simple and undefinable ideas. But that the
power perceiving them is properly a *sense* and not *reason*; that
these ideas denote nothing *true* of actions, nothing in the
nature of actions; this, he has left entirely without proof. He
appears, indeed, to have taken for granted, that if virtue and
vice are *immediately* perceived, they must be perceptions of
an *implanted* sense. But no conclusion could have been more
hasty. For will any one take upon him to say, that all powers
of immediate perception must be arbitrary and implanted;
or that there can be no simple ideas denoting any thing
besides the qualities and passions of the mind?—In short.
Whatever some writers have said to the contrary, it is certainly a point not yet decided, that virtue is wholly factitious,
and to be *felt* not *understood*.

As there are some propositions, which, when attended to,
necessarily determine all minds to *believe* them: And as
(which will be shewn hereafter) there are some ends, whose
natures are such, that, when perceived, all beings immediately and necessarily *desire* them: So is it very credible,
that, in like manner, there are some actions whose natures
are such, that, when observed, all rational beings immediately
and necessarily *approve* them.

I do not at all care what follows from Mr. *Hume*'s assertion,
that all our ideas are either *impressions, or *copies of impressions*;
or from Mr. *Locke*'s assertion that they are all *deducible from*

* See Mr. *Hume*'s *Treatise of Human Nature*, and *Philosophical Essays*.
[1 Hutcheson.]

42

SENSATION *and* REFLEXION.—The first of these assertions is, I think, destitute of all proof; supposes, when applied in this as well as many other cases, the point in question; and, when pursued to its consequences, ends in the destruction of all truth and the subversion of our intellectual faculties.—The other wants much explication to render it consistent with any tolerable account of the original of our moral ideas: Nor does there seem to be any thing necessary to convince a person, that all our ideas are not deducible from sensation and reflexion, except taken in a very large and comprehensive sense, besides considering how Mr. *Locke* derives from them our *moral ideas.* He places them among our ideas of relations, and represents *rectitude* as signifying the conformity of actions to some rules or laws; which rules or laws, he says, are either *the will of God,* the *decrees of the magistrate, or the fashion of the country*: From whence it follows, that it is an absurdity to apply *rectitude* to rules and laws themselves; to suppose the *divine* will to be directed by it; or to consider it as *itself* a rule and law. But, it is undoubted, that this great man would have detested these consequences; and, indeed, it is sufficiently evident, that he was strangely embarrassed in his notions on this, as well as some other subjects. But,

Secondly, I know of no better way of determining this point, than by referring those who doubt about it to common sense, and putting them upon considering the nature of their own perceptions.—Could we suppose a person, who, when he perceived an external object, was at a loss to determine whether he perceived it by means of his organs of sight or touch; what better method could be taken to satisfy him? There is no possibility of doubting in any such cases. And it seems not more difficult to determine in the present case.

Were the question; what that perception is, which we have of number, diversity, causation or proportion; and whether our ideas of them signify truth and reality perceived by the understanding, or impressions made by the objects to which we ascribe them, on our minds; were, I say, this the question would it not be sufficient to appeal to every man's consciousness?—These perceptions seem to me to have no greater pretence to be denominated perceptions of the understanding than *right* and *wrong*.

It is true, some impressions of pleasure or pain, satisfaction or disgust, generally attend our perceptions of virtue and vice. But these are merely their effects and concomitants, and not the perceptions themselves, which ought no more to be confounded with them, than a particular truth (like that for which *Pythagoras* offered a Hecatomb) ought to be confounded with the pleasure that may attend the discovery of it. Some emotion or other accompanies, perhaps, all our perceptions; but more remarkably our perceptions of right and wrong. And this, as will be again observed in the next chapter, is what has led to the mistake of making them to signify nothing but impressions, which error some have extended to all objects of knowledge; and thus have been led into an extravagant and monstrous scepticism.

But to return; let any one compare the ideas arising from our *powers of sensation*, with those arising from our *intuition of the natures of things*, and enquire which of them his ideas of right and wrong most resemble. On the issue of such a comparison may we safely rest this question. It is scarcely conceiveable that any one can impartially attend to the nature of his own perceptions, and determine that, when he thinks gratitude or beneficence to be *right*, he perceives nothing *true* of them, and *understands* nothing, but only receives an impression from a *sense*. Was it possible for a person to question, whether his idea of *equality* was gained from sense or intelligence; he might soon be convinced, by considering, whether he is not sure, that certain lines or figures are *really* equal, and that their equality must be perceived by all minds, as soon as the objects themselves are perceived.—In the same manner may we satisfy ourselves concerning the origin of the idea of

44

ight: For have we not a like consciousness, that we discern he one, as well as the other, *in* certain objects? Upon what possible grounds can we pronounce the one to be *sense*, and he other *reason*? Would not a Being purely intelligent, having happiness within his reach, *approve* of securing it for himself? Would not he *think* this right; and would it not *be* right? When we contemplate the happiness of a species, or of a world, and pronounce concerning the actions of reasonable beings which promote it, that they are *right*; is this judging erroneously? Or is it no determination of judgment at all, but a species of mental taste?—Are not such actions *really ight*? Or is every apprehension of rectitude in them false and delusive, just as the like apprehension is concerning the effects of external and internal sensation, when taken to belong to the causes producing them?

It seems beyond contradiction certain, that every being must *desire* happiness for himself; and can those natures of things, from which the *desire* of happiness and *aversion* to misery necessarily arise, leave, at the same time, a rational nature totally indifferent as to any *approbation* of actions procuring the one, or preventing the other? Is there nothing that any *understanding* can perceive to be amiss in a creature's bringing upon himself, or others, calamities and ruin? Is there nothing truly wrong in the absolute and eternal misery of an innocent being?—'It *appears* wrong to us.'—And what reason can you have for doubting, whether it appears what *it is*?—Should a being, after being flattered with hopes of bliss, and having his expectations raised by encouragements and promises, find himself, without reason, plunged into irretrievable torments; would he not *justly* complain? Would he want a *sense* to cause the idea of *wrong* to arise in his mind?—Can goodness, gratitude, and veracity, appear to any mind under the same characters, with cruelty, ingratitude, and treachery?—Darkness may as soon appear to be light.

It would, I doubt, be to little purpose to plead further here,

the natural and universal apprehensions of mankind, that ou
ideas of right and wrong belong to the understanding, an
denote real characters of actions; because it will be easy t
reply, that they have a like opinion of the *sensible qualities* c
bodies; and that nothing is more common than for men t
mistake their own sensations for the properties of the object
producing them, or to apply to the object itself, what the
find always accompanying it, whenever observed. Let i
therefore be observed,

Thirdly, That if right and wrong denote effects of sensation
it must imply the greatest absurdity to suppose them appl
cable to actions: That is; the ideas of *right* and *wrong* and c
action, must in this case be incompatible; as much so, as th
idea of pleasure and a regular form, or of pain and th
collisions of bodies.—All sensations, as such, are modes c
consciousness, or feelings of a sentient being, which must b
of a nature totally different from the particular causes whic
produce them. A *coloured body*, if we speak accurately, is th
same absurdity with a *square sound*. We need no experiment
to prove that heat, cold, colours, tastes, &c. are not rea
qualities of bodies; because the ideas of matter and of thes
qualities, are incompatible.*—But is there indeed any suc

* It is chiefly from hence; from our own ideas, and the reason of the thing
from the *unintelligibleness* of colour and other secondary qualities, when cor
sidered as modifications of matter, or from the repugnancy to coexistence i
the same subject which we perceive between these qualities and solid extension
that we conclude they are not properties of matter, but different effects pre
duced in our minds by the action of matter upon them. Most of the fact
alledged in confirmation of this, are in themselves no sufficient proofs of i
because equally applicable, as may be easily seen, to the real and primar
qualities of matter.—It is a remark, I know not how to forbear adding; tha
sensible qualities being universally allowed not to be qualities inherent i
matter; it is strange, that any persons should not allow the same to be equall
evident with respect to thought and consciousness. Is the notion of *conscious
thinking, reasonable matter*, less absurd than that of *white* or *red matter*? Is ther
less repugnancy between the ideas? Is it less plain, that figure, solidity, magni
tude, motion, and juxta position of parts are not, and cannot be desire, volition
and judgment; than it is that they cannot be cold or sour, or that any one thing
is not and cannot be another?

ncompatibility between *actions* and *right*? Or any such
absurdity in affirming the one of the other?—Are the ideas
of them as different as the idea of a sensation, and its cause?

On the contrary; the more we enquire, the more indisputable, I imagine, it will appear to us, that we express
necessary truth, when we say of some actions, they are right;
and of others, they are wrong. Some of the most careful
enquirers think thus, and find it out of their power not to be
persuaded that these are real distinctions belonging to the
natures of actions. Can it be so difficult, to distinguish
between the ideas of sensibility and reason; between the
intuitions of truth and the *passions of the mind*? Is that a scheme
of morals we can be very fond of, which makes our perceptions of moral good and evil in actions and manners, to be
all vision and fancy? Who can help seeing, that right and
wrong are as absolutely unintelligible, and void of sense and
meaning, when supposed to signify nothing true of actions,
no essential, inherent difference between them; as the perceptions of the external and internal senses are, when thought
to be properties of the objects that produce them?

How strange would it be to maintain, that there is no
possibility of *mistaking* with respect to right and wrong;* that
the apprehensions of all beings, on this subject, are alike just,
since all sensation must be alike *true* sensation?—Is there a
greater absurdity, than to suppose, that the *moral rectitude* of
an action is nothing absolute and unvarying; but capable,
like all the modifications of pleasure and pain, of being
intended and remitted, of increasing and lessening, of rising
and sinking with the force and liveliness of our feelings?
Would it be less ridiculous to suppose this of the relations
between given quantities, of the equality of numbers, or the
figure of bodies?

In the last place; let it be considered, that all actions,

* It will be observed presently, that the antient sceptics asserted universally
there could be no such thing as *error*; and for the very reason here assigned.

undoubtedly, have a *nature*. That is, *some character* certainl belongs to them, and somewhat there is to be *truly* affirmee of them. This may be, that some of them are right, other wrong. But if this is not allowed; if no actions are, *in them selves*, either right or wrong, or any thing of a moral an obligatory nature, which can be an object to the under standing; it follows, that, in themselves, they *are* all indiffer ent. This is what is essentially true of them, and this is wha all understandings, that perceive right, must perceive then to be. But are we not conscious, that we perceive the con trary? And have we not as much reason to believe the con trary, as to believe or trust at all our own discernment?

In other words; every thing having a *nature* or *essence*, from whence such and such truths concerning it necessarily result and which it is the proper province of the understanding to perceive; it follows, that nothing whatever can be exempted from its inspection and sentence, and that of every thought sentiment, and subject, it is the natural and ultimate judge *Actions*, therefore, *ends* and *events* are within its province. O these, as well as all other objects, it belongs to it to judge.— What is this judgment?—One would think it impossible for any person, without some hesitation and reluctance, to reply; that the judgment he forms of them is this; that they are all essentially *indifferent*, and that there is no one thing fitter to be done than another. If this is judging truly; how obvious is it to infer, that it signifies not what we do; and that the determination to think otherwise, is an imposition upon rational creatures? Why then should they not labour to suppress in themselves this determination, and to extirpate from their natures all the delusive ideas of morality, worth, and virtue? What though the ruin of the world should follow?—There would be nothing *really* wrong in this.

A rational agent void of all moral judgment, incapable of perceiving a difference, in respect of fitness and unfitness to be performed, between actions, and acting from blind pro-ensions without any sentiments concerning what he does, is not possible to be imagined. And, do what we will, we shall find it out of our power, in earnest to persuade ourselves, that reason can have no concern in judging of and directing our conduct; or to exclude from our minds all notions of right and wrong in actions.

But what deserves particular consideration here is this. If all actions and all dispositions of beings are in *themselves indifferent*, the all-perfect understanding of the Deity, without doubt, perceives this; and therefore he cannot *approve*, or *disapprove* of any of his own actions, or of the actions of his creatures:[1] The end he pursues, and the manner in which he treats his creatures must appear to him what it *is—indifferent*. What foundation then is left for his moral perfections? How can we conceive him to pursue universal happiness as his end, when, at the same time, we suppose nothing *in* the nature of that end to engage the choice of any being? Is it no diminution of his perfect character, to suppose him guided by mere unintelligent inclination, without any direction from reason, or any *moral approbation*?

In short; it seems sufficient to overthrow any scheme, that such consequences, as the following, should arise from it:—That no one being can judge one end to be better than another, or believe a real moral difference between actions; without giving his assent to an impossibility; without mistaking the *affections of his own mind* for *truth*, and *sensation* for *knowledge*.—That there being nothing intrinsically proper or improper, just or unjust; there is nothing *obligatory*;* but all

---

* Moral right and wrong, and moral obligation or duty, must remain, or vanish together. They necessarily accompany one another, and make but as it were one idea. As far as the former are fictitious and imaginary, the latter must be so too. This connexion or coincidence between moral rectitude and obligation, will be at large considered hereafter.
[1 Ed. 2, following a similar addition in ed. 1, adds: 'It being a contradiction to approve or disapprove, where it is known that there is nothing in itself right or wrong.' See Price's definition of approval on pp. 104–5.]

beings enjoy, from the reasons of things and the nature of actions, liberty to act as they will.

The following important corollary arises from these arguments:

That morality is *eternal and immutable*.

Right and wrong, it appears, denote what actions *are*. Now whatever any thing *is*, that it is, not by will, or decree, or power, but by *nature and necessity*. Whatever a triangle or circle is, that it is unchangeably and eternally. It depends upon no will or power, whether the three angles of a triangle and two right ones shall be *equal*; whether the periphery of a circle and its diameter shall be *incommensurable*; or whether matter shall be *divisible, moveable, passive*, and *inert*. Every object of the understanding has an indivisible and invariable essence; from whence arise its properties, and numberless truths concerning it. Omnipotence does not consist in a power to alter the nature of things, and to destroy necessary truth (for this is contradictory, and would infer the destruction of all wisdom, and knowledge) but in an absolute command over all *particular, external* existences, to create or destroy them, or produce any possible changes among them. —The natures of things then being immutable; whatever we suppose the natures of actions to be, they must be immutably. If they are indifferent, this indifference is itself immutable, and there neither is nor can be any one thing that, *in reality*, we *ought* to do rather than another. The same is to be said of right and wrong, of moral good and evil, as far as they express *real characters* of actions. They must immutably and necessarily belong to those actions of which they are *truly* affirmed.

No will, therefore, can render *any thing* good and obligatory, which was not so antecedently, and from eternity; or any action right, that is not so in itself; meaning by *action*, not the bare external effect produced, but the ultimate principle of conduct, or the determination of a reasonable being, considered as arising from the perception of some motives and reasons and intended for some end. According to this sense of the word *action*, whenever the principle from which we act is different, the action is different, though the external effects produced, may be the same. If we attend to this, the meaning and truth of what I have just observed, will be easily seen.— Put the case of any action, the performance of which is *indifferent*, or attended with no circumstances of the agent that render it better or fitter to be done than omitted. Is it not plain that, *while all things continue the same*, it is as impossible for any will or power to make acting obligatory here, as it is for them to make two equal things unequal without producing any change in either? It is true, the doing of any indifferent thing may become obligatory, in consequence of a command from a being possessed of rightful authority over us: But it is obvious, that in this case, the command produces a change in the circumstances of the agent, and that what, in consequence of it, becomes obligatory, is not the same with what *before* was indifferent. The external effect, that is, the *matter of the action* is indeed the same; but nothing is plainer, than that actions in this sense the same, may in a moral view be totally different according to the ends aimed at by them, and the principles of morality under which they fall.

When an action, otherwise indifferent, becomes obligatory, by being made the subject of a *promise*; we are not to imagine, that our own will or breath alters the nature of things by making what is indifferent not so. But what was indifferent *before* the promise is still so; and it cannot be supposed, that, *after* the promise, it becomes obligatory, without a contradiction. All that the promise does, is, to alter the connexion of a particular effect; or to cause that to be an *instance* [1]of right conduct[1] which was not so before. There are no effects producible by us, which may not, in this manner, fall

[1 Eds. 1 and 2 read 'of a general and eternal duty'.]

under different principles of morality; acquire connexion sometimes with happiness, and sometimes with misery; an thus stand in different relations to the eternal rules of duty

The objection, therefore, to what is here asserted, take from the effects of positive laws and promises, has no weigh It appears, that when an obligation to particular indifferen actions arises from the command of the Deity, or positiv laws; it is by no means to be inferred from hence, tha obligation is the creature of will, or that the nature of wha is indifferent is changed: nothing then becoming obligatory which was not so from eternity; that is, *obeying the divine wil and just authority.* And had there been nothing right in this had there been no reason from the natures of things fo obeying God's will; it is certain, it could have induced n obligation, nor at all influenced an intellectual nature a such.—Will and laws signify nothing, abstracted from some thing previous to them, in the character of the law-giver an the relations of beings to one another, to give them force an render disobedience a crime. If mere will ever obliged, wha reason can be given, why the will of one being should oblige and of another not; why it should not oblige alike to ever thing it requires; and why there should be any difference between *power* and *authority*? It is truth and reason, then that, in all cases, oblige, and not mere will. So far, we see, i it from being possible, that any will or laws should creat right; that they can have no effect, but in virtue of natura and antecedent right.

Thus, then, is morality fixed on an immoveable *basis*, and appears not to be, in any sense, *factitious*; or the *arbitrary pro duction* of any power human or divine; but *equally everlasting* and *necessary* with all *truth* and *reason*. And this we find to be as evident, as that right and wrong signify a *reality** in what is so denominated.

* Οὐ γὰρ ἔχω ἔγωγε οὐδὲν οὕτω μοι ἐναργὲς ὄν, ὡς τοῦτο, τὸ *EINAI* ὡς οἷόν τε μάλιστα καλόν τε καὶ ἀγαθόν. *Plat.* in *Phaed.* Sect. 18.

of Moral Right and Wrong

I shall conclude this chapter, with observing; that the opinion of those, who maintain that our ideas of morality are derived from sense, is far from being entirely modern. There were among the antients, philosophers, (*Protagoras*, in particular, and his followers) who entertained a like opinion; but extended it much further; that is, to *all science*; denied all absolute and immutable truth; and asserted every thing to be relative to perception. And indeed it seems not a very unnatural transition, from denying absolute *moral* truth, to denying *all truth*; from making right and wrong, just and unjust, dependent on perception, to asserting the same of whatever we commonly rank among the objects of the understanding. Why may not he who rejects the reality of rightness in beneficence, and of wrong in producing needless misery, be led, by the same steps, to deny the certainty of other self-evident principles? Why may he not as well deny the reality, for example, of *straitness* in a line drawn the shortest way between two points; or of aptness and unaptness, of connexion and proportion between certain objects and quantities? He that distrusts his reason in the one case, why should he not also in the other? He that refers the former perceptions to a sense; why should he not, with the before-mentioned philosopher, make *all knowledge to be sense*? —Consequences much worse cannot follow from making all the principles of knowledge arbitrary and factitious, than from making morality so; from supposing all we perceive of the natures and relations of things, to denote modes of sensation in our minds,[1] than from supposing this of the objects of our moral discernment. If the one overthrows *all* truth, the other overthrows that *part* of truth which is most important and interesting. If the one destroys the necessary wisdom and intelligence of the Deity (the very idea of a mind and of knowledge, being impossible, if there is nothing permanent

[1 Ed. 1 adds 'and not resemblances of any distinct and independent reality in things'. So ed. 2 also, but omitting 'resemblances of' and 'in things'.]

in the nature of things, nothing *necessarily* true, and therefore nothing to be *known*) the other equally destroys his moral perfections.*

One argument which, it seems, *Protagoras* made great use of in maintaining his opinions, was, that colours, tastes, and sounds, and the other sensible qualities of bodies exist only when perceived, and therefore are not qualities inherent in bodies, but sensations ever-varying, begot between the sensible object and organ, and produced by the action of the one on the other; the same object, as he reasoned, often appearing to have different qualities to different persons; and no two persons having exactly the same ideas of any one sensible quality of any object.† From hence, and from a notion, not very consistent with it, that consciousness and understanding were to be resolved into matter and motion; he concluded, that all things are in a perpetual flux;‡ and that nothing is

---

* Let us suppose an enquiry, similar to that which is the subject of this chapter, concerning that *necessity* which is meant when we say, 'that it is *necessary* there should be a cause of whatever begins to exist.' When we speak thus, do we only express a *feeling* of *sense*, or some *modification* of our own thoughts, and not a *judgment* of the *understanding*? Is it indeed true that there is no such *necessity* in the natures of things?—If these questions are to be answered in the affirmative, there is an end of all knowledge, and we are plunged into the abyss of atheism.—Modern scepticism has not stuck at this; and it is no inconsiderable apology for it, that in doing this, it has only extended further what some writers of the best character have contended for, with respect to *moral rectitude*.—While, however, men retain common sense, it cannot be possible for such opinions to gain ground. The faculty by which we distinguish between self-evident truth and palpable contradiction may be puzzled by the refinements and subtleties of men of genius, but it must for ever preserve its authority, nor can any real and lasting conviction be produced in opposition to it.

† This opinion was rejected by *Plato* and *Aristotle*; its being abused to scepticism and the taking away the natural discrimination of good and evil, begetting in the former, as Dr. *Cudworth* says, a prejudice against it. Vid. *Eternal and immutable Morality*, Chap. IV. 21.

‡ Ἐγὼ ἐρῶ, καὶ μάλ' οὐ φαῦλον λόγον, &c. 'I will say, (nor will it be said amiss) that nothing is any thing in itself; and that we never justly say of any object, that it *is* this or that. If we call an object great, it appears also little; if heavy, it is also light; and so of all objects; nothing being any one thing more than another. But all things, of which we wrongly say, that they *are*, spring out of motion, and the mixture and composition of things with one another;

true or false (any more than sweet or sour) in itself, but relatively to the perceiving mind. That he applied this particularly to moral good and evil, appears from several passages in *Plato*'s* *Theætetus*, where these notions of *Protagoras*'s are at large explained and confuted.—He that would have a fuller view of what is here said, may consult this Dialogue of *Plato*'s or Dr. *Cudworth*'s *Treatise* of *Immutable and Eternal Morality*.

Such is the agreement, in this instance, between the opinions of modern times and those of *Socrates*'s time. Such the tendency of the account of morality I have opposed; and it is astonishing how far some, who have embraced it, have extended it to our other perceptions, and revived, perhaps even exceeded, the wildest doctrines of ancient scepticism. The *primary* as well as *secondary* qualities of matter, cause,

---

for nothing ever absolutely *is*, but is always generated.' ἔστι μὲν γὰρ οὐδέ ποτ' οὐδέν. ἀεὶ γίγνεται. Vid. *Plat.* in *Theaet.*—οἷα ἕκαστα ἐμοὶ φαίνεται, τοιαῦτα μὲν ἔστιν ἐμοί. οἷα δὲ σοί, τοιαῦτα αὖ σοί. 'What a thing *appears* to me, that it is *to me*.' 'What it appears to you, that it is to *you*.'—αἴσθησις ἄρα τοῦ ὄντος αἰεί ἐστιν καὶ ἀψευδὴς ὡς ἐπιστήμη οὖσα. 'The object of sense is always truth, not can it deceive; for it is knowledge.' *Ibid.*—It was a controversy much agitated among the antient philosophers; whether all things stood still, or whether all things flowed. *Parmenides* held the former; *Heraclitus*, and, after him, *Protagoras* and others, the latter. The meaning of this controversy (in part at least) was, whether there was or was not any thing permanent and necessary in the natures of things; or, 'as *Aristotle* declares (*Arist. Met.* Lib. iii. cap. 5.) whether there were any other objects of the mind, besides singular sensibles, that were immutable; and, consequently, whether there was any such thing as proper science.' The former denied this, and asserted φερομένην οὐσίαν, a moveable essence. 'The *Parmenideans* and *Pythagoreans*, on the contrary, maintained, that, besides singular sensibles, there were other objects of the mind universal, eternal, and immutable, which they called the intelligible ideas, all originally contained in one Archetypal mind or understanding.' Vid. *Intellectual System* by Dr. *Cudworth*, p. 387. 2d. Edit.

◆ * Λέγε τοίνυν πάλιν, εἴ σοι ἀρέσκει τὸ μήτι ΕΙΝΑΙ ἀλλὰ ΓΙΓΝΕΣΘΑΙ ἀεὶ ἀγαθὸν καὶ καλόν. *Soc.* Tell me, is it your opinion, that nothing ever *is*, but is *made* good and virtuous? ἀλλ' ἐκεῖ οὐ λέγω, ἐν τοῖς δικαίοις καὶ ἀδίκοις, καὶ ὁσίοις καὶ ἀνοσίοις, ἐθέλουσιν ἰσχυρίζεσθαι ὡς οὐκ ἔστι φύσει αὐτῶν οὐδὲν οὐσίαν ἑαυτοῦ ἔχον, ἀλλὰ τὸ κοινῇ δόξαν τοῦτο γίγνεται ἀληθές, τότε ὅταν δόξῃ, καὶ ὅσον ἂν δοκῇ χρόνον, &c. *i.e.* They more especially asserted, that nothing is just or unjust, holy or unholy, naturally and essentially, but relatively to opinion or sense.

effect, connexion, extension, duration, identity, and almost all about which knowledge is conversant, have been represented as only qualities of our minds: the idea confounded with its object: The *esse* and the *percipi* maintained to be *universally* the same; and the impossibility asserted of every thing except *impressions*. Thus, is there neither matter, nor morality, nor Deity, nor any kind of external existence left. All our discoveries and boasted knowledge vanish, and the whole universe is reduced into a creature of fancy. Every sentiment of every being is equally just. Nothing being present to our minds besides our own ideas, there can be no conception of any thing distinct from them; no beings but* ourselves; no distinction between past and future time; no possibility of remembering wrong, or foreseeing wrong. He is the wisest man, who has the most fertile imagination, and whose mind is stored with the greatest number of notions, their conformity to the truth of things being incapable of being questioned.—When speculative men have proceeded to these lengths, or avow principles directly implying them, it becomes high time to leave them to themselves.†

* Nor ourselves neither; for to *exist*, and to *be perceived*, being the same, perceptions themselves can have no existence, unless there can be perceptions of perceptions *in infinitum*. Besides, by this system, the only idea of what we call *ourselves* is the contradictory and monstrous one of a series of successive and separable perceptions, not one of which *continues*, that is, *exists* at all; and without any substance that perceives.—It might be further remarked; that the very scheme that takes away the distinction between past and future, and admits of no real existence independent of perception, is itself derived from and founded upon the supposition of the contrary; I mean, the supposition that there have been *past* impressions, of which all ideas are copies; and that certain objects have been observed to have been conjoined in *past* instances, and by this means produced that customary transition of the imagination from one of them to the other, in which *reasoning* is said to consist. It would have been abusing the reader to mention these extravagancies, had not some of them been started by Bishop *Berkeley*; and his principles adopted and pursued to a system of scepticism, that plainly includes them all, by another writer of the greatest talents, to whom I have often had occasion to refer. See *Treatise of Human Nature*, and *Philosophical Essays*, by Mr. *Hume*.

† See Note D Appendix.

CHAP. II.

Of our Ideas of the Beauty and Deformity of Actions.

HAVING considered our ideas of *right* and *wrong*; I come now to consider our ideas of *beauty*, and its contrary.

This is the *second* kind of sentiment, or perception, with respect to actions, which I noticed at the beginning of the preceding chapter. Little need be said to shew, that it is different from the former. We are plainly conscious of more than the bare discernment of right and wrong, or the cool judgment of reason concerning the natures of actions. We often say of some actions, not only that they are *right*, but that they are *amiable*; and of others, not only that they are *wrong*, but *odious* and *shocking*. Every one must see, that these epithets denote the *delight*; or on the contrary, the *horror* and *detestation felt* by ourselves; and, consequently, signify not any real qualities or characters of actions, but the *effects in us*, or the particular pleasure and pain, attending the consideration of them.

'What then is the true account of these perceptions? Must they not arise entirely from an arbitrary structure of our minds, by which certain objects, when observed, are rendered the occasions of certain sensations and affections? And therefore, in this instance, are we not under a necessity of recurring to a *sense*? Can there be any connexion, except such as arises from implanted principles, between any perceptions and particular modifications of pleasure and pain in the perceiving mind?'

I answer; That there *may* be such a connexion; and that I think, there *is* such a connexion in many instances; and particularly in this instance.

Why or how the impressions made by *external objects* on our bodily organs, produce the sensations constantly attending them, it is not possible for us to discover. The same is true of the sensations and affections of mind produced by the objects of many of the *internal senses*. In such instances, we can conceive of no connexion between the effects in us and their apparent causes; and the only account we can give is, that 'such is our frame; so God has seen fit to adapt our faculties and particular objects to one another.' But this is far from being true *universally*. There are objects which have a *natural aptitude* to please or displease our minds. And thus in the *spiritual* world, the case is the same, as in the *corporeal*; where, though there are events which we cannot explain, and numberless causes and effects of which, for want of being acquainted with the inward structure and constitution of bodies, we know no more than their existence: There are also causes the manner of whose operation we understand; and events, between which we discern a necessary connexion.

One account, therefore, of the sentiments we are examining, is; 'that such are the *natures* of certain actions, that, when perceived, there must result certain emotions and affections.'

That there are objects which have a natural aptitude to please or offend, and between which and the contemplating mind there is a necessary congruity or incongruity, seems to me unquestionable.—For, what shall we say of supreme and complete excellence? Is what we mean by this only a particular kind of sensation; or, if something real and objective, can it be contemplated without emotion? Must there be the aid of a sense to make the character of the *Deity* appear *amiable*; or, would pure and abstract reason be indifferent to it? Is there any thing more necessary to cause it to be loved and admired besides *knowing* it? The more it is known, and the better it is understood, must it not the more delight?

Again, a reasonable being, void of all superadded determinations or senses, who knows what order and happiness are, would, I think, unavoidably, receive *pleasure* from the survey of an universe where perfect order prevailed; and the contrary prospect of universal confusion and misery would *ffend* him.

But his own happiness and misery are, undeniably, objects, which no being can contemplate with indifference. Of which in the next chapter.

What is thus true, in these and other instances, is particularly evident in the present case. It is not indeed plainer, that, in any instances, there are correspondencies and connexions of things among themselves; or that one motion has a tendency to produce another; than it is, that virtue is naturally adapted to *please* every observing mind; and vice the contrary.—I cannot perceive an action to be right, without *approving* it; or *approve* it, without being conscious of some degree of *satisfaction* and complacency. I cannot perceive an action to be wrong, without *disapproving* it; or *disapprove* it, without being *displeased* with it. Right actions then, as such, must be *grateful*, and wrong ones *ungrateful* to us. The one must appear *amiable*, and the other *unamiable* and *base*.— Goodness, faithfulness, justice, and gratitude, on the one hand; and cruelty, treachery, injustice, and ingratitude on the other, cannot appear alike to any mind. On all who perceive and compare them, they must have opposite effects. The *first* must be liked, the *last* disliked; the *first* must be loved, the *last* hated. Nor is it possible that these sentiments should be reversed. To *behold* virtue, is to *admire* it. To behold it in its intrinsic and complete importance, dignity, and excellence, is to possess supreme affection for it. On the contrary; to *perceive vice*, is the very same as to *blame and condemn*. To perceive it in its naked form and malignity, is to dread and detest it above all things.

Self-approbation and self-reproach are the chief sources of private happiness and misery. These are connected with, and entirely dependent upon, our consciousness of practising or not practising virtue. Self-approbation cannot be separated from the remembrance of having done *well*; nor self-condemnation from the remembrance of having done *wrong*. Nothing can be of more consequence to a being, who i obliged to be perpetually reflecting on himself, than to be a peace with himself, and able to bear the survey of his actions Virtue and vice, therefore, from the *natures of things*, are the immediate and principal, and the most constant and intimate causes of private happiness and misery.

It should be remembered here, that the effects produced by the consideration of virtue and vice, must be different in different beings, and in the same being in different circumstances of his existence. The pleasure received from virtuous actions, (that is the sense of *beauty* in them) must be varied by numberless causes, both in the circumstances of the actions, and in the understandings and conditions of the percipient beings. Pain or sickness; the influence of implanted byasses and propensions; many different dispositions of the temper, and associated ideas, may lessen or prevent the effects that would otherwise follow the perception of moral good and evil: But still the essential tendencies continue the same; and to every rational mind properly disposed, morally good actions must for ever be *acceptable*, and can never *of themselves* offend; and morally evil actions must for ever be *disagreeable*, and can never *of themselves* please.—The effects produced by all causes depend on the particular circumstances in which they operate, and must differ as these differ. And, agreeably to this general observation, the same objects of moral discernment, whatever may be their natural aptitude, must affect reasonable beings differently, according to the different dispositions they are in, and the different clearness of their perceptions.

These observations seem to lead to an idea of the happiness of the Deity, that may deserve to be just mentioned. Were the foundations of happiness of a nature entirely factitious, it would be impossible to conceive, how that Being, who is himself the cause of all things, and can derive nothing from any foreign source, could be happy. But it has been shewn, that there are objects of contemplation naturally productive of delight; and perfections or qualities implying blessedness. A *reasonable* being is capable of greater happiness than a being merely *sensitive*. He has, *in himself*, the sources of superior enjoyment. And as much more wisdom and reason as any being possesses; so much the higher bliss he is capable of. There is, therefore, in the natures of things, a stable and permanent foundation of happiness. And that of the Deity may result necessarily and wholly from what he *is*;* from his possessing in himself all truth, all good, all perfection, all that is *beatifying*.—But this is a subject much above us; and I suspect, that in thinking of God as a happy being we fall into some gross mis-conceptions.

To return therefore from this digression. The observations now made will not account for all our feelings and affections with respect to virtue and vice. Our intellectual faculties are in their infancy. The lowest degrees of reason are sufficient to discover *moral distinctions* in general; because these[1] are self-evident, and included in the ideas of certain actions and characters. They must, therefore, appear to all who are capable of making actions the objects of their reflexion. But the extent to which they appear, and the accuracy and force with which they are discerned; and, consequently, their influence, must, so far as they are the objects of pure intelligence, be in proportion to the strength and improvement of the rational faculties of beings and their acquaintance with truth and the natures of things.

From hence, it must appear, that in men it is necessary that the *rational principle*, or the *intellectual discernment* of *right*

---

* Ὅς εὐδαίμων μέν ἐστι καὶ μακάριος, δι᾽ οὐθὲν δὲ τῶν ἐξωτερικῶν ἀγαθῶν, ἀλλὰ δι᾽ αὐτὸν αὐτός, καὶ τῷ ποιός τις εἶναι τὴν φύσιν. *Arist. de Rep.* Lib. vii. cap. 1.
[1 Ed. 1 adds 'in their capital branches'.]

and *wrong*, should be aided by *instinctive determinations*.—The dictates of mere reason, being slow, and deliberate, would be otherwise much too weak. The condition in which we are placed, renders many urgent passions necessary for us; and these cannot but often interfere with our sentiments of rectitude. Reason alone, (imperfect as it is in us) is by no means sufficient to defend us against the danger to which, in such circumstances, we are exposed. Our Maker has, therefore, wisely provided remedies for its imperfections; and established a due balance in our frame by annexing to our intellectual perceptions sensations and instincts, which give them greater weight and force.

In short. The truth seems to be that, 'in contemplating the actions of moral agents, we have both a *perception of the understanding*, and a *feeling of the heart*; and that the latter, or the effects in us accompanying our moral perceptions, depend on two causes. Partly, on the positive constitution of our natures: But principally on the essential congruity or incongruity between moral ideas and our intellectual faculties.'*

It may be difficult to determine the precise limits between these two sources of our mental feelings; and to say, how far the effects of the one are blended with those of the other. It is undoubted, that we should have felt and acted otherwise than we now do, if the decisions of reason had been left entirely without support; nor is it easy to imagine how pernicious to us this would have proved. On this account it cannot be doubted, but that both the causes I have mentioned unite their influence: And the great question in morality is, not whether we owe *much* to implanted senses and determinations; but whether we owe *all* to them.

It was, probably, in consequence of not duly considering the difference I have now insisted on between the *honestum* and *pulchrum* (the δίκαιον and καλόν); or of not carefully

---

* *Placet suapte natura—virtus.* SEN.
   Etiamsi a nullo laudetur, natura est laudabile. TULLY.

listinguishing between the discernment of the mind, and the sensations attending it in our moral perceptions; that the Author of the *Enquiry into the Original of our Ideas of Beauty and Virtue*, was led to derive all our ideas of virtue from an implanted sense. Moral good and evil, he every where describes, by the effects accompanying the perception of them. The *rectitude* of an action is, with him, the same with its *gratefulness* to the observer; and wrong, the contrary. But what can be more evident, than that *right* and *pleasure, wrong* and *pain,* are as different as a cause and its effect; what is *understood,* and what is *felt*; absolute truth, and its *agreeableness* to the mind?—Let it be granted, as undoubtedly it must, that some degree of pleasure is inseparable from the observation of virtuous actions:* It is just as unreasonable to infer from hence, that the discernment of virtue is nothing distinct from the reception of this pleasure; as it would be to infer, as some have done, that solidity, extension, and figure are only *particular modes of sensation*; because attended, whenever they are perceived, with some sensations of sight or touch, and impossible to be conceived by the imagination without them.

An able writer on these subjects, tells us that, after some† doubts, he at last satisfied himself, that all beauty, whether natural or moral, is a species of absolute truth; as resulting from, or consisting in, the necessary relations and congruities of ideas. It is not easy to say what this means. *Natural beauty* will be considered presently. And as to *moral beauty,* one would think, that the meaning must be, that it denotes a real quality of certain actions. But the word *beauty* seems always to refer to the reception of pleasure; and the *beauty,* therefore, of an action or character, must signify its being such as *pleases us,* or has an aptness to *please* when perceived: Nor can it be just to conceive more in the action itself, or to

---

* The virtue of an action, Mr *Hume* says, is its *pleasing* us after *a particular manner. Treatise of Human Nature,* Vol. iii. page 103.
† See Mr. *Balguy's Tracts on the Foundation of Moral Goodness,* p. 61.

affirm more of it, than *this aptness*, or that objective goodness or rectitude on which it depends. Beauty and loveliness are synonimous; but an object *self-lovely* can only mean an object by its nature, fitted to engage love.

But it may be farther worth observing, that the epithets *beautiful* and *amiable* are, in common language, confined to actions and characters that please us *highly*, from the peculiar degree of moral worth and virtue apprehended in them. All virtuous actions must be pleasing to an intelligent observer, but they do not all please to the degree necessary to entitle them to these epithets, as we generally apply them.—The nature and origin of our ideas of the different degrees of virtue and vice in actions will be the subject of a particular enquiry hereafter.

These observations are applicable with a little variation to *natural beauty*. The general source of it, as observed by Dr. *Hutcheson*, is UNIFORMITY AMIDST VARIETY. If we ask, why this *pleases*? The proper answer, I think, is, that by its nature it is adapted to please.—There seems no more occasion in this case to have recourse to an *implanted sense* than in the former. —Some objects, I have shewn, are necessarily satisfactory to our thoughts, and carry in themselves a power to give pleasure when surveyed. And though this pleasure in many circumstances is lost; and regular and harmonious forms, through the influence of counter-acting causes, may sometimes even offend; yet they are incapable of offending *as such*, or under the conception of regular and harmonious: That is, it is not in any instance *they* give pain, but some malady in the mind, or some disagreeable idea associated with them.

The following facts deserve notice, and may be considered as contributing greatly towards producing the complacency of our minds in regular objects, and the preference we give them.

First, They are more easily viewed and comprehended by our minds. Every one knows how much more difficult it is to retain in the memory, a multitude of things which are unconnected and lie in confusion, than of things disposed according to a rule and plan. It is order that unites the parts of a complicated object, so that we can survey it at once with distinctness and satisfaction; whereas, if it wanted order it would become not one, but a multiplicity of objects; our conceptions of it would be broken and embarrassed, between many different* parts, which had no correspondence to one another, and each of which would require a distinct idea of itself. By *regularity, variety* is measured and determined, and infinity itself, as it were, conquered by the mind, and subjected to its view. The justness of these observations will appear to any one, by considering abstract truths, and the general laws of nature; or by thinking of a thousand equal lines, as ranged into the form of a regular Polygon, or, on the contrary, as joined to one another at adventures without any order.

Farther. Order and symmetry give objects their stability and strength, and subserviency to any valuable purpose. What strength would an army have, without order? Upon what depends the health of animal bodies, but upon the due order and adjustments of their several parts? What happiness could prevail in the world, if it was a *chaos*?

Thirdly. Regularity and order evidence art and design. The objects in which they appear bear the impresses of intelligence upon them; and this, perhaps, is one of the principal causes of their agreeableness.

Confusion denotes only the negation of regularity and order, and it is not positively displeasing except where we expected order; or where it appears to be owing to impotence and want of skill.

It is scarcely needful to observe, that brutes are incapable

* See *The Enquiry into the Original of our Ideas of Beauty*, Sect. viii. 2.

of the pleasures of beauty, because they proceed from a *comparison* of objects, and a discernment of *analogy, design,* and *proportion,* to which their faculties do not reach.

It has been asserted that it is *variety* alone that pleases in beautiful objects; and the *uniformity* only as necessary to make it distinctly perceivable by the mind. It might, perhaps with equal reason, be affirmed that it is *uniformity* alone that pleases, and *variety* only as requisite to its being exhibited and displayed in a greater degree.

I have already noticed the opinion that *natural beauty* is a real quality of objects.—It seems impossible for any one to conceive the objects themselves to be endowed with more than a particular order of parts, and with *powers,* or an *affinity* to our perceptive faculties, thence arising; and, if we call this *beauty,* then it is an absolute, inherent quality of certain objects; and equally existent whether any mind discerns it or not. But, surely, order and regularity are, more properly, the *causes* of beauty than *beauty itself.*

It may be farther worth the reader's consideration, how far the account given of the pleasures received from the contemplation of moral good and of natural beauty may be applied to the pleasures received from many other sources; as the *approbation of our fellow-creatures, greatness of objects, discovery of truth* and *increase of knowledge.*

I will only add, that in such enquiries as these, we are necessarily led to consider the nature and origin of our notions of *perfection* and *excellency.*

Those who think there is no distinction, in point of real *objective* excellence and worth, between *actions* and *characters,* may be expected to fly to a *sense* to account for any *preference* we give in our ideas to any objects.* We have ideas of

---

* We have the ideas of greater decency and dignity in some pleasures than in others; as, in the pleasures of the imagination or the understanding, when compared with those of the bodily senses. Dr. *Hutcheson,* after observing this,

different degrees of perfection in different objects; but, upon this scheme, they are all an *illusion*. The whole compass and possibility of being is, to the eye of right reason, in this respect entirely on a level. The very notion of *intrinsic* excellence, *self*-worth and different degrees of *objective* perfection and imperfection, implies an impossibility and contradiction.— How can it be possible for any person to acquiesce in such an opinion? When we conceive of an intelligent being as a more *noble and perfect* nature than a clod of earth; do we then err? Is it owing to an implanted power, that we make such a distinction; or that, in particular, we give the preference in our esteem to the divine nature, as surpassing infinitely in *excellence and dignity*, all other natures? The truth is; these, like the other ideas taken notice of in the preceding chapter, are ideas of the understanding. They are derived from the cognizance it takes of the comparative essences of things; and arise necessarily in our minds upon considering certain objects and qualities because they denote *not* what we *feel*, but what such objects and qualities *are*.

There is in nature an infinite variety of existences and objects, which we as unavoidably conceive endowed with various degrees of *perfection*, as we conceive of them at all, or consider them as *different*. It is not possible to contemplate and compare dead matter and life; brutality and reason; misery and happiness; virtue and vice; ignorance and knowledge; impotence and power; the deity and inferior beings; without acquiring the ideas of *better* and *worse*; *perfect* and *imperfect*; *noble* and *ignoble*; *excellent* and *base*.—The first remove from nothing is unwrought matter. Next above this is vegetative life; from whence we ascend to sensitive and animal life, and from thence to happy and active intelligence;

seems uncertain whether it ought to be ascribed to a constant opinion of innocence in the former pleasures; which would reduce the preference we give them, as he says, to the *moral sense*; or whether there be not in these cases a different sort of perceptions to be reckoned another class of sensations. See *Treatise of the Passions*, Sect. I. Art. I.

which admits of an infinite variety of degrees, and of different orders and classes of beings, rising without end, above one another. Every successive advance of our thoughts in this gradation, conveys the notion of higher and higher excellence and worth; till at last we arrive at uncreated and complete excellence. If this is not *intellectual* perception, but *sensation* merely; then may all nature as it now stands in our ideas be reversed; and the dust we tread be conceived to possess supreme excellence, as justly and truly as now the contrary is conceived.

I am pleased to find an excellent writer expressing fully my sentiments on this subject.* 'We cannot (says he) avoid observing, that of things which occur to our thoughts, the idea of superior excellence accompanies some upon a comparison with others. As the external senses distinguish between pleasant and painful in their objects, and the internal sense perceives a difference between the beautiful and the deformed; so the *understanding* not only separates truth from falsehood, but discerns a dignity in some beings and some qualities beyond others. It is not possible for a man to consider inanimate nature and life, the brutal and the rational powers, or virtue and vice, with a perfect indifference, or without preferring one before the other in his esteem. And the idea of a difference in the degrees of their perfection, as necessarily arises in his mind, as that of a difference in their being.'

* See Mr. Abernethy's Sermons Vol. II. p. 219.

CHAP. III.

Of the Origin of our Desires and Affections.

WHAT comes next to be enquired into, according to the order proposed in page 13, is our perception of GOOD and ILL-DESERT. But before I enter on this enquiry, I must turn the reader's attention to another subject closely connected with the subject already examined, and the consideration of which, my design in this work will not allow me to omit. I mean, the origin of our affections in general; and, particularly, of *self-love* and *benevolence*.

Each of our affections has its particular end. SELF-LOVE leads us to desire and pursue *private*, and BENEVOLENCE, *public* happiness. AMBITION is the love of fame, and distinction; and CURIOSITY is the love of what is new and uncommon. The objects of these and all our other affections, are desired for their own sakes; and constitute so many distinct principles of action. What is not at all desired *for itself*, but only as a means of something else, cannot, with any propriety, be called the object of an affection. If, for example, according to the opinion of some, we desire every thing merely as the means of our own good, and with an ultimate view to it, then in reality we desire nothing but our own good, and have only the one single affection of self-love.

As all moral approbation and disapprobation, and our ideas of beauty and deformity, have been ascribed to an INTERNAL SENSE; meaning by this, not '*any inward* power of perception,' but 'an *implanted power*, different from *reason*;' so, all our desires and affections have, in like manner, been ascribed to INSTINCT, *meaning by instinct, not merely* '*the immediate desire of an object*,' but '*the reason* of this desire; or an *implanted propension*.'—The former opinion I have already at large examined. I am now to examine the latter.

'Is then all desire to be considered as *wholly instinctive*? Is it, in particular, owing to nothing but an original bias given our natures, which they might have either wanted or have received in a contrary direction; that we are at all concerned for our own good, or for the good of others?'

As far as this enquiry relates to *private* good, we may without hesitation answer in the negative. The desire of happiness for *ourselves*, certainly arises not from INSTINCT.[1] The full and adequate account of it, is, *the nature of happiness*. It is impossible, but that creatures capable of pleasant and painful sensations, should *love and chuse* the one, and *dislike and avoid* the other. No being, who knows what happiness and misery are, can be supposed indifferent to them, without a plain contradiction. Pain is not a *possible* object of *desire*; nor happiness, of *aversion*. No power whatsoever can cause a creature, in the agonies of torture and misery, to be pleased with his state, to like it for itself, or to wish to remain so. Nor can any power cause a creature rejoicing in bliss to *dislike* his state, or be *afraid* of its continuance. Then only can this happen, when pain can be *agreeable*, and pleasure *disagreeable*; that is, when pain can be pleasure; and pleasure, pain.

From hence I infer, that it is by no means, in general, an absurd method of explaining our affections, to derive them from the natures of things and of beings. For thus without doubt we are to account for one of the most important and active of all our affections. To the preference and desire of *private happiness* by all beings, nothing more is requisite than to *know* what it *is*.—'And may not this be true, likewise, of *public* happiness? May not benevolence be *essential* to *intelligent* beings, as well as self-love to *sensible beings*?'

But to enter a little more minutely into the discussion of this point. Let us, again, put the case of a being *purely* reasonable. It is evident, that (though by supposition void

[1 Ed. 2, following a similar addition in ed. 1, adds 'in the sense in which I have just defined it'.]

of *implanted* byasses) he would not want all principles of action, and all inclinations. It has been shewn he would perceive VIRTUE, and possess affection to it, in proportion to the degree of his knowledge. The nature of *happiness* also would engage him to chuse and desire it for *himself*. And is it credible that, at the same time, he would be necessarily indifferent about it for *others*? Can it be supposed to have that in it, which would determine him to seek it for *himself*; and yet to have nothing in it, which could engage him to approve of it for *others*? Would the nature of things, upon this supposition, be consistent? Would he not be capable of seeing, that the happiness of others is to them as important as his is to him; and that it is in itself equally valuable and desirable, whoever possesses it?

Let us again enquire; would not this being assent to this proposition; 'happiness is *better* than misery?'—A definition has been asked of the word *better* here. With equal reason might a definition be asked of the word *greater*, when the whole is affirmed to be *greater* than a part. Both denote simple ideas, and both *truth*. The one, what happiness is, compared with misery; and the other, what the whole is, compared with a part. And a mind that should think happiness not to be better than misery, would mistake as grossly, as a mind that should believe the whole not to be *greater* than a part. It cannot therefore be reasonably doubted, but that such a being, upon a comparison of happiness and misery, would as unavoidably as he perceives their difference, *prefer* the one to the other; and *chuse* the one rather than the other, for his fellow-beings.

If the idea the word *better* stands for, in the before-mentioned proposition, is indeed to be referred to a *sense*, and implies nothing *true*; if to the judgment of right reason, happiness and misery are objects in themselves indifferent, this must be perfectly understood by the Deity. There can, in him, therefore, be no preference of one to the other. There is nothing *in* happiness to engage or justify his choice of it. What account, then, is to be given of his *goodness?*—Some will say; the same account that is to be given of his *existence*; meaning no account at all. But there is an account to be given of his existence; even the same with that which is to be given of all necessary truth: And this account is fully applicable to his *benevolence*, as the origin of it has been now explained. But were this, universally, an implanted and factitious principle; it would be unavoidable to conclude, that it cannot exist in a nature from which must be excluded every thing implanted and factitious. How much, therefore, upon this supposition, will our evidences for this attribute be lessened? Can we admit a supposition which obliges us to conceive God as good, *without* the approbation of his understanding?—This is a similar argument to that used before in the first chapter; and it may be farther proper to hint, though it can scarce escape observation, that, what I have endeavoured to shew in that chapter, infers what I have said on the present subject; and that if either be right, both must be so.

It is confessed, that, in our inward sentiments, we are determined to make a distinction between publick happiness and misery; and to apprehend a preferableness of the one to the other. But it is asserted, that this is owing to our frame; that it arises from senses and instincts *given* us, and not from the *nature* of happiness and misery.—But why is this asserted? It *may be* owing to the latter cause. The instance of self-love *demonstrates* this.—Let any thing equivalent be offered to prove the contrary.

In the same manner in which self-love and benevolence have been explained, may we account for some of our other affections. But these being of less importance, and the consideration of them not so much in my way, I shall only just touch upon the love of fame and of knowledge.

Approbation and disapprobation of ourselves and others,

as our own actions and dispositions, or those of others, are observed to be right or wrong, are unavoidable. Intelligence therefore, alone, being sufficient for the perception of morality, lays the foundation of fame and honour. And it is not much less evident that it will, likewise, give rise to the desire and pursuit of them.

Can a reasonable being be indifferent about *his own* approbation? If not about *his own*; why should we think him necessarily so about that of others? Is there nothing in the *good opinion* and *esteem* of his fellow-beings which can incline him to chuse them, rather than their *contempt* and *aversion*?

The desire of *knowledge* also, and the preference of TRUTH, must arise in every intelligent mind. TRUTH is the proper object of mind, as light is of the eye, or harmony of the ear. To this it is, by its nature, fitted, and upon this depends its existence; there being no idea possible of *mind*, or *understanding*, without something to be *understood*. Truth and Science are of infinite extent; and it is not conceivable, that the understanding can be indifferent to them; that it should want inclination to search into them; that its progress, in the discovery of them, should be attended with no satisfaction; or that, with the prospect before it of unbounded scope for improvement and endless acquisitions, it should be capable of being equally contented with error, darkness, and ignorance.

Why, therefore, reasonable beings love *truth, knowledge, and honour*, is to be answered in the same manner with the enquiry; why they love and desire *happiness*?

In the method now pursued, we might go on to give a particular explication of the causes and grounds of the various sentiments of veneration, awe, love, wonder, esteem, &c. produced within us by the contemplation of certain objects. As some objects are adapted to *please*, and as others necessarily excite *desire*; so almost every different object has a different effect on our minds, according to its different nature and qualities. And these emotions, or impressions, are almost as different and various, as the objects themselves of our consideration. Why should we scruple ascribing them to a necessary correspondence between them and their respective objects?—It cannot be true, that, antecedently to arbitrary constitution, *any* affections of our minds are equally and indifferently applicable to *any* objects and qualities: Nor can any one assert this, without going so far as to deny all *real* connexion between causes and effects.

But it must not be forgotten, that, in men, the sentiments and tendencies of our intelligent nature are, in a great degree, mingled with the effects of arbitrary constitution. It is necessary this observation, before insisted on, should be here called to mind. Rational and dispassionate benevolence would, in us, be a principle much too weak, and utterly insufficient for the purposes of our present state. And the same is true of our other rational principles and desires.

And this, perhaps, will afford us a good reason for distinguishing between *affections* and *passions*. The former, which we apply indiscriminately to all reasonable beings, may most properly signify the desires founded in the reasonable nature itself, and essential to it; such as self-love, benevolence, and the love of truth.—These, when strengthened by instinctive determinations, take the latter denomination; or are, properly; *passions*.—Those tendencies within us that are merely instinctive, such as hunger, thirst, &c, we commonly call *appetites* or *passions* indifferently, but seldom or never *affections*.

I cannot help, in this place, stepping aside a little to take notice of an opinion already referred to; I mean, the opinion of those who will allow of no *ultimate* object of desire besides *private* good. What has led to this opinion has been inattention to the difference between *desire*, and the *pleasure* implied in the gratification of it. The latter is subsequent to the former, and founded in it: That is, an object, such as *fame*, *knowledge*, or the *welfare of a friend*, is desired, not because we foresee that when obtained, it will give us pleasure; but, *vice versa*; obtaining it gives us pleasure, because we previously desired it or had an *affection* carrying us to it and resting in it. And, were there no such affections, the very foundations of happiness would be destroyed. It cannot be conceived, that obtaining what we do not desire, should be the cause of pleasure to us; or that what we are perfectly indifferent to, and is not the end of any affection, should, upon being possessed, be the means of any kind of gratification.*

Besides; if every object of desire is considered—merely as the cause of pleasure; one would think, that, antecedently to experience, no one object could be desired more than another; and that the first time we contemplated fame, knowledge, or the happiness of others; or had any of the objects of our natural passions and desires proposed to us, we must have been absolutely indifferent to them, and remained so, till, by some means, we were convinced of the connexion between them and pleasure.

For farther satisfaction on this point, nothing can be more proper than to consider; whether, supposing we could enjoy the same pleasure *without* the object of our desire, we should be indifferent to it. Could we enjoy pleasures equivalent to those attending knowledge, or the approbation of others, without them, or with infamy and ignorance, would we no longer wish for the one or be averse to the other? Would a person lose all curiosity, and be indifferent whether he stirred a step to gratify it, were he assured he should receive equal sensations of pleasure by staying where he is? Did you believe, that the prosperity of your nearest kindred, your friends or your country, would be the means of no greater happiness to

---

* 'The very idea of happiness or enjoyment, (as Dr. *Butler* says) is this, an appetite or affection having its object.' See Sermons preached at the *Roll*'s chapel.

you, than their misery; would you lose all love to them, and all desires of their good?—Would you not chuse to enjoy the same quantity of pleasure *with* virtue, rather than *without* it. —An unbiassed mind must spurn at such enquiries; and any one, who would, in this manner, examine himself, might easily find, that all his affections and appetites (self-love itself excepted) are, in their nature, *disinterested*; and that though the seat of them be *self*, and the effect of them the gratification of *self*, their direct tendency is always to some particular object different from private pleasure, beyond which they carry not our view. So far is it from being true that, in following their impulses, we aim at nothing but our own interest; that we continually feel them drawing us astray from what we *know* to be our interest; and may observe men every day carried by them to actions and pursuits, which they acknowledge to be ruinous to them.

But to return from this digression.—Of our several passions and appetites, some are subordinate to self-love, and given with a view to the preservation and welfare of *individuals*. Others are subordinate to benevolence, and given in order to secure and promote the happiness of the *species*. The occasion for them arises entirely from our deficiencies and weaknesses. Reason alone, did we possess it in a higher degree, would answer all the ends of them.—Thus; there would be no need of the *parental affection*, were all parents sufficiently acquainted with the reasons for taking upon them the guidance and support of those whom nature has placed under their care, and were they virtuous enough to be always determined by those reasons. And, in all other instances of implanted principles, it is plain, that there is a certain degree of knowledge and goodness, by which they would be rendered superfluous.

It is incumbent on those who see this, and can regard *appetite*, as, in the design of nature, merely ministerial and

upplemental to *reason*, and necessary only on the account of
ts imperfections, to labour to improve it, and to extend its
nfluence as much as possible; to learn more and more, in all
nstances, to substitute it in the room of *appetite*, and to
liminish continually the occasion for instinctive principles in
hemselves.—All the inferior orders of creatures, and men
hemselves during their first years, have no other guide than
nstinct. The farther men advance in existence, and the wiser
and better they grow, the more they are disengaged from
t. And there may be numberless orders of superior beings,
who are absolutely above it, and under the sole influence
and guidance of reason.

We cannot, indeed, considering the present weak and imperfect state of human reason, sufficiently admire the wisdom
and goodness of God, in the provision he has made against
the evils which would arise from hence, by particular, instinctive determinations. As long as men have not that wisdom which would secure their taking regularly the sustenance
necessary for their support, upon barely knowing it to be
proper at certain intervals; how kind is it to remind them of
it, and urge them to it, by the solicitations of *hunger*? As it is
probable, they would not be sufficiently engaged to the relief
of the miserable, without the sympathies and impulses of
compassion; how properly are *these* given them? And as, in
like manner, if left to mere reason, the care of their offspring
would be little attended to; how wisely are they bound to
them by the *parental fondness*, and not suffered to neglect them
without doing violence to themselves?

In general; were we trusted wholly with the care of ourselves, and was our benevolence determined alike to all mankind, or no farther to particular persons according to our
different relations to them, than unassisted reason would
determine it; what confusion would ensue? What misery
would be soon introduced into human affairs?

How evidently, therefore, do the wisdom and benevolence

of our Maker appear in the frame of our natures?—It is true that these very principles, the necessity of which to the preservation and happiness of the species, we so evidently see often prove, in event, the causes of many grievous evils. But they are plainly *intended* for *good*. These evils are the *accidental* not the *proper* consequences of them. They proceed from the unnatural abuse and corruption of them, and happen entirely through our own fault, contrary to what appears to be the constitution of our nature and the will of our Maker. It is impossible to produce one instance in which the *original* direction of nature is to evil, or to any thing not, upon the whole, best.

I am not at all solicitous about determining nicely, in all cases, what in our natures is to be resolved into *instinct*, and what not. It is sufficient, if it appears, that the most important of our desires and affections have a higher and less precarious original.

CHAP. IV.

Of our Ideas of good and ill Desert.

IT is needless to say any thing to shew that the ideas of good and ill desert necessarily arise in us upon considering certain actions and characters; or, that we conceive virtue as always *worthy*, and vice as the contrary. These ideas are plainly a species of the ideas of right and wrong. There is, however, the following difference between them, which may be worth mentioning. The epithets, *right* and *wrong*, are, with strict propriety, applied only to *actions*; but *good* and *ill desert* belong rather to the *agent*. It is the *agent* alone, that is capable of happiness or misery; and, therefore, it is he alone that properly can be said to *deserve* these.

I apprehend no great difficulty in explaining these ideas. They suppose virtue practised, or neglected; and regard the treatment due to beings in consequence of this. They signify the propriety which there is in making virtuous agents happy, and in discountenancing the vicious. When we say, a man *deserves* well, we mean, that his character is such, that we *approve* of shewing him *favour*; or that it is *right* he should be happier than if he had been of a contrary character. We cannot but love a virtuous agent, and desire his happiness above that of others. Reason determines at once, that he *ought* to be the better for his virtue.—A vicious being, on the contrary, as such, we cannot but hate and condemn. Our concern for his happiness is necessarily diminished; nor can any truth appear more self-evidently to our minds, than that it is improper he should prosper in his wickedness, or that happiness should be conferred on him to the same degree that it is on others of worthy characters; or that it would have been conferred on himself, had he been virtuous.

Different characters require different treatment. Virtue

79

affords a *reason* for communicating happiness to the agent Vice is a *reason* for withdrawing favour, and for punishing.— This seems to be very intelligible. But in order farther to explain this point, it is necessary to observe particularly, tha the *whole* foundation of the sentiments now mentioned is by no means this; 'the tendency of virtue to the happiness of the world, and of vice to its misery; or the publick utility of the one, and perniciousness of the other.'—We have an im mediate approbation of making the virtuous happy, and dis couraging the vicious, abstracted from all consequences Were there but two beings in the universe, one of whom wa virtuous, the other vicious; or, were we to conceive two such beings, in other respects alike, governed apart from the rest of the world, and removed for ever from the notice of al other creatures; we should still approve of a different treat ment of them. That the good being should be less happy, or a greater sufferer, than his evil fellow being, would appear to us wrong.

Suppose a person had any particular benefit to communicate, and that the only consideration to determine which of two competitors shall have it, is their contrary moral characters; what room would there be for hesitation? Who would not immediately determine in favour of the virtuous character? Can it be said it would be indifferent which of the competitors was preferred, if there were no other beings in the world; or if all memory of the fact was to be immediately obliterated? The virtuous person, every one would think, is *worthy* of the benefit; the other *unworthy*: That is, their respective characters are such, that it is right it should be conferred on the one *rather* than the other. But, why *right*? Not merely on account of the effects; (which, in these instances, we are far from taking time always to consider) but *immediately and ultimately right*; and, for the same reason that beneficence is right, and that objects and relations, in general, are what they are.

The moral worth or MERIT of an agent, then, is, 'his virtue considered as implying the fitness, that good should be communicated to him preferably to others; and as disposing all observers to esteem, and love him, and study his happiness.' —Virtue naturally, and of itself, recommends to favour and happiness, qualifies for them, and renders the being possessed of it the proper object of encouragement and reward. It is, in a like sense, we say that a person, who has been a benefactor to another, *deserves* well of him; that benefits received ought to be acknowledged and recompensed; and, that the person who bestows them is, preferably to others, the proper object of our regard and benevolence.

I deny not, but that one circumstance of great importance, upon which is grounded the fitness of countenancing virtue and discountenancing vice among reasonable beings, is, the manifest tendency of this to prevent misery, and to preserve order and happiness in the world. What I assert is, that it is not *all* that renders such a procedure right; but that, setting aside the consideration of publick interest, it would still remain right to make a distinction between the lots of the virtuous and vicious. Vice is of ESSENTIAL DEMERIT; and virtue is *in itself rewardable*. For, once more, let us imagine an order of reasonable beings made to pass through a particular stage of existence, at the end of which they are annihilated: Among whom, during the period they existed, no distinction was made on account of their different characters: Virtue was not favoured, nor vice punished: Happiness and misery were distributed promiscuously; the guilty often prosperous, and flourishing; the good, as often afflicted and distressed, and sometimes brought to untimely ends by the oppression of their more happy, though wicked fellow-beings: The *most* wicked, generally, the *least* sufferers; and the *most* upright, the *least* happy. Notwithstanding all this, the quantity of happiness enjoyed may be conceived to exceed the ill. But will any one say, that, were there no connexion between such beings and the rest of the universe, there would be nothing in th. disposition of its affairs that would be wrong?—It will b. said, for nothing else can be said, 'that such a state c. reasonable beings cannot be approved because there woul. have been *more* happiness among them, had their differen. lots been ordered agreeably to the rules of distributive justice. But is it so unavoidable to see this, that every one's disappro. bation must be always immediately determined by it? I there no other kind of wrong in so governing a system o. beings, than in producing a *smaller* quantity of happines. rather than a *greater*? Or can the view of such beings give a. much satisfaction to an unbiassed mind, as if there had bee. among them, upon the whole, the same quantity of happi. ness, but distributed with a regard to their moral characters'

In the case of a single, solitary evil being, it may perhap. be very true, that the only thing that could justify putting him into a state of absolute misery, would be its conducive. ness to his reformation. But the reason why we approve o' using methods to accomplish his reformation, is not merely this; 'that it is expedient to his happiness.' For were thi. true, it would, in a moral view, be indifferent whether he was made happy in consequence of being *punished* and thus reformed, or in consequence of such an extraordinary com. munication of advantages as should counter-act and over. balance any sufferings necessarily occasioned by his vices. Can we equally approve these opposite methods of treating such a being? Supposing the same quantity of happiness enjoyed, is it indifferent whether a being enjoys it in a course of wickedness, or of virtue?—It would be extravagant to assert, that there is no *possible* method whereby a being can, in any degree, escape the hurtful effects of his vices, or lose the beneficial effects of his virtue. We see enough in the present world to convince us of the contrary.

Several questions which I cannot answer may be asked on

his subject. There are many particular cases and different
circumstances of agents and of guilt, in which it may be
difficult to determine what is right to be done; nor is it at all
necessary to my present purpose that I should take notice of
such cases. It is sufficient, if I have given a just account of
good and ill desert in general; and shewn, that virtue is
essentially a *proper* object of *favour*, vice of *discouragement*; and
that the *rewardableness* of the one, and the *demerit* of the other,
are instances of absolute and eternal rectitude, the ideas of
which arise in us *immediately* upon the consideration of virtuous and vicious characters, appear always along with them,
and are, by no means, wholly coincident with or resolvable
into views of publick *utility* and *inutility*.

Upon this perception of good and ill desert is founded the
passion of resentment; the hopes unavoidably springing up
in every virtuous mind; and the presaging terrors and anticipations of punishment accompanying a consciousness of
guilt.

Let me add; that there is no perception of our minds
which it becomes us more to attend to. It points out to us
clearly, the *way* to happiness and the *conditions* of it. It is
seeing, that according to just order and equity, sin is the for-
feiture of our expectations of good; and virtue, the ground of
the highest hope.—Considered merely, as a principle of the
natures which God has given us, or a determination inter-
woven with our frame, it implies a declaration from the
author of our minds, informing us how he will deal with us,
and upon what the exercise of his goodness to us is suspended.
—But, considered as a necessary perception of reason, it
proves with the evidence of demonstration what the *supreme
reason* will do; what laws and rules it observes in carrying on
the happiness of the universe; and that its end is, not simply
happiness, but 'happiness enjoyed with virtue.'*

* 'Perhaps divine goodness, with which, if I mistake not, we make very free
in our speculations, may not be a bare single disposition to produce happiness;

Of our Ideas of Desert

Before I proceed to the next chapter, I cannot help desiring the reader, once more, to reflect on that reverse of nature which is possible, and which might have obtained, if the opinion concerning the foundation of morals which I have opposed be true. Let him try to conceive of the world, and of all our ideas of good, of morality, of perfection, and of the Deity as inverted; the principal objects of the consideration of our minds as not *being* what they now *seem* to be, but as perceived by all intelligent beings *under notions* entirely contrary: what is now approved and esteemed, as disapproved and hated: all that is now contemplated as *fit*, as *worthy*, as *amiable and excellent*, appearing *evil and base*: cruelty, impiety, ingratitude and treachery apprehended to be *virtue*; and beneficence, piety, gratitude and faithfulness, to be *wickedness*: The very aversion arising in us in considering the former, produced by the latter: respect and love excited by ill offices; contempt and resentment by acts of kindness: misery prevailing throughout the world, as happiness now does, and chosen and pursued with the same universal approbation and ardour: *virtue*, conceived as having *demerit*; and *vice*, as well-deserving and rewardable.—Can these things be? Is there nothing in any of them repugnant to the natures of things?

but a disposition to make the good, the faithful, the honest man happy. Perhaps an infinitely perfect mind may be pleased, with seeing his creatures behave suitably to the nature he has given them; to the relations in which he has placed them to each other; and to that which they stand in to himself: that relation to himself, which, during their existence, is even necessary, and which is the most important one of all: perhaps, I say, an infinitely perfect mind may be pleased with this moral piety of moral agents, in and for itself; as well as upon account of its being essentially conducive to the happiness of his creation.' See *Butler*'s *Analogy*, Part I. Chap. 2.

CHAP. V.

Of the relation of Morality to the Divine Nature; the Rectitude of our Faculties; and the Grounds of Belief.

MORALITY has been represented as necessary and immutable. There is an objection to this, which to some has appeared of considerable weight, and which it will be proper to examine.

It may seem 'that this is setting up something distinct from God, which is independent of him, and equally eternal and necessary.'

It is easy to see that this difficulty affects morality, no more than it does all truth. If for this reason, we must give up the unalterable natures of right and wrong, and make them dependent on the Divine will; we must, for the same reason, give up all necessary truth, and assert the possibility of contradictions.

What I have hitherto aimed at has been, to prove that morality is a branch of *necessary truth*, and that it has the same foundation with it. If this is acknowledged, the main point I contend for is granted, and I shall be very willing that truth and morality should stand and fall together. This subject however cannot be pursued far enough, and morality traced to its source, without entering into the consideration of the difficulty now proposed; which naturally occurs in all enquiries of this sort.

In the first place, therefore, let it be observed, that something there certainly is which we must allow not to be dependent on the will of God. For instance; this will itself; his own existence; his eternity and immensity; the difference between power and impotence, wisdom and folly, truth and falsehood, existence and non-existence.

To suppose these dependent on his will, is so extravagant that no one can assert it. It would imply, that he is a change able and precarious being, and render it impossible for us to form any consistent ideas of his existence and attributes. But these must be the creatures of will, if all truth be so.—There is another view of this notion, which shews that it overthrows the Divine attributes and existence. For,

Secondly, Mind supposes truth; and intelligence, something intelligible. Wisdom supposes certain *objects* about which it is conversant; and knowledge, *knowables.*—An eternal, necessary *mind* supposes eternal, necessary *truth*; and infinite knowledge, infinite knowables. If then there were no infinity of knowables; no eternal, necessary, independent* truths; there could be no infinite, independent, necessary *mind* or *intelligence*; because there would be nothing to be certainly and eternally known. Just as, if there were nothing *possible,* there could be no *power*; or, if there were no necessary *infinity* of possibles, there could be no necessary, *infinite* power; because power supposes objects, and eternal, necessary, infinite power, an infinity of eternal and necessary *possibles.*

In like manner it may be said, that if there were no *moral distinctions,* there could be no *moral attributes in the Deity.* If there were nothing eternally and unalterably right and wrong, there could be nothing meant by his eternal, unalterable rectitude or holiness.—It is evident, therefore, that annihilating truth, possibility, or moral differences, is indeed annihilating all mind, all power, all goodness; and that so far as we make the former precarious, dependent, or limited; so far we make the latter so too.

Hence we see clearly, that to conceive of truth as depending on God's will, is to conceive of his intelligence and knowledge as depending on his will. And is it possible, that any one can think this as reasonable, as, on the contrary, to conceive of his *will* (which, from the nature of it, *requires something* to

---

* Ἀΐδια νοητά, in *Plato's* language.

guide and determine it) as dependent on and regulated by his *understanding*?—What can be more preposterous, than to make the Deity nothing but will; and to exalt this on the ruins of all his attributes?

But it may still be urged, that these observations remove not the difficulty; but rather strengthen it. We are still left to conceive of 'certain objects, distinct from Deity, which are necessary and independent; and on which too his existence and attributes are founded; and without which, we cannot so much as form any idea of them.' I answer; we ought to distinguish between the *will* of God and his *nature*. It by no means follows, because they are independent of his *will*, [1]that they are also independent[1] of his *nature*. To conceive thus of them would indeed involve us in the greatest inconsistencies. Wherever, or in whatever objects, *necessity* and *infinity* occur to our thoughts, the divine, eternal nature is to be acknowledged.[2]

We shall, I believe, be more willing to own this, when we have attentively considered what abstract truth and possibility are. Our thoughts are here lost in an unfathomable abyss where we find room for an everlasting progress, and where the very notion of arriving at a point, beyond which there is nothing farther, implies a contradiction. There is a proper infinity of ideal objects and verities *possible* to be known; and of systems, worlds, and scenes of being, perception, order, and art, wholly inconceivable to finite minds, *possible* to exist. This infinity of truth and possibility we

[1 Ed. 1 reads 'that they are properly distinct from him, and independent'.]

[2 Ed. 1, followed fairly closely by ed. 2, adds: 'to which nothing of this kind can be unallied.—The truth, therefore, is that the objects we are now contemplating, are not things detached from, or independent of, the Deity; but different views, modes, or attributes of his nature.' Perhaps Price dropped this statement, and that given in footnote 1 above, because, until we have understood his full account of the nature of God, they appear to suggest Spinoza's pantheism, from which he dissociates himself in his own footnote to the next paragraph. Price differs from pantheists in holding that God is the whole of necessary existence or truth, but not of all existence.]

cannot in thought destroy. Do what we will, it always returns upon us. Every thought and every idea of every mind; every kind of agency and power, and every degree of intellectual improvement and pre-eminence amongst all reasonable beings, imply its necessary and unchangeable existence.—Can this be any thing besides the divine, un-created, infinite *reason and power*, from whence all other reason and power are derived, offering themselves to our minds, and forcing us to see and acknowledge them?—What is the true conclusion from such considerations, but that there is an incomprehensible *first* wisdom, knowledge, and power *necessarily existing*, which contain in themselves all things, from which all things sprung,* and upon which all things depend? —There is nothing so intimate with us, and one with our natures, as *God*. He is included, as appears, in all our con-ceptions, and necessary to all the operations of our minds: Nor could he be *necessarily existent*, were not this true of him. For it is implied in the idea of *necessary existence*, that it is *fundamental* to all other existence, and pre-supposed in every *notion* we can frame of every thing.—In short, it seems very plain, that truth having always a reference to MIND; infinite, eternal truth implies an infinite, eternal MIND: And that, not being itself a *substance*, nor yet *nothing*, it must be a *mode of a substance*; or the *essential wisdom and intelligence of the one, necessary Being*.

It is worth observing that this gives us a kind of intuition of the *unity* of God. Infinite, abstract truth is essentially *one*. This is no less clear of truth, than it is of space or duration. When we have fixed our thoughts on infinite truth, and try to imagine a *second* or *another* infinity of it; we find ourselves endeavouring absurdly to imagine *another* infinity of the

* It was, in all probability, something of this kind, and not modern *Pantheism*, or *Spinozism*, that some of the ancients meant, when they represented God as being all things; as the unchangeable and infinite τὸ ὄν and ἓν ὄν. See Dr. *Cudworth's Intellectual System*, Vol. I.

ame truth. It is self-evident, then, that there can be but one nfinite mind. Infinite truth supposes and infers the existence f one infinite essence, as its *substratum*, and but one. Were here more, they would not be *necessary*.—Particular truths, contemplated at the same time by many different minds, are n this account, no more different, than the present moment f duration is different in one place from what it is in another; r, than the sun is different, because viewed at the same time by myriads of eyes.

Let it be remembered here, that in necessary truth, is included the comparative natures of happiness and misery; the *right* in producing the one, and the *wrong* in producing the other; and, in general, *moral* truth, moral fitness and excellence, and all that is *best* to be done in all cases, and with respect to all the variety of actual or possible beings and worlds.—This is the necessary GOODNESS of the divine nature.—It demonstrates, that, in the divine intelligence, absolute rectitude is included; and that eternal, infinite power and reason are in essential conjunction with, and imply complete, moral excellence, and particularly perfect and boundless *Benevolence.** It shews us, that whenever we transgress truth and right, we immediately affront that God who *is* truth and right; and that, on the contrary, whenever we determine ourselves agreeably to them, we pay immediate homage to him.

From the whole it is plain, that none have reason to be offended, when *morality* is represented as eternal and immutable; for it appears that it is only saying that God himself is eternal and immutable, and making his nature the high and sacred original of virtue, and the sole fountain of all that is true and good and perfect.

---

* *Ratio profecta à rerum natura, & ad recte faciendum impellens, à delicto avocans: quae non tum denique incipit lex esse, cum scripta est, sed tum cum orta est: orta autem simul est cum mente divina.* Cic. de Leg. Lib. ii.—*Ita principem legem illam & ultimam, mentem esse omnia ratione aut cogentis aut vetantis Dei.* Ibid.—λόγῳ ὀρθῷ πείθεσθαι καὶ θεῷ ταὐτόν ἐστι. Hier. Carm. Pythag.

Of the relation of

The same kind of reasoning with some that I have here used has been, by Dr. *Clark*, applied, (and I think justly) to *space and duration*: But these sentiments are more particularly countenanced by Dr. *Cudworth*, who, at the end of his Treatise on *Eternal and immutable Morality*, has considered the same difficulty, and given a like answer to it.*

* The authority of the admirable *Plato* might also have been here mentioned. Those who are acquainted with his writings, know that he represents IDEAS, or the intelligible essences of things, as the only seat of truth and the only object of knowledge and *mind*. Here only, according to him, can we find *unity*; it being plainly impossible to conceive of more than *one species* or abstract essence of a triangle, or of any other object of the understanding. These likewise he represents as the originals and examplars of all created existences; as eternal and incorruptible; above all motion and mutation, and making up together the *one infinite, first intelligence*, or *TO ON*. Particular sensible existences, on the contrary, he represents as being nothing fixed, or permanent in themselves but the seats of multiplicity, generation, and motion; the objects not of *knowledge*, but of *opinion and imagination*; and to be looked upon as rather *shadows*, than *realities*.—He ridicules those *earth-born men*, (γηγενεῖς, in *Sophista*) as he styles them, who rejecting all invisible, incorporeal essences, and abstract ideas, (νοητά, ἀμετακίνητα, ἀσώματα, καὶ ἀόρατα εἴδη. *Ibid.*) allow nothing to have existence besides the objects of sense and fancy, or what they can see and handle: and says, that those who have not learnt to look above all sensibles and individuals to abstract truth and the natures of things, to beauty or good itself, are not to be ranked amongst true philosophers, but among the ignorant, the vulgar, and blind.—What he has delivered to this purpose has been carried into mysticism and jargon, by the *latter Platonists*; but this is no reason for rejecting it.—See the note at the end of the first chapter.

I cannot help particularly recommending to the reader's perusal here, the two last chapters of Mr. *Harris*'s HERMES.

This writer has entered far into this part of *Plato*'s philosophy; and I am glad to find that I can mention him as one of its patrons and friends.

'These etymologies (says he, page 371, 2d edition) prove their authors to have considered SCIENCE and UNDERSTANDING, not as fleeting powers of perception, like *sense*; but rather as steady, permanent, and durable COMPREHENSIONS. But if so, we must, somewhere or other, find for them *steady, permanent, and durable* OBJECTS, &c.—The following, then, are questions worth considering. *What* these objects are? *Where* they reside? And *how* they are to be discovered?—Not by *experimental philosophy* it is plain, for that meddles with nothing but what is tangible, corporeal, and mutable, &c.'—'May we be allowed (page 389) to credit those speculative men, who tell us, *it is in these permanent and comprehensive* FORMS, that the DEITY views at once, without looking abroad, all possible productions, both present, past, and future.—That this great and stupendous view is but the view of himself, &c.'

There is, perhaps, no subject where more must be trusted to every person's own reflexion; where the deficiencies of language are more sensible; or on which it is more difficult to write, so as to be entirely understood.

A great deal might have been added to what has been said; and the whole argument, now very imperfectly touched, explained at large and pursued throughout, would, I think, contain one of the highest of all speculations.—Some farther account of it may be found in the Dissertation on the Being and attributes of God, at the end of this Treatise.

There has been another difficulty started,* in which morality is concerned, which will be proper for our present examination. It has been asked, 'whether the truth of all our knowledge does not suppose the right make of our faculties? whether it is not possible, that these might have been so constituted, as unavoidably to deceive us in all our apprehensions? and how we can know that this is not actually the case?'

Some may imagine that these enquiries propose difficulties which are impossible to be surmounted, and that they bind us down to universal and invincible scepticism. For, 'how are we to make out the truth of our faculties, but by these very suspected faculties themselves? and how vain would be such an attempt? where could it leave us but where it found us?'—It may be observed, that it is not only us, but all reasonable creatures, who are thus reduced to a state of everlasting scepticism: Nay, that it must be impossible, God should make any creature, who shall be able to satisfy himself on any point, or believe even his own existence. For what satisfaction can he obtain, in any case, but by the intervention of his faculties? and how shall he know that they are not

---

* It is probable I should not have taken notice of this objection, had I not found it considered by Dr. *Cudworth* at the end of his treatise of *eternal and immutable morality*; and answered in a manner, I judged not quite clear and satisfactory.

delusive?—These are very strange consequences; but let us consider,

First, That we are informed of this difficulty *by* our faculties, and that, consequently, if we do not know that any regard is due to their information, we likewise do not know that there is any regard due to *this* difficulty.—It will appear presently to be a contradiction, to suppose that our faculties can teach us universally to suspect themselves.

Secondly, Our natures are such, that whatever we see, or *think* we see evidence against, we *cannot* believe. If then there should appear to us, on the whole, any evidence against the supposition, that our faculties are so contrived as always to deceive us, we are obliged to reject it. Evidence must produce conviction proportioned to the imagined degree of it; and conviction is inconsistent with suspicion. It will signify nothing to urge that no evidence in this case can be regarded, because discovered by our suspected faculties; for, we cannot suspect, we cannot in any case doubt *without* reason, or *against* reason. Doubting supposes evidence; and there cannot, therefore, be any such thing as doubting, whether evidence itself is to be regarded. A man who doubts of the veracity of his faculties, must do it on their own authority; that is, *at the very time, and in the very act of suspecting them,* he must *trust* them. As nothing is more plainly self-destructive, than to attempt to *prove* by reason, that reason deserves no credit, or to assert that we have *reason* for thinking, that there is no such thing as *reason*; it is, certainly, no less so, to pretend, that we have reason to *doubt* whether reason is to be regarded; or, which comes to the same, whether our faculties are to be regarded. And, as far as it is acknowledged there is no reason to doubt, so far it will be ridiculous to pretend to doubt.

These observations might be sufficient on this subject, for they shew us that the point in debate is a point we are obliged to take for granted, and which is not capable of being questioned. But yet, however trifling it may seem after what has been said, it will be of some use to point out more particularly the meaning of this enquiry, 'Do not our faculties always deceive us?' And to shew what the evidence really is which we have for the contrary.

Let it be considered then farther, that it is impossible what is not *true*, should be *perceived*.—Now, it is certain, that there is a great variety of truths which we *think* we perceive; and, the whole question, consequently, is, whether we *really* perceive them, or not. The existence of absolute truth is supposed in the objection. Suspicion of our faculties and fear of being deceived evidently imply it; nor can we deny, that it exists, without contradicting ourselves; for it would be to assert, that it is true, that nothing is true. The same may be said of *doubting* whether there is any thing true; for doubting denotes a hesitation or suspense of the mind about the truth of what is doubted of; and, therefore, a tacit acknowledgment that there is somewhat true. Take away this, and there is no idea of it left.* So impossible is universal scepticism; and so necessarily does truth remain, even after we have taken it away. There being then truth perceivable, we are unavoidably led to believe, that we *may*, and that, in many instances, we *do* perceive it. But what I meant here to observe was, that to doubt of the rectitude of our faculties, is to doubt, whether our reason is not so formed and situated, as to misrepresent every object of science to us; whether we ever *know*, or only *imagine* we know; whether, for example, we *actually perceive*, or only *fancy* that we perceive a circle to be *different* from a triangle, or the whole to be *bigger* than a part.

As far as we cannot doubt of these things, or find ourselves forced to think we *perceive* them; so far we cannot doubt our faculties: So far we are forced to think them right.—It appears, therefore, that we have all the reason for believing our faculties, which we have for assenting to any self-evident

---

* Thus ignorance implies something to be known, and doubting about the way to a place, that there is a way.

propositions; or for believing that we have any real perceptions.—Whatever we perceive, we perceive as it *is*; and to
perceive nothing as it is, is to perceive nothing at all. A mind
cannot be without ideas, [1]and as far as it has ideas they must
be *true* ideas; a *wrong* idea of an object being the same with
no idea of it, or the idea of some *other* object.[1]

Observations of this kind may shew us the truth of the
following conclusions.

First, No being can be made who shall perceive falsehood.
What is false, is nothing. Error is always the effect, not of
perception, but of the want of it. As far as our perceptions
go, they must correspond to the truth of things.

Secondly, No being can be made who shall have *different*
ideas, and yet not see them *different*. This would be to *have*
them, and at the same time not to have them.* There can,
therefore, be no rational beings, who do not assent to all the
truths which are included in the apprehended difference
between ideas.—Thus; To have the ideas of a whole and a
part, is the same with seeing the one to be *greater* than the
other. To have the ideas of two figures, and an exact coincidence between them when laid on one another, is the
same with seeing them to be *equal*. The like may be observed
of many of the truths which we make out by demonstration;
for demonstration is only the self-evident application of self-
evident principles.

* We may mis-name our ideas, or imagine that an idea present at one time
in our minds, is the same with one different from it, that was present at another.
But no one can conceive, that a being, contemplating at the *same* time two ideas,
can then think them not two but the same. He cannot have two ideas before
his mind without being *conscious* of it; and he cannot be *conscious* of it, without
knowing them to be different, and having a complete view and discernment of
them, as far as they are *his* ideas.

[1 Ed. 1 reads: 'and ideas it cannot have without perceiving them; and as
far as it perceives them, it perceives truth; it being impossible that it should
perceive them to be what they are not. It makes no difference what these ideas
are, for though they represent nothing actually existing, yet they are still
equally subjects of truth, equally adequate and complete in themselves, and of
perfect and determined natures.']

In a word; either there are truths, which we are forced to think we know, or there are not. None probably will assert the latter; and declare seriously, there is nothing they find themselves under any necessity of believing. Were there any such persons they would be incapable of being reasoned with; nor would it be to any purpose to tell them, that this very declaration gives itself the lye.—If, therefore, there are truths which we *think* we perceive, it is the greatest folly to pretend, at the same time, to doubt of the rectitude of our understandings with respect to them; that is, to *doubt* whether we perceive them or not.—Thinking we are right, believing, and thinking our faculties right, are one and the same. He that says, he doubts whether his eyes are not so made as always to deceive him, cannot without contradicting himself, say, he *believes* he ever sees any external object. If we have a necessary determination to believe at all, we have a necessary determination to believe our faculties; and in the degree we *believe* them, we cannot *distrust* them. An expression then which has been used should be inverted, and instead of saying, 'upon supposition my faculties are duly made, I am sure of such and such things;' it should be said, 'I am sure of such and such truths; and, therefore, I am in the same degree sure my faculties inform me rightly.'

Shall it still be objected; 'I have found myself mistaken in *many* cases; and how shall I know but I may be so in *all*?'—I answer; look into yourself and examine your own conceptions. Clearness and distinctness of apprehension, as you have or want it, will and must satisfy you, when you are right, and when it is possible you may be wrong. Do not you really know, that you are not deceived, when you think, that if equals are taken from equals, the remainders will be equal? Can you entertain the least doubt, whether the body of the sun is bigger than it appears to the naked eye? or is it any reason for questioning this, that you once may have thought otherwise? Is it reasonable, because you have judged wrong in *some cases*, through ignorance, haste, prejudice, or partial views, to suspect that you judge wrong *in all cases*, however clear? Because, through bodily indisposition or other causes, our senses *sometimes* misrepresent outward objects to us, are they *for ever* to be discredited? Because we sometimes dream, must it be doubtful whether we are ever awake? Because one man imposed upon us, are we to conclude that no faith is due to any human testimony? or because our memories have deceived us with respect to some events, must we question whether we remember right what happened the last moment?*

But let it, for this or any other reason, be granted *possible*, that all our recollections are wrong, all our opinions false, and all our knowledge delusion; still there will be only a bare *possibility* against all reason and evidence, and the whole weight and bent of our minds obliging us to think the contrary. It is not in our power to pay the least regard to a simple *may be*, in opposition to *any* apparent evidence,† much

---

* Conclusions of this sort, (strange as they may seem) have been actually drawn; and it has been asserted, that because in adding together a long series of numbers, we are liable to err, we cannot be sure that we are right in the addition of the smallest numbers; and, therefore, not in reckoning twice two to be four.

Another sceptical argument which has been insisted on, is this. In every judgment we can form, besides the uncertainty attending the original consideration of the subject itself; there is another derived from the consideration of the fallibility of our faculties, and the past instances in which we have been mistaken; to which must be added a third uncertainty, derived from the possibility of error in this estimation we make of the fidelity of our faculties; and to this a fourth of the same kind, and so on *in infinitum*; till at last the first evidence, by a constant diminution of it, must be reduced to nothing. See Mr. *Hume's Treatise of Human Nature*, Vol. I. p. 315, &c. As much of this strange reasoning as is not above my comprehension, proves just the reverse of what was intended by it. For let it be acknowledged, that the consideration of the fallibility of our understandings, and the instances in which they have deceived us, necessarily diminishes our assurance of the rectitude of our sentiments; the subsequent reflection on the uncertainty attending this judgment which we make of our faculties, diminishes not, but contributes to restore to its first strength, our original assurance; because the more precarious a judgment or probability unfavourable to another appears, the less must be its effect in weakening it.

† How trifling then is it to alledge against any thing, for which there appears

less in opposition to the *strongest*.—Let it be admitted farther, that there may be a set of rational beings in a state of necessary and total deception, or to whom nothing of truth and reality ever appears; though this be absolutely impossible, and the same, as I have before observed, with supposing them to be void of all intellectual perception, and inconsistent with the very idea of their existence, as thinking and reasonable beings; yet, granting this, we cannot help thinking, that it is not the case with *us*; and that such beings can by no means think and perceive as we do.

In a word: What things *seem* to us, we must take them to *be*; and whatever our faculties inform us of, we must give credit to.—A great deal, therefore, of the scepticism, which some have professed and defended, can be nothing but affectation and self-deception.

I shall conclude this chapter with a few observations on the general grounds of belief and assent. These may be all comprehended under the three following heads.

The first is immediate consciousness or FEELING. It is absurd to ask a reason for our believing what we *feel*, or are inwardly conscious of. A thinking being must necessarily have a capacity of discovering some things in this way. It is from hence particularly we acquire the knowledge of our own existence, and of the several operations, passions, and sensations of our minds. [1]And it is also under this head I would comprehend the information we derive from our powers of recollection or memory.[1]

The *second* ground of belief is INTUITION; by which I mean the mind's survey of its own ideas, and the relations between

to be an overbalance of evidence, that, did we know more of the case, *perhaps* we might see equal evidence for the contrary. It is always a full answer to this, to say; *perhaps* not.—What we are wholly unacquainted with, may, for aught we know, make as much *for* any of our opinions, as *against* them.

[1 This sentence is not in eds. 1 and 2.]

them, and the notice it takes of what[1] is or is not true and false, consistent and inconsistent, possible and impossible in the natures of things. It is to this, as has been explained at large in the first chapter, we owe our belief of all self-evident truths; our ideas of the general, abstract affections and relations of things; our moral ideas, and whatsoever else we discover, without making use of any process of reasoning.—It is on this power of intuition, essential, in some degree or other, to all rational minds, that the whole possibility of all reasoning is founded. To it the last appeal is ever made. Many of its perceptions are capable, by attention, of being rendered more clear; and many of the truths discovered by it, may be illustrated by an advantageous representation of them, or by being viewed in particular lights; but seldom will admit of proper proof.—Some truths there must be, which can appear only by their own light, and which are incapable of proof; otherwise nothing could be proved, or known; in the same manner as, if there were no letters, there could be no words, or if there were no simple and undefinable ideas, there could be no complex ideas.—I might mention many instances of truths discernible no other way than *intuitively*, which learned men have strangely confounded and obscured, by supposing them subjects of *reasoning and deduction*. One of the most important instances, the subject of this treatise affords us; and another we have, in our notions of the necessity of a *cause* of whatever begins to exist, and our general ideas of *power and connexion*:* And, sometimes, reason has been ridiculously employed to prove even our own existence.

The *third* ground of belief is ARGUMENTATION *or* DEDUCTION. This we have recourse to when intuition fails us; and it is, as just now hinted, highly necessary, that we carefully distinguish between these two, mark their differences and

* See the second section of the first chapter, p. 25, &c.
[1 Eds. 1 and 2 add 'absolutely and necessarily'.]

limits, and observe what information we owe to the one or the other of them.—Our ideas are such, that, by comparing them amongst themselves, we can find out numberless truths concerning them, and, consequently, concerning actually existent objects, as far as correspondent to them, which would be otherwise undiscoverable. Thus, a particular relation between two ideas, which cannot be discerned by any immediate comparison, may appear, to the greatest satisfaction, by the help of a proper, intermediate idea, whose relation to each is either self-evident, or made out by some precedent reasoning.—It is very agreeable here to consider, how one truth infers other truths; and what vast accessions of knowledge may arise from the addition of one new idea, by supplying us with a proper medium for discovering the relations of those we had before; which discoveries might themselves help to further discoveries, and these to yet further, and so on without end.—If one *new idea* may have this effect; what inconceivable improvements may we suppose possible to arise from the unfolding of one *new sense* or *faculty*?

It would be needless to give any instances of knowledge derived from *Argumentation*. All is to be ascribed to it, which we have not received from either of the preceding sources.

It may be worth observing, that all we believe on any of these grounds is not equally evident to us. This is obvious with respect to the last, which supplies us with all the degrees of evidence, from that producing full certainty, to the lowest probability. *Intuition*, likewise, is found in very various degrees. It is sometimes clear and perfect, and sometimes faint and obscure.[1] Several propositions in geometry would appear very likely to it, though we had no demonstrations of them.—Neither do *consciousness, memory*, and *reflexion on ourselves* convince us equally of all we discover by them. They

[1 Ed. 1 reads 'wavering'; ed. 2 'obscure'.]

give us the utmost assurance of our own existence, and also our identity as far as clear and distinct recollection can reach; but they do not give the same assurance of a great deal that has passed within us, of the springs of our actions, and the particular nature, ends, tendencies, and workings of our passions and affections, which is sufficiently proved by the disputes on these subjects.

It may also be worth mentioning, that some things we discover only in one of these ways, and some in more, or in all of them. All that we now prove by *Reasoning* might be still equally thus proved, though it were in the same degree *intuitive* to us, that it may be to beings above us. Intuition is not always incompatible with argumentation, though, when perfect, it supersedes it; and, when imperfect, is often incapable of receiving any aid from it; and, therefore, in such cases, ought to be rested entirely on its own evidence. Every process of reasoning is composed of intuitions, and all the several steps in it are so many distinct intuitions; which, when clear and unquestionable, produce *demonstration and certainty*; when otherwise, give rise to *opinion and probability*. Nothing would be a greater advantage to us, in the search of truth, than taking time often to resolve our reasonings into their constituent intuitions; and to observe carefully, what light and evidence attend each, and in what manner, and with what degree of force, they infer the conclusion. Such a custom of analysing our sentiments, and tracing them to their elements and principles, would prevent much error and confusion, and shew us what degree of assent is due to the conclusions we receive, and on what foundation our opinions really stand.

An instance of what is discovered in all the ways above-named, is the existence of matter. *Immediate feeling* discovers to us our own organs, and the modifications of them. These the soul perceives by being *present* with them.—We have the ideas of matter, and of a material world; and we, therefore, see *intuitively* the *possibility* of their existence; for *possibility* of existing is implied in the idea of every object; what is impossible being nothing, and no object of reflexion.—We are conscious of certain impressions made upon us, and of certain notices transmitted to us from without, and know they are produced by some foreign cause. We touch a solid substance, and feel resistance. We see certain images drawn on our organs of sight, and know they are acted upon by *something*. The resistance made *may be* owing to a resisting body; and the scenes painted before us *may be* derived from a correspondent, external scene, discovering itself to us by means of intermediate matter. Supposing an external world, in what better manner could the information of it be communicated to us? What is more incredible, than that all the notices conveyed to us by our senses, and all the impressions made upon them, corresponding in all respects to the supposition of an external world, and confirming one another in numberless ways, should be entirely visionary and delusive? It is, I own, still *possible*, that matter may not exist.[1] So likewise is it *possible*, that the *planets* may not be inhabited, though every particle of matter on the *earth* abounds with inhabitants; that gravity may not be the power that keeps them in their orbits, though it be certainly the power that keeps the *moon* in its orbit; and that we may be the *only* beings in the world, and the only productions of divine power, though the greatest reason to conclude the contrary offers itself to us, from the consideration barely of our own existence, and the consequent *possibility and likelihood* of the existence of numberless other beings. Analogy and intuition, in these cases, immediately inform us what is fact, and produce conviction which we cannot resist.—In short, it is *self-evident*,

[1 Ed. 1 adds: 'and that all these appearances and notices may be derived immediately and solely from the regular and constant action of the Deity, or of some other invisible and intelligent cause, upon our minds.' So ed. 2 also, but omitting 'immediately and solely'.]

that a *material world*, answerable to our ideas, and to what we feel and see, is *possible*. We have no reason to think that it does not exist. Every thing appears as if it did exist; and against the reality of its existence there is nothing but a bare possibility, against actual feeling, and all the evidence which our circumstances and condition, as embodied spirits, seem capable of.

It is well known what controversies have of late been raised on this subject; some denying the existence of a material world; while others, not finding it possible seriously to doubt, resolve their conviction into a determination given us to believe, which cannot be accounted for.[1] I should go too far out of my way, were I to say much more of the nature and grounds of our conviction in this instance. I shall therefore only observe farther, that the same principles on which the existence of *matter* is opposed, lead us equally to deny the existence of *spiritual* beings. And those who reject the one, while they believe the other, should tell us, 'on what grounds they believe there exist any beings whatsoever besides themselves.'

This dispute, after all, turns chiefly on the question; whether matter, considered as something actually existing *without the mind* and *independent of its perceptions*, be *possible*, or not? For there are few, probably, who will deny its existence for any reason besides an apprehension of the impossibility of it, in any other sense, than as an idea, or sensation in the mind.—One would think that there can be no occasion for spending time in refuting this. What is indisputable, if it be not so, that whatever is *conceivable* cannot be *impossible*? What pretence can there be for asserting, that *figure*, *motion*, and *solid extension* are *sensations*, which cannot, any more than [2]*pleasure* and *pain*,[2] have any real existence *without the mind*,

[1 Ed. 1 adds: 'Indeed, the nature and grounds of our conviction in this instance, have not, perhaps, been yet sufficiently explained.']
[2 Ed. 1 reads '*colour and sound*'. Cf. p. 15.]

that will not imply the same of the *object* of every idea, and of *all that is commonly thought to have a distinct and continued existence*?—But it is time to proceed to what has a nearer relation to the design of this treatise.*

* See Note E at the Conclusion.

CHAP. VI.

Of Fitness, and Moral Obligation, and the various Forms of
Expression, which have been used by different Writers in
explaining Morality.

AFTER the account that has been given of the nature and
origin of our ideas of morality; it will be easy to perceive
the meaning of several terms and phrases, which are commonly used in speaking on this subject.

Fitness and *unfitness* most frequently denote the congruity
or incongruity, aptitude or inaptitude of any means to
accomplish an end. But when applied to actions, they
generally signify the same with *right* and *wrong*; nor is it often
hard to determine in which of these senses[1] these words are
to be understood. It is worth observing, that *fitness*, in the
former sense, is equally undefinable with *fitness* in the latter;
or, that it is as impossible to express, in any other than
synonymous words, what we mean, when we say of certain
objects, 'that they have a *fitness* to one another; or are *fit* to
answer certain purposes,' as it is when we say, 'reverencing
the Deity is *fit*, or beneficence is *fit* to be practised.' In the
first of these instances, none can avoid owning the absurdity
of making an arbitrary sense the source of the idea of *fitness*,
and of concluding that it signifies nothing real in objects, and
that no one thing can be properly the *means* of another. In
both cases the term *fit*, signifies a simple perception of the
understanding.

Morally good and *evil*, *reasonable* and *unreasonable*, are
epithets also commonly applied to actions, evidently meaning
the same with *right* and *wrong*, *fit* and *unfit*.

Approving an action is the same with discerning it to be

[1 Ed. 1 adds 'the relative or the absolute'.]

right; as *assenting* to a proposition is the same with discerning it to be *true*.[1]

But *Obligation* is the term most necessary to be here considered; and to the explication of it, the best part of this chapter shall be devoted.

Obligation to action, and *rightness* of action, are plainly coincident and identical; so far so, that we cannot form a notion of the one, without taking in the other. This may appear to any one upon considering, whether he can point out any difference between what is *right, meet* or *fit* to be done, and what *ought* to be done.* It is not indeed plainer, that figure implies something figured, solidity resistance, or an effect a cause, than it is that *rightness* implies *oughtness* (if I may be allowed this word) or *obligatoriness*. And as easily can we conceive of figure without extension, or motion without a change of place, as that it can be *fit* for us to do an action, and yet that it may not be what we *should* do, what it is our *duty* to do, or what we are under an *obligation* to do.—*Right, fit, ought, should, duty, obligation*, convey, then, ideas necessarily including one another. From hence it follows,

First, That virtue, *as such*, has a real obligatory power antecedently to all positive laws, and independently of all will; for obligation, we see, is involved in the very nature of it. To affirm, that the performance of that, which, to omit, would be wrong, is not obligatory, unless conducive to private good or enjoined by a superior power, is a manifest contradiction. It is to say, that it is not true, that a thing is what it is; or that we are *obliged* to do what we *ought* to do; unless it be the object of a command, or, in some manner, privately useful.—If there are any actions fit to be done by an agent, besides such as tend to his own happiness, those

---

* *Obligatory* answers to *oportet, decet, debitum*, in Latin; and to δεῖ, δέον ἐστί, θεμιτόν, καθῆκον, δίκαιον, in Greek.

[1 Eds. 1 and 2 add: "'Tis, however, to be remembered, that the word *approbation* conveys likewise, particularly, an idea of the *pleasure and satisfaction* generally accompanying the discernment of right.']

actions, by the terms, are *obligatory*, independently of their influence on his happiness.—Whatever it is *wrong* to do, that it is our *duty* not to do, whether enjoined or not by any positive law.*—I cannot conceive of any thing much more evident than this.—It appears, therefore, that those who maintain that all obligation is to be deduced from positive laws, the Divine will, or self-love, assert what (if they mean any thing contrary to what is here said) implies, that the words *right* and *just* stand for no real and distinct characters of actions; but signify merely what is *willed* and *commanded*, or conducive to private advantage, whatever that be; so that any thing may be both right and wrong, morally good and evil, at the same time and in any circumstances, as it may be commanded or forbidden by different laws and wills; and any the most pernicious effects will become just, and fit to be produced by any being, if but the smallest degree of clear advantage or pleasure may result to him from them.

Those who say, nothing can oblige but the will of God, generally resolve the power of this to oblige to the annexed rewards and punishments. And thus, in reality, they subvert entirely the independent natures of moral good and evil; and are forced to maintain, that nothing can *oblige*, but the prospect of pleasure to be obtained, or pain to be avoided. If this be true, it follows that *vice* is, properly, no more than *imprudence*; that nothing is right or wrong, just or unjust, any farther than it affects self-interest; and that a being, independently and completely happy, cannot have any moral perceptions. The justness of these inferences cannot be denied by one, who will attend to the coincidence here insisted on between obligation and virtue.

But to pursue this point farther; let me ask, would a

---

* It is obvious, that this is very different from saying (what it would be plainly absurd to say) that every action, the performance of which, in certain circumstances is wrong, will continue wrong, let the circumstances be ever so much altered, or by whatever authority it is commanded.

person who either believes there is no God, or that he does not concern himself with human affairs, feel no *moral obligations*, and therefore not be at all *accountable*? Would one, who should happen not to be convinced, that virtue tends to his happiness here or hereafter, be released from every *bond* of duty and morality? Or, would he, if he believed no future state, and that, in any instance, virtue was against his *present* interest, be truly *obliged*, in these instances, to be wicked?—These consequences must follow, if obligation depends entirely on the knowledge of the will of a superior, or on the connexion between actions and private interest.— But, indeed, the very expression, *virtue tends to our happiness*, and the supposition that, in certain cases, it may be inconsistent with it, imply that it may exist independently of any connexion with private interest; and would have no sense, if it signified only the relation of actions to private interest. For then, to suppose virtue to be inconsistent with our happiness, would be the same with supposing, that what is *advantageous* to us, may be *disadvantageous* to us.

It is strange to find those who plead for self-interest, as the only ground of moral obligation, asserting that, when virtue clashes with present enjoyments, all motives to it cease, supposing no future state. For, upon their principles, the truth is not, that all motives to practise virtue, would, in these circumstances, cease, but that virtue itself would cease; nay, would be changed into vice; and what would otherwise have been fit and just, become unlawful and wrong: For, being under an obligation in these circumstances not to do what appeared to us fit, it could not in reality *be* fit; we could not do it without violating our duty, and therefore certainly, not without doing wrong. Thus, all who find not their *present* account in virtue, would, upon these principles (setting aside another world) be under an obligation to be wicked. Or, to speak more properly, the subject-matter of virtue and vice (that is, the relation of particular actions to private good) would be altered; what was before *wickedness* would become *virtue*, and what was before *virtue* would become *wickedness*.— It should be carefully minded that, as far as another world creates *obligation*, it creates *virtue*; for it is an absurdity too gross to be maintained, that we may act contrary to our obligations, and yet act virtuously.

Another observation worthy our notice in this place, is that rewards and punishments suppose, in the very idea of them, moral obligation, and are founded upon it. They do not *make* it, but *enforce* it. They are the *sanctions* of virtue, and not its *efficients*. A reward supposes something done to *deserve* it, or a conformity to *obligation subsisting previously to it*; and punishment is always inflicted on account of some breach of *obligation*. Were we under no obligations, antecedently to the proposal of rewards and punishments, it would be a contradiction to suppose us subjects capable of them.—A person without any light besides that of nature, and supposed ignorant of a future state of rewards and punishments and the will of the Deity, might discover these by reasoning from his natural notions of morality and duty. But were the latter dependent on the former, and not *vice versa*; this could not be said, nor should we have any principles left, from which to learn the will of the Deity, and the conditions of his favour to us.

Secondly, From the account given of *obligation*, it follows that *rectitude* is a *law* as well as a *rule* to us; that it not only *directs*, but *binds* all, as far as it is perceived.—With respect to its being a *rule*, we may observe, that a rule of action signifying some measure or standard to which we are to conform our actions, or some information we possess concerning what we ought to do, there can, in this sense, be no *other* rule of action; all besides, to which this name can be properly given, implying it, or signifying only helps to the discovery of it. To perceive or to be informed how it is *right* to act, is the very notion of a *direction* to act. And it must be lded, that it is such a direction as implies *authority*, and hich we cannot disregard or neglect without remorse and ain. Reason is the guide, the *natural* and *authoritative* guide f a rational being. Where he has no discernment of right nd wrong, there, and there only, is he (morally speaking) *ee*. But where he has this discernment, where *moral good* ppears to him, and he cannot avoid pronouncing concerning n action, that it is fit to be done, and evil to omit it; here he tied in the most strict and absolute manner, in bonds that o power in nature can dissolve, and from which he can at o time, or in any single instance, break loose, without offer- ig the most unnatural violence to himself; without making n inroad into his own soul, and immediately pronouncing is own sentence.

That is properly a *law* to us, which we always and un- voidably feel and own ourselves *obliged* to obey; and which, s we obey or disobey it, is attended with the immediate anctions of inward triumph and self-applause, or of inward hame and self-reproach, together with the secret appre- ensions of the favour or displeasure of a superior righteous ower, and the anticipations of *future* rewards, and punish- nents.—That has proper *authority* over us, to which, if we efuse submission, we transgress our duty, incur guilt, and xpose ourselves to just vengeance. All this is certainly true f our moral judgment, and contained in the idea of it.

Rectitude then, or virtue, is a LAW.* And it is the *first* and *upreme* law, to which all other laws owe their force, on which hey depend, and in virtue of which alone they oblige. It is n *universal* LAW. The whole creation is ruled by it: under it nen and all rational beings subsist. It is the source and guide f all the actions of the Deity himself, and on it his throne and ;overnment are founded. It is an *unalterable and indispensible* .AW. The repeal, suspension or even *relaxation* of it, once for moment, in any part of the universe, cannot be conceived

* Τὸ μὲν ὀρθὸν νόμος ἐστὶ βασιλικός. *Plat. Minos.*

without a contradiction. Other laws have had a date; time when they were enacted, and became of force. The are confined to particular places, rest on precarious found tions, may lose their vigour, grow obsolete with time, an become useless and neglected. Nothing like this can be tru of this law. It has no date. It never was made or enacte It is prior to all things. It is self-valid and self-originate and must for ever retain its usefulness and vigour, withou the possibility of diminution or abatement. It is coeval wit eternity; as unalterable as necessary, everlasting truth; independent as the existence of God; and as sacred an awful as his nature and perfections.—The *authority* it po sesses is native and essential to it, underived and absolute It is superior to all other authority, and the basis and pare of all other authority. It is indeed self-evident that, proper speaking, there is no other authority; nothing else that ca claim our obedience, or that *ought* to guide and rule heave and earth.—It is, in short, the *one* authority in nature, th same in all times and in all places; or, in one word, th DIVINE authority.

Thirdly, From the account given of obligation, it appea how absurd it is to enquire, what *obliges* us to practise virtue as if obligation was no part of the idea of virtue, but somethin adventitious and foreign to it; that is, as if what was *du* might not be our *duty*, or what was *wrong, unlawful*; or as if might not be true, that what it is *fit* to do, we *ought* to do, an that what we *ought* to do, we are *obliged* to do.—To ask, wh are we *obliged* to practise virtue, to abstain from what wicked, or perform what is just, is the very same as to ask why we are *obliged* to do what we are *obliged* to do?—It is no possible to avoid wondering at those, who have so unaccount ably embarrassed themselves, on a subject that one woul think was attended with no difficulty; and who, because the cannot find any thing in *virtue and duty themselves*, which ca induce us to pay a regard to them in our practice, fly t

:lf-love, and maintain that from hence alone are derived all
iducement and obligation.

Fourthly, From what has been observed, it may appear, in
/hat sense obligation is ascribed to God. It is no more than
scribing to him the perception of rectitude, or saying, that
here are certain ends, and certain measures in the admini-
tration of the world, which he approves, and which are
etter to be pursued than others.—Great care, however,
hould be taken, what language we here use. *Obligation* is a
vord to which many persons have affixed several ideas,
vhich should by no means be retained when we speak of
Jod. Our language and our conceptions, whenever he is the
ubject of them, are *always* extremely defective and inade-
|uate, and *often* very erroneous.—There are many who think
t absurd and shocking to attribute any thing of *obligation* or
aw to a being who is necessarily sufficient and independent,
nd to whom nothing can be prior or superior. How, I con-
eive, we are to frame our apprehensions on this subject, has
ilready, in some measure, appeared. It should, methinks,
e enough to satisfy such persons, that the obligations ascribed
o the Deity arise entirely from and exist in his own nature;
nd that the eternal, unchangeable LAW, by which it has
een said, he is directed in all his actions, is no other than
HIMSELF; *his own infinite, eternal, all perfect understanding.*

Fifthly, What has been said also shews us, on what the
obligations of religion and the Divine will are founded. They
are plainly branches of universal rectitude. Our obligation
to obey God's will means nothing, but that obedience is *due*
to it, or that it is *right and fit* to comply with it. What an
absurdity is it then, to make obligation *subsequent* to the
Divine will, and the *creature* of it? For why, upon this supposition, does not *all* will oblige equally? If there be any
thing which gives the preference to one will above another;
that, by the terms, is *moral rectitude.* What would any laws or
will of any being signify, what influence could they have on

the determinations of a moral agent, was there no goo
reason for complying with them, no obligation to regar
them, no *antecedent right* of command?—To affirm that w
are *obliged* in any case, but not in virtue of *reason and right,*
to say, that in that case we are not obliged at all.—Beside
nothing could be ever commanded by the Deity, was ther
no prior reason for commanding it. To which add, that on
ground of our obligation to obey His will is this, its bein
under the direction of reason, or always a wise, righteou
and good will. Thus, therefore, on all accounts, and i
every view of things, do will and law presuppose reason an
right. And it is upon the whole, unquestionable, that if w
take away the latter, the former lose all support and efficacy
and that were there nothing in itself just and obligatory
nothing could be made so by law, will, commands, com
pacts, or any means whatever. See observations to the sam
purpose, Chap. I. at the conclusion.

One cannot but observe on this occasion, how the ideas o
right and wrong force themselves upon us, and in some forn
or other, always remain, even when we think we have anni
hilated them. Thus, after we have supposed all actions an
ends to be in themselves indifferent, it is natural to conceive
that it is *right* to give ourselves up to the guidance of un
restrained inclination, and *wrong* to be careful of our actions
or to give ourselves any trouble in pursuing any ends. Or, i
with *Hobbs* and the orator in *Plato's Gorgias*, we suppose tha
the strongest may oppress the weakest, and take to themselves
whatever they can seize; or that unlimited power confers an
unlimited right; this plainly still leaves us in possession of the
idea of *right*, and only establishes *another species* of it.—In like
manner, when we suppose all the obligations of morality to
be derived from laws and compacts, we at the same time find
ourselves under a necessity of supposing something *before*
them, not absolutely indifferent in respect of choice; something good and evil, right and wrong, which gave rise to

ιem and occasion for them; and which, after they are made,
ιakes them regarded.

But to return to the subject under consideration. The
ecessary perfections of the Deity; the infinite excellencies
ʼ his nature as the fountain of reason and wisdom; the
ιtire dependence of all beings upon him, and their deriving
om his bounty existence and all its blessings and hopes—
ʼom hence, and not merely from his almighty power, arises
is SOVEREIGN AUTHORITY. These are the reasons that render
im the proper object of our supreme homage, constitute his
ight of government, vest him with universal and just domi-
ion, and make it the first duty of the whole intelligent world
ɔ obey, to please, and honour him in all they think and do.—
ʼhose who will allow of no other motive to regard the Deity,
ιo other meaning of the obligation to obey him, besides what
ɟ implied in his power to make us happy or miserable,
ιaintain what it is wonderful how any human mind can
eriously embrace. They maintain, that were it possible to
ιuppose that we had nothing to hope or fear from him, we
ɦould not have the least desire of his approbation, or the
east concern about his expectations from us, or any reason
ʼor paying him any kind of regard; that setting aside the
ɔonsideration of our own interest, it is entirely indifferent
vhat our dispositions and behaviour are with respect to him;
ɟhat his nature, attributes and benefits, however glorious, are,
ιn themselves, incapable of having any effect upon any
ɾational nature; and that though (retaining power) we were
ɛver so much to change or reverse his character, it would still
be equally incumbent upon us to love, revere, and obey him,
ɟo resign our wills to his, and to endeavour to approve our-
ɟelves to him.

Farther, what has been said will shew us, what judgment to
form concerning several accounts and definitions, which
have been given of obligation. It is easy here to perceive the

perplexity arising from attempting to define words expressin
simple perceptions of the mind.—An ingenious and ab.
writer* defines obligation to be *a state of the mind into which
is brought by perceiving a reason for action.* Let this definition b
substituted wherever the words *duty, should, obliged,* occur
and it will soon be seen how defective it is. The meaning o
it is plainly, that obligation denotes that attraction or excite
ment which the mind feels upon perceiving right and wron;
But this is the *effect* of obligation perceived, rather tha
obligation itself. Besides, it is proper to say, that the duty o
obligation to act is a reason for acting; and then this definitio
will stand thus: *obligation is a state of the mind into which it*
brought by perceiving obligation to act.—This author divide
obligation into *external* and *internal*; by the former, meanin
the excitement we feel to pursue pleasure as *sensible agents*
and, by the latter, the excitement we feel to pursue virtue a
reasonable and moral agents. But, as merely sensible beings, w
are incapable of obligation; otherwise it might be properl
applied to brutes, which, I think, it never is. What, in thes
instances, produces confusion, is not distinguishing betwee
perception and the effect of it; between *obligation* and a
motive. All motives are not obligations; though the contrar
is true, that wherever there is obligation, there is also a
motive to action.—Some perhaps, by *obligation,* may onl
mean such a motive to act, as shall have the greatest influence
and be most likely to determine us, and as far as this is al
that is intended, it may be allowed, that the obligation to
practise virtue depends greatly, as mankind are now situated
on its connexion with private interest, and the views o
future rewards and punishments.

Obligation has, by several writers, been styled, the *necessit*
of doing a thing in order to be happy.† I have already taken

* *Mr. Balguy. See his tracts on the foundation of moral goodness and the law of truth.*
† 'The whole force of obligation (says Bishop *Cumberland* in his *treatise* of the
laws of nature, chap. v. sect. ii.) is this, that the legislator hath annexed to the

ufficient notice of the opinion from which this definition is
derived; and therefore shall here only ask, what, if this be the

observance of his laws, good, to the transgression evil; and those natural: In
respect whereof men are moved to perform actions, rather agreeing than
disagreeing with the laws.'—Ibid. sect. 27. 'I think that moral obligation may
be thus universally and properly defined. Obligation is that act of a legislator,
by which he declares that actions conformable to his law are necessary to those
for whom the law is made. An action is then understood to be necessary to a
rational agent, when it is certainly one of the causes necessarily required to that
happiness, which he naturally and consequently necessarily desires.'—Again,
sect. xxxv. 'I cannot conceive any thing which could bind the mind of man with
any necessity (in which *Justinian's* definition places the force of obligation)
except arguments proving, that good or evil will proceed from our actions.'—
The remarks which Mr. *Maxwell*, the translator, makes on these passages, are
so good, that I cannot help transcribing some of them.—'If, says he, this (that
is, the necessity of the observance of the law as a means of our happiness) be
the whole of the law's obligation, the transgression of the law is not *unrighteous-
ness*, *sin* and *crime*, but only *imprudence* and *infelicity*, for the sanction of the law
importeth no other evil. But the obligation or bond of the law is the *jural
restraint* which is expressed by *non licet, you may not do it*; but because a bare
non licet or prohibition is not sufficient to enforce the law, therefore the *sin* and
punishment, the *precept* and the *sanction* both concur to make the *jural restraint*,
which must be thus fully expressed, *non licet impune, you may not do it with impunity*. But though sin and punishment are closely connected, yet the obligation
of *non licet, it may not be done*, is distinct from the obligation of *non impune, not
with impunity*, as sin and punishment are of distinct consideration. But a man
is *bound*, both when he cannot do a thing *without sin*, and when he cannot do a
thing *without punishment*; and *both* these *obligations* are in every law, and both
concur to make the obligation of it. But because the obligation of *non licet*, is
antecedent to the obligation of *non impune*, the precept to the sanction, and the
sin is made by the law, the law hath so much obligation, as to make the sin
before the penalty is enacted; therefore, the law hath an obligation antecedently to the sanction of it. For every one is *bound* to avoid what is sin,
because none can have a right to do what is unrighteous.—No ingenuous man
looks upon himself as obliged to be grateful to his benefactors, to love his wife
and children, or to love and honour his God and Saviour, merely by the sanction of rewards and punishments. Is there no obligation on men from right and
wrong, due and undue, sanctity and sin, righteousness and wickedness, honesty
and dishonesty, conscience or crime, virtue or villainy, but merely from a
prudent regard to their own happiness?—The vulgar say, *I am bound in duty, in
justice, in gratitude*; and the schools say, *that the obligation of the law of nature is a
bond of conscience.*—It is not possible to deduce a conscientious obligation, merely
from a *politick and prudential regard to our own happiness.*—The legislator annexes
to his law the sanction of the *good of pleasure*, for the sake of the *good of virtue*,
which the law enjoineth; this, therefore, is the principle in the estimation of the

only sense of obligation, is meant when we say, a man *obliged* to study his own happiness? Is it not obvious tha *obliged*, in this proposition, signifies, not the necessity c doing a thing in order to be happy, which would make i ridiculous; but only, that it is *right* to study our own happiness and *wrong* to neglect it?

A very learned author* maintains, that moral obligatio always denotes some object of will and law, or implies som obliger. Were this true; it would be mere jargon to mentio our being *obliged* to obey the Divine will; and yet, this is a proper language as any we can use. But his meaning seem to be, that the word *obligation* signifies only the *particula fitness* of obeying the Divine will, and cannot properly b applied to any other fitness; which is restraining the sense o the word, in a manner which the common use of it by n means warrants.

The sense of obligation given by Dr. *Hutcheson,*† agrees i some measure, with the account here given of it. Then, h says, a *person is obliged to an action, when every spectator, or h himself, upon reflexion, must approve his action and disapprov omitting it.* This account, however, is not perfectly accurate for though obligation to act, and reflex approbation anc disapprobation do, *in one*‡ *sense*, always accompany anc

lawgiver; whose will, if it be made known, is, without a sanction, a bond o obligation upon us; for we *owe* obedience thereto, and every one is bound t pay what he oweth.' See the *Appendix to Cumberland's treatise of the laws of nature* page 55.—'A virtuous practice (says the same writer, page 83.) is, in the nature and reason of the thing, indispensably requisite in all intelligent agents, and i to them *matter of law and obligation.* For *law* or *obligation* (in a large, but very proper sense) is nothing else, but a *non licet,* or a boundary to licence.'

* *See Dr. Warburton's Divine Legation, Vol. I. page 50.*

† *Illustrations on the Moral Sense.* Sect. I.

‡ The reason of adding this restriction is this. A man may, through involuntary error, approve of doing what he *ought* not to do, or think that to be his duty, which is really contrary to it; and yet it is too, in this case, really his duty to act agreeably to his judgment.—There are then two views of obligation, which, if not attended to, will be apt to produce confusion.—*In one sense,* a man's being *obliged* to act in a particular manner depends on his knowing it; and in

mply one another; yet they seem as different as an *act* and
n *object* of the mind, or as perception and the truth perceived.
t is not exactly the same to say, it is our *duty* to do a thing;
nd to say, we *approve* of doing it. The one is the quality of
he action, the other the *discernment* of that quality. Yet, such
s the connexion between these, that it is not very necessary
o distinguish them; and, in common language, the term
bligation often stands for the sense and judgment of the mind
concerning what is fit or unfit to be done. It would, never-
heless, I imagine, prevent some confusion, and keep our
deas more distinct and clear, to remember, that a man's
consciousness that an action ought to be done, or the
judgment concerning obligation and inducing or inferring it,
cannot, properly speaking, be *obligation itself*; and that, however variously and loosely this word may be used, its primary
and original signification coincides with *rectitude*.*

another sense, it does not. Was not the *former* true, we might be contracting guilt,
when acting with the fullest approbation of our consciences: And was not the
latter true, it would not be sense ever to speak of *shewing* another what his
obligations are, or how it is *incumbent upon him* to act.—This entirely coincides
with the distinction of virtue into *absolute* and *relative*, hereafter to be explained,
Chap. VIII.

* I observe that Dr. *Adams*, in an excellent Sermon on the *Nature and Obligation of Virtue*, agrees with me in the account he gives of obligation.—To the
question, in what does the obligation to virtue and right action consist? he
answers, 'that *right* implies *duty* in its idea; that to perceive an action to be right,
is to see a reason for doing it in the action itself, abstracted from all other considerations whatsoever; and that this perception, this acknowledged rectitude
in the action, is the very essence of obligation, that which commands the
approbation and choice, and binds the conscience of every rational being,'
page 11.—'Nothing (he says, *p.* 14.) can bring us under an obligation to do what
appears to our moral judgment wrong. It may be supposed our interest to do
this; but it cannot be supposed our duty: For, I ask, if some power, which we
are unable to resist, should assume the command over us, and give us laws
which are unrighteous and unjust; should we be under an obligation to obey
him? Should we not rather be obliged to shake off the yoke, and to resist such
usurpation, if it were in our power? However then we might be swayed by hope
or fear; it is plain, that we are under an obligation to right, which is antecedent,
and, in order and nature, superior to all other. Power may compel, interest may
bribe, pleasure may persuade; but reason only can oblige. This is the only
authority which rational beings can own, and to which they owe obedience.'—

I shall leave the reader to judge how far these remarks ar applicable to what Dr. *Clarke* says on this head, who give much the same account of obligation with that last mentioned and some of whose words it may not be amiss to quote. Se his *Evidences of Natural and revealed Religion*, page 43, 6th Edit 'The judgment and conscience of a man's own mind, concern ing the reasonableness and fitness of the thing, that his action should be conformed to such or such a rule or law, is th truest and formallest obligation, even more properly and strictly so, than any opinion whatsoever, of the authority o the giver of a law, or any regard he may have to its sanction by rewards and punishments; for whoever acts contrary to this sense and conscience of his own mind, is necessarily self condemned; and the greatest and strongest of all obligations is that which a man cannot break through without condemn ing himself.—The original obligation of all is the eterna reason of things; that reason which God himself, who has no superior to direct him, and to whose happiness nothing car be added, nor any thing diminished from it, yet constantly obliges himself to govern the world by.—So far, therefore, as men are conscious of what is right and wrong, so far they are under an obligation to act accordingly; and, consequently, that eternal rule of right which I have been hitherto describ ing, it is evident, ought as indispensably to govern men's actions, as it cannot but necessarily determine their assent.' Page 51, he says, 'The minds of men cannot but acknowledge the reasonableness and fitness of their governing all their actions by the rule of right or equity: And this assent is a formal obligation upon every man actually and constantly to conform himself to that rule.'

Dr. *Butler*, likewise, in his Sermons on *Human Nature*, and

The coincidence which, in other instances, I have found between the sentiments of this most judicious writer, on the subject of virtue, and those delivered in this treatise, has very agreeably surprized me, and given me a degree of confidence in some of the opinions I have maintained, which I should otherwise have wanted.

he explanatory remarks upon them in the *Preface*, insists
strongly on the obligation implied in reflex approbation; the
supremacy belonging to the principle of reflexion within us;
and the authority and right of superintendency which are
constituent parts of the idea of it. From this incomparable
writer, I beg leave to borrow one observation more of considerable importance, on this subject.

Every being endowed with reason, and conscious of right
and wrong, is, as such, necessarily a *law* to himself:* It
follows, therefore, that the greatest degree of ignorance or
scepticism possible, with respect to the tendencies of virtue,
the authority of the Deity, a future state, and the rewards
and punishments to be expected in it, leaves us still truly and
fully accountable, guilty, and punishable, if we transgress
this law; and will, by no means, exempt us from justice, or
be of any avail to excuse or save us, should it prove true that
such authority and future state really exist. For what makes
an agent ill-deserving is not any opinion he may have about
a superior power, or positive sanctions; but his doing wrong,
and acting contrary to the conviction of his mind. 'What
renders obnoxious to punishment, is not the fore-knowledge
of it, but merely violating a known obligation.'

There is an objection to what has been now said of obligation, which deserves to be considered.†—It may be asked, 'Are
there not many actions, of which it cannot be said, that we are
bound to perform them, which yet are *right* to be performed;
and the actual performance of which appears to us even more
amiable, than if they had been strictly our duty; such as re-
quital of good for evil, and acts of generosity and kindness?'

I answer, that allowing this, the most that can follow from
it is, not that rectitude does not imply obligation, but that it

---

* I have not here copied Dr. *Butler*, but given the sense of his observations in
other words. See the *Preface* to his sermons, *p.* 20.
† See *Essays on the Principles of Morality and natural Religion*, Part I. Essay ii.
Chap. 3.

does not imply it absolutely and universally, or so far as tha there can be no sense in which actions are denominatec *right*, which does not carry in it *obligation*. The nature o rectitude may vary, according to the objects or actions to which it is ascribed. All right actions are not so in precisely the same sense; and it might, with little prejudice to what is above asserted, be granted, that some things are right in such a sense as yet not to be our indispensable duty. But then let it be remembered: That it holds universally and incontestably, that whatever is right in such a sense, as that the omission of it would be wrong, is always and indispensably obligatory. And, in the next place, that though the idea of *rightness* may be more general than that of *fitness*, *duty*, or *obligation*; so that there may be instances to which we apply the one, but not the other; yet this cannot be said of *wrong*. The idea of this, and of obligation, are certainly of the same extent; I mean, that though there may be cases in which it cannot be said, that what we approve as right, *ought* to have been done; yet there are no cases in which it cannot be said, that what is wrong to be done, or omitted, *ought not* to be done or omitted.

But, not to dwell on this: It will be found on careful enquiry that the objection now mentioned does not require any such restrictions of what has been advanced as, at first sight, may appear to be necessary; and the following observations will, perhaps, shew this.

In the *first* place, Beneficence, *in general*, is undoubtedly a duty; and it is only with respect to the *particular* acts and instances of it that we are at liberty. A certain person, suppose, performs an act of kindness to another: We say, he *might* not have done it, or he was not *obliged* to do it; that is, he was not obliged to do this *particular* kind act. But to be kind in some instances or other; to do all the good he can to his fellow-creatures, every one is obliged; and we necessarily look upon that person as blame-worthy and guilty who aims

ot at this; but contents himself with barely abstaining from
njury and mischief. A certain part of our fortunes and
labour we *owe* to those about us, and *should* employ in doing
good; but the particular objects and methods of beneficence
are not absolutely fixed. Here we are left to our own choice,
and may not be in any sense bound; that is, there may be
nothing in any particular objects or methods of beneficence,
which render it fit and right *they* should be chosen rather than
others. If a man endeavours to do all the good which is
suitable to his station and abilities, we never condemn him
for not doing it in a particular way, or for rejecting particular
objects that are offered to him; except these objects are such,
that it is right he should *prefer* them. As far as this happens,
so far, even here, *duty* takes place. Thus, *cæteris paribus*, it is
right, friends, relations, and benefactors should be preferred
to strangers; and, whoever does otherwise, acts contrary to
his *duty*.

Again; the precise limits of some general duties cannot be
determined by us. No one can tell *exactly* to what degree he
ought to be beneficent, and how far he is obliged to exert
himself for the benefit of other men. No person, for instance,
can determine accurately, how far, in many cases, his own
good ought to give way to that of another, what number of
distressed persons he ought to relieve, or what portion *precisely* of his fortune he ought to lay out in charity, or of his
time and labour in direct endeavours to serve the publick.

In order to form a judgment in these cases, there are so
many particulars to be considered in our own circumstances
and abilities, and in the state of mankind and the world,
that we cannot but be in some uncertainty. There are indeed
degrees of *defect* and *excess*, which we easily and certainly see
to be wrong: But there is a great variety of intermediate
degrees, concerning which we cannot absolutely pronounce,
that one of them rather than another ought to be chosen.—
The same is true of the *general* duty of worshipping God.

Many of the *particular* circumstances attending it, and the precise degree of frequency with which it should be performed, are not distinctly marked out to us. In this, as well as the preceding instance, our consciences, within certain limits, are *free*,* and for a very good reason; namely, because we have no distinct apprehensions of *rectitude* to guide us. To the same degree and extent that we see this, we are *bound*, in these as much as in any other cases. Whenever any degree of beneficence, or any particular circumstances and frequency of divine worship, or any behaviour in any possible instances, appear, *all things considered*, BEST; they become *obligatory*. It is impossible to put a case, in which we shall not be *obliged* to conform ourselves to the *right* of it, whatever that is. Even what, at any time, or in any circumstances, is, upon the whole, only more *proper* to be done, *ought* then to be done; and to suppose the contrary, would be to take away the whole sense and meaning of such an assertion.

In short, the following general reasoning will hold universally.—Let a person be supposed to have under his consideration, any action proposed to be performed by him. The performance of it must be either right, or wrong, or indifferent. Now it is self-evident, that, if it is not the last, it must be one of the other two, and that obligation will ensue: For what can be plainer than that it is a contradiction to say, we may act as we will, when it is not *indifferent* how we act?—If it is *wrong*, obligation to forbear is implied.—If *right*, this may be true only of such *kind* of actions, as relieving the miserable, or worshipping the Deity in general; and then, it is only these *general duties* that are obligatory, which may be consistent with complete liberty and perfect indifference, in regard to the *particular action* in view.—Or, it may be true of this

---

* The latitude here taken notice of is one thing that allows so much room and scope for unfairness and disingenuity; and which renders it generally certain, that a backward unwilling heart that is not strongly attached to virtue, and possessed with an inward relish for it, will err on the deficient side.

particular action, and then it is no longer indifferent; yet still, there may be liberty as to the time and manner of doing it. But if even the time and manner are not indifferent, then is he also as to these *obliged*.

'But what shall we say, to the *greater amiableness* of the actions under consideration? How can there be greater virtue, or any virtue at all, in doing particular actions which before-hand were indifferent, and which without any blame we might have omitted?'—The answer is very easy. What denominates an agent virtuous, and entitles him to praise, is his acting from a regard to goodness and right. Now, the performance of particular instances of duty, or producing particular effects which have nothing in them that requires our preference, may, as much as any actions whatsoever, proceed from this regard. Relieving a miserable object is virtue, though there may be no reason that obliges a person to select this object in particular out of many others. Worshipping God may arise from a general sense of duty, though it is known that the particular times and manner in which it is done, have nothing morally better in them.—And as to the *greater* merit we apprehend in many actions of this kind (as, in many instances of generosity, kindness, charity, and forgiveness of injuries) it is plainly to be accounted for, in the following manner.—As every action of an agent is *in him* so far virtuous, as he was determined to it by a regard to virtue; so the more of this regard it discovers, the more we must admire it. And it is plain, it is more discovered, and a stronger virtuous principle proved, by fixing (in cases where the limits of duty are not exactly defined) upon the greater rather than the less. A person acts more apparently from good motives, and shews a greater degree of benevolence, and is therefore deservedly more applauded, who chuses to devote *more* of his fortune, his time and his labour, to promote the happiness of his fellow-creatures, or to serve his neighbours or his country, when he knows not but that if he had devoted

less, he would have done all that was in reason incumben
upon *him,* and deserved just commendation. And even whe
there is *over*doing, and a person is led to visible extremes an
an undue neglect of his private concerns, we always approve
except we suspect the influence of some indirect motives
Some of these observations will be again more particularl
insisted on, when I come to consider the difference which
they imply and require us to keep in view, between the virtu
of the *action,* and the virtue of the *agent.*

I shall only say farther on this subject, that it appears to b
so far from being true, that the performance of *mere* duty
produces no love or friendship to the agent, (as has been
asserted) that, on the contrary, he who, however tempted
and opposed, discharges his whole duty, and endeavours
faithfully and uniformly to *be* and *do* in all respects just what
he *ought* to *be* and *do,* is the object of our highest love and
friendship: To aim at acting *beyond* obligation, being the
same with aiming at acting *contrary* to obligation; and doing
more than is fit to be done, the same with *doing wrong.*

Having now given, what appears to me, the true account
of the nature and foundation of moral good and evil and of
moral obligation, I will add, as a supplement to this chapter,
an examination of some of the forms of expression, which
several eminent writers have used on this subject.

The meaning and design of these expressions will appear,
after considering, that all actions being necessarily right, indifferent, or wrong; what determines which of these an
action should be accounted is the *truth of the case*; or the
relations and circumstances of the agent and the objects. In
certain relations there is a certain conduct right. There are
certain manners of behaviour which we unavoidably approve, as soon as these relations are known. Change the
relations, and a different manner of behaviour becomes right.
Nothing is clearer than that what is due or undue, proper or

improper to be done, must vary according to the different natures and circumstances of beings. If a particular treatment of *one* nature is right; it is impossible that the same treatment of a *different* nature, or of *all* natures, should be right.

From hence arose the expressions, *acting suitably to the natures of things*; *treating things as they are*; *conformity to truth*; *agreement and disagreement, congruity and incongruity between actions and relations*. These expressions are of no use, and have little meaning, if considered as intended to *define* virtue; for they evidently *presuppose* it. Treating an object as being what *it is*, is treating it as *it is right such* an object should be treated. Conforming ourselves to truth means the same with conforming ourselves to the true state and relations we are in; which is the same with doing what such a state and such relations *require*, or what is *right* in them. In given circumstances, there is something peculiar and determinate *best* to be done; which, when these circumstances cease, ceases with them, and other obligations arise. This naturally leads us to speak of *suiting* actions to circumstances, natures, and characters; and of the *agreement* and *repugnancy* between them. Nor, when thus considered, is there any thing in such ways of speaking, not proper and intelligible. But, at the same time, it is very obvious, that they are only different phrases for *right* and *wrong*; and it is to be wished that those who have made use of them had attended more to this, and avoided the ambiguity and confusion arising from seeming to deny an *immediate perception* of morality without any deductions of reasoning; and from attempting to give definitions of words which admit not of them. Were any one to define *pleasure*, to be the *agreement* between a faculty and its object; what instruction would such a definition convey? Would it be amiss to ask, what this *agreement* is; and whether any thing be meant by it, different from the *pleasure itself*, which the object is fitted to produce by its influence on the faculty?

It is well known that Mr. *Wollaston*, in a work which has

obtained great and just reputation, places the whole notion of moral good and evil in *signifying* and *denying* truth. Supposing his meaning to be, that all virtue and vice may be reduced to these *particular instances* of them; nothing can be more plain, than that it leaves the nature and origin of our ideas of them as much as ever undetermined: For it acquaints us not, whence our ideas of right in observing truth and wrong in violating it, arise; but supposes these to be perceptions of self-evident truths, as indeed they are, but not more so, than our ideas of the other principles of morality.—The evil of ingratitude and cruelty is not the same with that of denying truth, or affirming a lie: Nor can the *formal ratio and notion* of it (as Mr. *Wollaston* speaks) be justly said to consist in this; because there may be no intention to deny any thing true, or to produce an assent to any thing false. Ingratitude and cruelty would be wrong, though there were no rational creatures in the world besides the agent, and though he could have no design to declare a falshood; which is a quite distinct species of evil.—A person, who neglects the worship due to God, may have no thought of denying his existence, or of conveying any such opinion to others. It is true, he acts as if he did not exist, that is, in a manner which nothing else can justify, or which, upon any other supposition, is inexcuseable; and therefore, *figuratively speaking*, may be said to *contradict* truth, and to declare himself to be self-originated and self-sufficient.* It is probable, this eminent writer meant in reality but little more than this; and the language he has introduced, I would not, by any means, be thought absolutely to condemn. All I aim at, is to guard against making a wrong application of it.

* How plain is it here, that the very thing that gives ground for the application of this language in this instance, is our perceiving, antecedently to this application, that such a manner of acting, in such circumstances, is *wrong*? The same is true in all other instances: Nor, independently of this perception, could we ever know when to say, that an action affirms or denies truth. How then does such language explain and define right and wrong?

With the same view I must add, that when virtue is said to consist in *conformity to the relations of persons and things*; this must not be considered as a *definition of virtue*, or as intended to assign a *reason justifying the practice of it*. Nothing can be gained by such forms of expression, when used with these intentions: And, if we will consider why it is right to conform ourselves to the relations in which persons and objects stand to us; we shall find ourselves obliged to terminate our views in a *simple perception*, and something *ultimately approved* for which no justifying reason can be assigned.—Explaining virtue by saying, that it is the *conformity of our actions to reason*, is yet less proper; for this conformity signifying only, that our actions are such as our reason discerns to be right; it will be no more than saying, that virtue is doing right.*

It should be further considered, that neither do these forms of expression direct us to proper *criteria*, by which we may be enabled to judge in all cases what is morally good or evil. For if, after weighing the state and circumstances of a case, we do not perceive how it is proper to act; it would be

---

* To the same purpose Dr. *Adams* has observed, 'That when virtue is said to consist in a conformity to truth; in acting agreeably to the truth of the case; to the reason, truth, or fitness of things; there is, if not impropriety, something of obscurity or inaccuracy in the expression; and that the only meaning of such expressions will, in all cases, be found to be this; acting according to what reason, in the present circumstances of the agent, and the relations he stands in to the objects before him, pronounces to be right.' See his Sermon before quoted, p. 55–58.—'Truth (as he elsewhere says) is a term of wider extent than right. The characters of wisdom or prudence, of skill in any art or profession, *are*, as well as virtue, founded in a regard to truth, and imply the acting agreeably to the nature and reason of things; yet are these ideas certainly distinct from that of goodness, or moral rectitude. The man, who builds according to the principles of geometry, acts as agreeably to truth, and he who should transgress the rules of architecture, as much violates truth, as he who acts agreeably to the duty of gratitude, or contrary to it. But, in the former of these instances, the conformity to truth is not virtue but skill; the deflection from it is not vice, but ignorance or folly,' p. 29.—To these observations may be added, that to act *agreeably* to the character of an oppressor, or tyrant, is, in no improper sense, to act viciously; to injure and to destroy. So vague and loose is this way of speaking, and so liable to objections, when used to define and explain virtue.

trifling to direct us, for this end, to consider what is *agreeable* to them. When, in given circumstances, we cannot determine what is *right*, we must be also equally unable to determine what is *suitable* to those circumstances. It is indeed very proper and just to direct us, in order to judge of an action, to endeavour to discover the whole *truth* with respect to its probable or possible consequences, the circumstances and qualifications of the object, and the relations of the agent; for this, as was before said, is what determines its moral nature; and no more can be intended by representing *truth* and *relations* as *criteria* of virtue.

'The language we are considering then expressing neither *definitions* nor *proper criteria* of virtue, of what use is it? and what is designed by it?'—I answer, that it is evidently designed to shew, that morality *is founded* in truth and reason; or that it is equally necessary and immutable, and perceived by the same power, with the natural proportions and essential differences of things.

'But what, it may be again asked, is it more than bare assertion? What proof of this does it convey?' In reply to this, it might be observed, that the same questions may be put to those who have maintained the contrary; and it is, I think, necessary they should better examine this subject before they consider it, as they do, a decided point, that our ideas of morality are derived from an arbitrary sense, and not ideas of the understanding.

The agreement of *proportion* between certain quantities, is real and necessary; and perceived by the understanding. Why should we doubt, whether the agreement of *fitness* also between certain actions and relations, is real and necessary, and perceived by the same faculty? From the different natures, properties, and positions of different objects result necessarily different *relative* fitnesses and unfitnesses; different productive *powers*; different *aptitudes* to different ends, and agreements or disagreements amongst themselves. What is there absurd or exceptionable in saying, likewise, that from the various relations of beings and objects, there result different *moral* fitnesses and unfitnesses of action; different *obligations* of conduct; which are equally real and unalterable with the former, and equally independent of our ideas and opinions? For any particular natural objects to exist at all, and for them to exist with such and such mutual proportions, is the same. And, in like manner, for reasonable beings of particular natures and capacities to exist at all in such and such circumstances and relations, and for such and such conduct to be fit or proper is the same. And as the Author of nature, in creating the former, willed the proportions and truths implied in them to exist; so likewise, by the very act of creating the latter, and placing them in their respective relations to one another and to himself, he willed that such and such actions should be done, and such and such duties observed.—When we compare innocence and eternal misery, the idea of *unsuitableness* between them arises in our minds. And from comparing together many natural objects and beings, an idea of *unsuitableness*, likewise, but of a totally different kind, arises within us; that is, we perceive such a *repugnancy* between them, that the one cannot be made to correspond to the other; or, that their different properties cannot co-exist in the same subject; or, that they are not capable of producing such and such particular effects on one another. Why should one of these be taken to be less *real* than the other?—No one can avoid owning that he has the idea of *unsuitableness*; (that is, a sentiment of *wrong*) in the application of eternal misery to innocence. Let him, if he can, find out a reason for denying it to be a sentiment of his understanding, and a perception of truth.

To this purpose have the advocates for fitness, as the foundation of morality, argued. This, I think, has been the drift of their assertions and reasonings. It must, however, be allowed, that they have, by too lax a use of words, given occasion for the objections of those who have embraced and defended the contrary opinion.

It would not be difficult to shew, how the like dispute might be raised about the original of our ideas of *power* and *connexion*, the like objections started, and the same embarrassment produced.

But it will better help to illustrate some of these remarks, and give a clearer view of the state of this controversy, if, for *moral good and evil*, we substitute *equality* and *inequality*, and suppose these to be the objects of enquiry. He that should derive our ideas of them from a *sense*, would be undoubtedly mistaken, if he meant any thing more, than that they were *immediately* perceived. And another, who, in opposition to this, should assert them to be *founded on the natures and unalterable mutual respects and proportions of things*; and to denote *conformity to reason*, or the *agreement and disagreement, correspondency and repugnancy* between different quantities; would as plainly assert the truth; though in language liable to be misunderstood, and really trifling, if designed to set aside an *immediate power* of perception in this case, and to define *equality* and *inequality*: Nor, in this view of such language, would any thing be more proper than to observe, how much more determinate it is to say, that the *agreement* between two quantities is their *equality*, than that their *equality* is the *agreement* between them. But how unreasonable would it be to conclude, as in the parallel case has been done, that therefore *equality* and *inequality* are perceived by an *implanted sense*, and not at all objects of knowledge?

CHAP. VII.

*Of the Subject-matter of Virtue, or its
principal Heads and Divisions.*

THERE remain yet three questions to be considered in
relation to virtue.

First, To what particular course of action we give this
name, or what are the chief *heads* of virtue.

Secondly, What is the *principle* or *motive*, from which a
virtuous agent, as such, acts.

Thirdly, What is meant by the different *degrees* of virtue, in
different actions and characters, and how we estimate them.
—Each of these questions shall be examined in the order in
which they are here proposed.

There would be less occasion for the first of these enquiries,
if several writers had not maintained, that the *whole* of virtue
consists in BENEVOLENCE. Nothing better can be offered on
this point, than what is said under the fifth observation in
the *Dissertation on the Nature of Virtue*, annexed to Bishop
Butler's Analogy.—From hence, therefore, I shall borrow the
following passage:—'Benevolence and the want of it, singly
considered, are in no sort the whole of virtue and vice; for,
if this were the case, in the review of one's own character, or
that of others, our moral understanding and moral sense,
would be indifferent to every thing, but the degrees in which
benevolence prevailed, and the degrees in which it was
wanting: That is, we should neither approve of benevolence
to some persons rather than to others, nor disapprove injustice and falshood upon any other account, than merely as an
over-balance of happiness was foreseen likely to be produced
by the first, and of misery by the last. But now, on the contrary, suppose two men competitors for any thing whatever,

which would be of equal advantage to either of them. Though nothing indeed would be more impertinent, than for a stranger to busy himself to get one of them preferred to the other, yet such endeavour would be virtue in behalf of a friend, or benefactor, abstracted from all consideration of distant consequences; as, that examples of gratitude, and the cultivation of friendship, would be of general good to the world.—Again, suppose one man should by fraud or violence, take from another the fruit of his labour, with intent to give it to a third, who, he thought, would have as much pleasure from it, as would balance the pleasure which the first possessor would have had in the enjoyment, and his vexation in the loss of it; suppose again, that no bad consequences would follow, yet such an action would surely be vicious.'

The cases here put are clear and decisive, nor is it easy to conceive what can be said in reply to them. Many other cases and observations, to the same purpose, might be mentioned.—It cannot be true, for instance, that promises and engagements are not in any case binding upon any one, any further than he thinks the observance of them will be productive of good upon the whole to society; or, that we are released from all obligation to regard them, as soon as we believe, that violating them will not hurt the person to whom they have been made, or that, if detrimental to him, it will be equally beneficial to ourselves, or, in any other way, will be attended with advantages equivalent to the foreseen harm. He would be looked upon by all, as having acted basely, who, having any advantage to bestow which he had engaged to give to one person, should give it another; nor would it be regarded as any vindication of his conduct to alledge, that he knew this other would reap equal profit from it. Many particular actions, and omissions of action, become, in consequence of promises and engagements, highly evil, which otherwise would have been entirely innocent; and the degree of vice in any harm done, is always greatly increased, when done by means of deceit and treachery.—To treat a party of rebels, after they had surrendered themselves upon certain terms stipulated with them, in the same manner as if they had been reduced by force, would be generally disapproved: And yet it might be hard to shew, that the consequences of not keeping faith with them would have been very detrimental to the publick.—A general would be universally condemned, who, by means of any treacherous contrivance should engage his enemies to trust themselves in his power, and then destroy them. How different are our ideas of such conduct from those we have of the same end gained by open and fair conquest?

Would it be indifferent whether a person, supposed to be just returned from some unknown country or new world, gave a true or false account of what he had seen? Is there a man in the world who, in such a case, would not think it better to tell truth than needlessly and wantonly to deceive? Is it possible any one can think he may innocently (to save himself or another from some small inconvenience, which he can full as well prevent by other means) tell any lies or make any false protestations, if he *knows* they will never be found out? If he may thus impose upon his fellow-creatures by declaring one falsehood, why may he not in like circumstances declare any number of falsehoods, and with any possible circumstances of solemnity? Why is he not at liberty to make any declarations, however deceitful, to practise any kinds of dissimulation and commit perjuries, whenever he believes they are likely to hurt no one, and will be the means of introducing him to any degree of greater ease or usefulness in life?—Can we, when we consider these things, avoid pronouncing, that there is *intrinsick rectitude* in keeping faith and in sincerity, and *intrinsick evil* in the contrary; and that it is by no means true, that veracity and falshood appear *in themselves*, and *exclusive* of *their consequences*, wholly indifferent to our moral judgment? Is it a notion capable of being seriously defended, or even endured by an ingenuous mind, that the goodness of the end always consecrates the means; or that, *cæteris paribus*, it is as innocent and laudable to accomplish our purposes by lies, prevarication and perjury, as by faithful and open dealing and honest labour? wherein, upon such sentiments, would consist the wickedness of pious frauds; and why are they condemned and detested?

No worse mistake, indeed, can be well conceived than this; for, as the excellent author before-cited observes, 'it is certain, that some of the most shocking instances of injustice,* adultery, murder, perjury, and even persecution, may, in many supposable cases, not have the appearance of being likely to produce an overbalance of misery in the present state; perhaps, sometimes, may have a contrary appearance.'

A disapprobation in the human mind of ingratitude, injustice, and deceit, none deny. The point under examination is, the *ground* of this disapprobation; whether it arises solely from views of inconvenience to others and confusion in society occasioned by them; or whether there be not also *immediate wrong* apprehended in them, independently of their effects. The instances and considerations here produced seem sufficiently to determine this. It appears, that they are disapproved when productive of no harm, and even when in some degree beneficial.

'Shall it be still urged that, in cases of this kind, our disapprobation is owing to the idea of a plan or system of common utility established by custom in the mind with

* Is a man warranted to destroy himself, as soon as he believes his life is become useless or burthensome to those about him, and miserable to himself? How shocking in many circumstances would the most private assassination be of a person whose death all may wish for, and consider as a benefit to himself and to the world? Who would not severely reproach himself for reserving to himself the property of another which had been lost, and which he had accidentally found, however secretly he might do this, and whatever reason he might have for thinking that it would be of greater use to him than to the proprietor? There would be no end of mentioning cases of this sort, but I have chosen to instance particularly in veracity.

which these vices are apprehended to be inconsistent; or to a habit acquired of considering them as of general pernicious tendency, by which we are insensibly influenced, whenever, in any particular circumstances or instances, we contemplate them?'—But why must we have recourse to the influence of habits and associations in this case? This has been the refuge of those, who would resolve all our moral perceptions into views of private advantage, and may serve to evade almost any evidence which can be derived from the experience we have of the workings of our minds and the motives of our actions. In the cases which have been mentioned, we may remove entirely the idea of a publick, and suppose no persons existing whose state they can at all influence; or, we may suppose all memory of the action to be for ever lost as soon as done, and the agent to foresee this; and yet, the same ideas of the ingratitude, injustice, or violation of truth will remain. —If the whole reason for regarding truth arose from its influence on society, a primitive Christian would not have been blame-worthy for renouncing his religion, blaspheming Christ, and worshipping the Pagan gods (all which is no more than denying truth) whenever he could purchase his life by these means, and at the same time avoid a discovery, and thus prevent the prejudice to Christians and Pagans that might arise from his conduct?—*Peter* would not have been innocent in denying his Master with oaths and imprecations, though he had known that he should never be detected. A stranger, in a Pagan country, would not do right to comply with its superstitions, to worship and profess contrary to his sentiments, and abjure his faith, in order to secure his quiet or life, provided he judged the deceit would not be known, that he could do no good by a different conduct, or that his hypocrisy had no tendency to establish and perpetuate idolatry.

It is further to be observed on this argument, that in these cases it does not appear that mankind in general much attended to distant consequences. Children, particularly, cannot be supposed to consider consequences, or to have any fixed ideas of a public or a community; and yet, we observe in them the same aversion to falshood and relish for truth, as in the rest of mankind. There is indeed no less evidence, that, in the cases specified, we approve and disapprove *immediately*, than there is that we do so, when we consider benevolence or cruelty. It has been urged against those who derive all our desires and actions from self-love, that they find out views and reasonings for men, which never entered the minds of most of them; and which, in all probability, none attended to in the common course of their thoughts and pursuits.— The same may be urged against those, who derive all our sentiments of moral good and evil from our approbation of benevolence and disapprobation of the want of it; and both, in my opinion, have undertaken tasks almost equally impracticable. Any person, one would imagine, who will impartially examine his own mind, may feel, in his dislike of several vices, something different from the apprehension of their diminishing happiness or producing misery, and easily observe that it is not merely under these notions that he always censures and condemns. It is true, this apprehension, when it occurs, always heightens our disapprobation. Falshood, ingratitude, and injustice undermine the foundations of all social intercourse and happiness, and the consequences of them, were they to become universal, would be terrible.—For this reason, supposing morality founded on an arbitrary structure of our minds, there would be a necessity for distinct senses immediately condemning and forbidding them. Leaving them to the influence of a general disapprobation of all actions evidencing a neglect of publick good, or without any particular determination against them any farther than by every man they should be thought likely to produce more misery than happiness, would be attended with the worst effects. It would not, in all likelihood, by any means, be sufficient to secure tolerably the order of human society; especially, considering how many amongst mankind there are, who are incapable of enlarged reflexions, and whose thoughts are confined within the narrowest limits; and how little prone all men naturally are to be affected with or to regard remote events, as well as how liable they are to take up the wrongest opinions of the tendencies of their actions, and the good or ill to the world which they may occasion.

Perhaps, he who should maintain, that we have no affection properly resting in *ourselves*, but that all our desires and aversions arise from a prospect of advantage or detriment to *others*, would not assert what would be much less defensible than what those assert who maintain the reverse of this, and deny all *disinterested benevolence*.—In like manner, to assert that our approbation of *beneficence* is to be resolved into our approbation of *veracity*, or that the whole of morality consists in *signifying and denying truth*, would not be much more unreasonable than the contrary assertion, that our approbation of *veracity* and of all that is denominated virtue, is resolvable into the approbation of *beneficence*. But why must there be in the human mind approbation only of one sort of actions? Why must all moral good be reduced to one particular species of it, and kind affections, with the actions flowing from them, be represented, as alone capable of appearing to our moral faculty *virtuous*? Why may we not as well have an immediate relish also for truth, for candour, sincerity, piety, gratitude, and many other modes and principles of conduct?—Admitting all our ideas of morality to be derived from implanted determinations; the latter of these determinations is equally possible with the other; and what has been above hinted shews that there is the greatest occasion for them to secure the general welfare, and that therefore it might antecedently be expected that a good Being would give them to us.*

---

* Dr. *Hutcheson*, however he may in general have expressed himself, as if he thought the only object of the *moral sense* and the whole of virtue, was

Of the Subject-matter of Virtue

How unreasonable is that love of uniformity and simplicity which inclines men thus to seek them where it is so difficult to find them? It is this that, on other subjects, has often led men astray. What mistakes and extravagances in natural philosophy have been produced, by the desire of discovering *one* principle which shall account for all effects? I deny not but that in the human mind, as well as in the material world, the most wonderful simplicity takes place; but we ought to learn to wait, till we can, by careful observation and enquiry, find out wherein it consists; and not suffer ourselves rashly to determine any thing concerning it, or to receive any general causes and principles which cannot be proved by experience.

If the account of morality I have given is just, it is not to be conceived, that promoting the happiness of others should comprehend the whole of our duty, or that the consideration of publick good should be that alone in *all* circumstances which can have any concern in determining what is right or wrong. It has been observed, that every different situation of a reasonable creature requires a different manner of acting, and that concerning all that can be proposed to be done, something is to be affirmed or denied, which, when known, necessarily implies a *direction* to the agent in regard to his behaviour.

Having premised these observations, I shall now proceed to enumerate some of the most important *Branches of virtue*, or *heads of rectitude and duty*.

What requires the first place is our DUTY TO GOD, or the benevolence, yet appears to have been convinced of the necessity of allowing *a distinct sense*, recommending to us faithfulness and veracity.—See *Philosophiae moralis institutio compendiaria*, Cap. IX. lib. ii. *Facultatis hujus, sive orationis, comes est et moderator sensus quidam subtilior, ex veri etiam cognoscendi appetitione naturali non parum confirmatus, quo vera omnia, simplicia, fidelia comprobamus; falsa, ficta, fallacia odimus.* —Lib. ii. Cap. X. *Sensu enim cujusque* proxime *commendatur is sermonis usus, quem communis exigit utilitas.*—*Hoc vero stabile consilium eo tantum utendi sermone, qui cum animi sententia congruit, quique alios non decipit, comprobant et animi sensus* per se, *et utilitatis communis ratio.*

whole of that regard, subjection and homage we owe him. These seem unquestionably objects of moral approbation, independently of all considerations of utility. They are considered as indispensably obligatory, and yet the principle upon which they are practised cannot be an intention, in any manner, to be useful or profitable to the object of them. Those persons must be uncommonly weak and ignorant who mean, by their religious services, to make an addition to the happiness of the Deity, or who entertain any apprehensions, that it is on his own account, and to advance his own good, he expects their gratitude and prayers. I know, indeed, that some writers of great worth have expressed themselves, as if they doubted, whether the secret spring of all obedience to him, and concurrence with his ends, is not some desire of contributing to his satisfaction and delight. It would be trifling with most of my readers, to employ much time, in representing the prodigious absurdity of such an opinion.

Let any pious man of plain sense and free from gross superstition, be appealed to, and asked, whether he approves of piety to God as proceeding from a view to his felicity? whether he submits to his will, and worships and prays to him, from an opinion that these, in the literal sense, *please* or gratify him? He would undoubtedly at once disclaim any such sentiments and motives. Upon a little consideration he might say, 'he obeyed and worshipped God, because it was *right*—because he apprehended it his *duty*.'—Should he be asked, why he thought obedience and devotion to God his *duty*? the reply that would most naturally occur to him, would be; 'because God was the creator, governor, and benefactor of the whole world, and particularly was *his* creator, governor, and benefactor.' But should he be once more asked, why he thought it his duty to honour and worship his Maker, benefactor and governor? he would (as well he might) wonder at the question, as much as if he had been asked, why twenty was greater than two?—Why should we not admit here the

natural and unperverted sentiments of men, and acknowledge, what leaves no difficulty and seems so evident, that
submission, reverence, and devotion to *such* a being as God,
are, as much as any behaviour to our fellow-men, instances
of *immediate duty intuitively* perceived; the sense of which,
equally with kind affections, is a spring and motive of action.

That the state and happiness of the Deity, cannot be
affected by any thing we, or any other beings, can do, no
one surely, upon mature consideration, will deny. But let it
be only *supposed*, that this is the case; what alterations will
follow as to our duty to him? Would no behaviour on this
supposition, terminating solely in him as its object and end,
remain proper? Would it have any effect in releasing the
rational creation from their allegiance, and rendering impiety
and disobedience less shocking?

It is true, all the pious and virtuous are actuated by love
to God, which implies joy in his happiness; but this would
never produce any acts of acknowledgement and obedience,
or any study of the good of others in compliance with his
intentions; while there is no apprehension that they can affect
his happiness; and, at the same time, no perception of fitness
in them independent of this.

What has been now said, is, in some degree, applicable to
superiors and benefactors among created beings; and the
grounds of duty to them, are, in their general nature, the
same with those of our duty to the Deity. A fellow-man may
be raised so much above us in station and character, and so
little within the reach of any of the effects of what we can do,
that the reason of the respect and submission we pay him,
and of our general behaviour to him, cannot be any view to
his benefit, but *principally*, or *solely*, the sense of what is in
itself right, decent, or becoming.—To all beings, according
to their respective natures, characters, abilities, and relations
to us, there are suitable affections and manners of behaviour
owing, which, as long as their characters and relations to

ıs continue the same, are as invariable as the proportion between any particular geometrical figures or quantities.—The higher the rank of any being is, the more perfect his nature, the more excellent his character, the more near and intimate his connexions with us, and the greater our obligations to him; the more strict and indispensable duty, and the greater degree of regard, affection, and submission we owe him.

This last observation shews us, what ideas we ought to entertain of the importance of the duty we owe to God, and of the place it holds amongst our other duties. There can, certainly, be no proportion between what is due from us to *creatures* and to the *Creator*; between the regard and deference we owe to beings of precarious, derived, and limited goodness, and to him who possesses original, necessary, everlasting fulness of all that is amiable. As much as this Being surpasses other beings in perfection and excellence, so much is he the worthier object of our veneration and love. As much as we are more dependent upon him, and indebted to him, so much the more absolute subjection and ardent gratitude may he claim from us.—The whole universe, compared with God, is nothing in *itself*, nothing to *us*. He ought then to be *all* to us; his will our unalterable guide; his goodness the object of our constant praise and trust; the consideration of his all-directing providence our highest joy; the securing his favour our utmost ambition; and the imitation of his righteousness the great end of all our actions. He is the fountain of all power and jurisdiction, the cause of all causes, the disposer of the lots of all beings, the life and informing principle of all nature; from whose never-ceasing influence every thing derives its capacity of giving us pleasure; and in whom, as their source and centre, are united all the degrees of beauty and good that we can observe in the creation. On him then ought our strongest affection and admiration to be fixed, and to him ought our minds to be continually directed.

How shameful would it be to forget this Being amidst shadow
and vanities, to attend to his *works* more than *himself*, or t
regard any thing equally with him?—It is here, undoubtedly
virtue ought to begin: From hence it should take its rise
A regard to God, as our first and sovereign principle of con
duct, should always possess us, accompany us in the discharg
of all private and social duties, and govern our whole lives
Inferior authority we ought to submit to; but at the sam
time ultimately viewing that authority, which is the ground
of all other, and supreme in nature. Inferior benefactors w
should be grateful to, in proportion to our obligations to
them and dependence upon them; but yet considering them
as only instruments to his goodness, and reserving our firs
and chief gratitude for our first and chief benefactor. The
gifts of his bounty, the objects to which he has adapted ou
faculties, and the means of happiness he has provided for us
we should accept and enjoy; but it would be disingenuous
and base to do it with little consideration of the giver, o
with hearts void of emotion towards him. Every degree o
real worth we observe among inferior beings should be
properly acknowledged, and esteemed; but yet as being no
more than rays from his glory, and faint resemblances of his
perfections. Created excellence and beauty we may and
must admire; but it would be inexcusable to be so much
taken up with these, as to overlook him before whom all
other excellence vanishes. To him through all inferior causes
we ought to look; and his hand, it becomes us to own and
adore, in all the phænomena of nature, and in every event.
The consideration of his presence with us should affect us
more, and be a stronger check upon our behaviour, than if
we knew we were every moment exposed to the view of the
whole creation. We ought to love him above all things, to
throw open our minds, as much as possible, to his influence,
and keep up a constant intercourse with him by prayer and
devotion. We ought to refer ourselves absolutely to his

management, rely implicitly on his care, commit, with boundless hope, our whole beings to him *in well-doing*, and *wish* for nothing, at any time, but what is most acceptable to his wisdom and goodness.—In short; he ought to have, in all respects, the supremacy in our minds; every action and design should be sacred to him; reverence, admiration, hope, joy, desire of approbation, and all the affections suited to such an object, should exert themselves within us in the highest degree we are capable of them. An union to him, by a resemblance and participation of his perfections, we should aspire to, as our complete dignity and happiness, beyond which there can be nothing worthy the concern of any being. No rebellious inclination should be once indulged; no murmur, in any events, shew itself in our minds; and no desire or thought ever entertained by us, which is inconsistent with an inviolable and chearful loyalty of heart to his government.

These are some of the chief particulars of our duty to the Deity; and it naturally here offers itself to our observation, how extremely defective the characters of those persons are, who, whatever they may be in other respects, live in the neglect of God. Nothing, indeed, can be more melancholy, than to see so many persons capable of maintaining a good opinion of themselves, though they know themselves to be regardless of piety, and inattentive to the Author of all good. Can any one seriously think, that a misbehaviour of this kind is not as truly inconsistent with goodness of temper and sound virtue, and in the same manner destructive of the foundations of hope and bliss, as any other misbehaviour? Do neglect and ingratitude, when men are the objects of them, argue *great* evil of temper, but *none* when the author of the world is their object? Why should *impiety* be less criminal than *dishonesty*?

Every man, as far as he discharges private and social duties, is to be loved and valued, nor can any thing be said that ought in reason to discourage him. Whatever good any

person does, or whatever degree of real virtue he possesses
he is sure, in some way or other, to be the better for. Tho
it should not be such as will save him from just condemna
tion; yet it will at least, render him so much the less guilty
and unhappy.—But, in truth, as long as men continue void
of religion and piety, there is great reason to apprehend they
are destitute of the genuine principle of virtue, and possess but
little true moral worth. Their good behaviour in other
instances, may probably flow more from the influence of
instinct and natural temper, or from the love of distinction
credit, and private advantages, than from a sincere regard
to what is *reasonable* and *fit as such*. Were this the principle
that chiefly influenced them, they would have an equal
regard to *all* duty; they could not be easy in the omission of
any thing they know to be right, and especially not in the
habitual neglect of him, with whom they have infinitely more
to do, than with all the world.—He that forgets God and his
government, presence, and laws, wants the main support and
the living root of genuine virtue, as well as the most fruitful
source of tranquillity and joy: Nor can he, with due exactness, care, and faithfulness, be supposed capable of performing his duties to himself and others. He that is without the
proper affections to the Author of his being, or who does not
study to cultivate them by those acts and exercises, which are
the natural expressions of them, should indeed be ashamed
to make any pretensions to integrity and goodness of character.—'The knowledge and love of the Deity, the universal
mind, is as natural a perfection to such a being as man, as
any accomplishment to which we arrive by cultivating our
natural dispositions; nor is that mind come to the proper
state and vigour of its kind, where religion is not the main
exercise and delight.'*

* *Illustrations on the Moral Sense* by Dr. *Hutcheson*, Sect. 6. See also his *System
of Moral Philosophy*, Chap. X. Book I. Vol. I. where may be found an excellent
account of the worship and affections due to God, and of their importance to

It must, however, be added, that the persons who fall into the contrary extreme, are, upon all accounts, the most inexcusable and wicked; I mean, those who pretend to *religion* without *benevolence*, without honesty; who are zealously devout, but at the same time envious, peevish, perverse, spiteful, and can cheat and trick, lie and calumniate. Nothing can be conceived more inconsistent, or shameful than this. The solemn worship of such is the highest possible aggravation of their guilt. The regard they pretend for God is an abuse and mockery of him; and their religion the worst sort of *blasphemy*. Religion furnishes us with the strongest motives to social duties; it lays us under additional obligations to perform them; and it is the nature of it to improve our zeal for all that is just and good, to increase our love of all men, and to render us more gentle, mild, fair, candid, and upright, in proportion to the degree in which it truly possesses our hearts. He, therefore, who, while under any influence from religion, and with the idea of God in his mind, does any thing wrong, is so much the more blameable, and shews proportionably greater degeneracy and viciousness of character.

Before we quit this subject, I cannot help begging the reader to pause a-while, and to consider particularly, what is

our perfection and happiness.—See likewise the *Characteristicks*, Vol. II. p. 76. 'Hence we may determine justly the relation which virtue has to piety; the first being not complete but in the latter: Since where the latter is wanting, there cannot be the same benignity, firmness, or constancy; the same good composure of the affections, or the same uniformity of mind. And thus the perfection and height of virtue must be owing to the belief of a God.'—And elsewhere, 'Man is not only born to virtue, friendship, honesty, and faith, but to religion, piety, adoration, and a generous surrender of his mind to whatever happens from that supreme cause, or order of things, which he acknowledges entirely just and perfect.' Vol. III. p. 224.—'My design is this, to make you free and happy, always looking unto God in every small and in every great matter.' Εἰς τὸν θεὸν ἀφορῶντας ἐν παντὶ μικρῷ καὶ μεγάλῳ. *Epict.* apud *Arr.* Lib. ii. cap. 19.— 'Nothing, says *M. Antoninus*, is well done, that is done without a respect to the Divine nature.' Οὐκ ἀνθρώπινόν τι ἄνευ τῆς ἐπὶ τὰ θεῖα συναναφορᾶς εὖ πράξεις. Lib. iii. Sect. 13.

meant by the will of God, and how important and awful a motive to action it implies.

What can have a tendency to impress an attentive mind so deeply, or strike it with so much force, as to think, in any circumstances, 'God *wills* me to *do*, or to *bear* this?'—One such reflexion should be enough at all times to disarm the strongest temptations, to silence every complaint, to defeat all opposition, and to inspire us with the most inflexible courage and resolution. Did we take more leisure to attend to this, we could not possibly behave as we often do. He that, when solicited to any thing unlawful, will but stop, till he has duly attended to the *sense* and felt the *weight* of this truth; 'the Deity disapproves and forbids my compliance, must tremble at the thought of complying, and lose all inclination to it. When we think rightly who God is, nothing can appear so shocking as that helpless, indigent beings, his own offspring, and the objects of his constant care and bounty, should counteract his intentions, and rebel against his authority, or be dissatisfied with what he appoints. The most loud applauses and general friendship of our fellow-creatures are nothing, and can have no effect, when separated from his. All opposition is impotence, when not approved by him: And the threats of all the world, could they be supposed to interfere with what we know he requires from us, would, if we had a just sense of things, be as much lost to us as a whisper in the midst of thunder, or the attention to a toy in the moment of instant death.

What it is he wills, we can in general be at no loss to know. Whatever afflictions or disappointments happen to us; whatever pains we feel, or unavoidable inconveniencies are mingled with the lot assigned us; these it is as certain that he wills us to bear, and to acquiesce in, as it is that we at all suffer by them: Since it is demonstrable, that in his world and under his eye, nothing can befal us either *contrary* to, or *without* his consent and direction. Whatever opportunities fall in our way of doing good, it is his will that we embrace and improve. Whatever our consciences dictate to us, and we know to be *right* to be done, *that* he commands more evidently and undeniably, than if by a voice from heaven we had been called upon to do it.—And, when conscious of faithful endeavours to be and do every thing that we ought to be and do, with what joy of heart may we look up to him, and exult in the assurance of his approbation? When employed in acts of kindness, in forming good habits, and practising truth and righteousness; how resolute and immoveable must it render an upright person, and with what fortitude and ardour may it possess his breast, to consider; 'I am doing the will of Him to whom the world owes its birth, and whom the whole creation obeys: I am imitating the perfections, and securing the friendship of that Being, who *is* everlasting truth and righteousness; who cannot, therefore, be conceived to be indifferent to those who practise them; and who possesses infinite power, and can cause all nature to furnish out its stores to bless me?'

Thus does religion elevate the mind; and such is the force and majesty it gives to virtue. The most effectual means of forming a good temper and establishing good dispositions, is the contemplation of the divine administration and goodness. We cannot have our minds too intent upon them, or study enough to make every thought pay homage to the Divinity, and to hallow our whole conversation by an habitual regard to him whose prerogative it is, as the first cause and the original of all perfection, to be the guide and end of all the actions of his creatures.

It will, I suppose, scarcely be thought by the most cursory reader, that what has been now said, lays greater stress upon *will*, than is consistent with the foundation of morals I have been defending.

It has not been asserted, that, *of itself*, it can have any effect on morality, or be an end and rule of action. If we consider it as denoting either the general *power* of producing effects, or the *actual* exertion of this power; it is most manifest, that it implies nothing of a *rule*, *direction*, or *motive*, but is entirely ministerial to these, and supposes them. UNDERSTANDING is, in the nature of it, before WILL: KNOWLEDGE before POWER: it being necessary, that every intelligent agent, in exerting his power, should *know* what he does, or design some effect, which he *understands* to be possible. The general idea of *will* is applicable alike to all beings capable of design and action; and, therefore, merely as will, it can never have any influence on our determinations.

What renders obedience to the will of God a duty of so high and indispensable a nature, is this very consideration, that it is the *will of God*: the will of the universal and almighty Parent, benefactor, and ruler; a will which is in necessary union with perfect rectitude, which always executes the dictates of it, and which, whenever made known, directs to what is absolutely *best*. When we obey this then, it is *unerring rectitude*, it is the *voice of eternal wisdom* we obey; and it is then, therefore, we act most wisely.

The *second* branch of virtue, which we may take notice of, is that which has *ourselves* for its object. There is, undoubtedly, a certain manner of conduct terminating in ourselves, which is properly matter of *duty* to us. It is too absurd to be maintained by any one, that no relation which an action may have to our own happiness or misery, can (supposing other beings unconcerned) have any influence in determining, whether it is or is not to be done, or make it appear to rational and calm reflexion otherwise than *morally indifferent*. —It is contradictory to suppose, that the same necessity which makes an end to us, and determines us to the choice and desire* of it, should be unaccompanied with an approbation of using the means of attaining it. It is, in reality, no

* See last Section of Chapter I. page 45.

more morally indifferent, how we employ our faculties, and what we do relating to our own interest, than it is how we behave to our fellow-creatures. If it is my duty to promote the good of *another*, and to abstain from hurting him; the same, most certainly, must be my duty with regard to *myself*. It would be contrary to all reason to deny this; or to assert that I *ought* to consult the good of another, but not my own; or that the advantage an action will produce to another makes it right to be done, but that an equal advantage to myself leaves me at liberty to do or omit it.—So far is this from being true, that it will be strange, if any one can avoid acknowledging that it is right and fit that a being should, when all circumstances on both sides are equal, *prefer* himself to another; reserve, for example, to *himself*, a certain means of enjoyment he possesses rather than part with it to a *stranger*, to whom it will not be *more* beneficial.

It is evident, that this affords us another instance of right behaviour, the principle of which is not kind affection, and which no views of public utility, or sympathy with others can possibly explain. What can prove more incontestably that actions evidencing kind affections are not the only ones we approve, than our approving in many cases of the prevalency of self-love against them, and our being conscious that in these cases it *should* thus prevail? Private interest affords us, indeed, the fullest scope for virtue; and the practice of this branch of duty is no less difficult, and requires no less resolution and zeal, than the practice of any other branch of duty. Our lower principles and appetites are by no means always friendly to true self-love. They almost as often interfere with this as with benevolence. We continually see men, through the influence of them, acting in opposition to their own acknowledged interest, as well as to that of others, and sacrificing to them their fortunes, healths, and lives.—Now, in cases of this kind, when a person is tempted to forego his own happiness by an importunate appetite, it is as really praiseworthy to overcome the temptation, and preserve a steady regard to his own interest, as it is to perform any acts of justice, or to overcome temptations to be dishonest or cruel. Restraining licentious passions; strict temperance, sobriety, and chastity; rejecting *present* for *future greater* good; governing all our inferior powers so as that they shall never disturb the order of our minds; acting up to the dignity and hopes of reasonable and immortal beings; and the uniform and sted- fast pursuit of our own true perfection in opposition to what- ever difficulties may come in our way: This is high and true virtue. We have it not in our power to avoid approving and admiring such conduct.—On the contrary; an undue neglect of our own good; folly and imprudence; intemperance and voluptuousness; sensuality and extravagance; acting beneath our characters and expectations; confining our ambition to low and transitory objects, when we might fix them on objects of inestimable worth and eternal duration; following blind passions to beggary and distress, and yielding to them our liberty, independence, and self-enjoyment, the principal blessings of this life, and the prospect of future happiness: All this, however hurtful to none but the agent himself, is vicious and criminal: The guilty person deserves the severest reproaches, and necessarily appears to himself and others base and despicable.—The *selfishness* we blame is such a regard to our own gratification, and such an attention to a narrow and partial private interest, as engrosses too much of our labour, contracts our hearts, excludes a due concern for others and a proper regard to their good, and stifles or checks the exercise of benevolence, friendship and generosity. Where nothing of this sort takes place, the care of *self* is never cen- sured, but always expected and praised.

It should not, however, be overlooked, that acting with a view to private advantage does not so generally and certainly prove a virtuous intention, as acting with a view to publick good; and that, in rejecting an evil, or embracing a good to ourselves, when it is sensible and at hand, and no opposition arises from any interfering desires and propensions, the virtuous effort and design, and consequently the degree of virtue in the agent, can be but small. But of this more will be said hereafter.

For the reason, why we have not so sensible an indignation against the neglect of private good, as against many other instances of wrong behaviour, see what is said under the fourth observation in *The Dissertation on Virtue*, at the end of *Butler's Analogy*.

Thirdly, Another part of rectitude is BENEFICENCE, or the study of the good of others. Publick happiness is an object that must necessarily determine all minds to prefer and desire it. It is of essential and unchangeable value and importance; and there is not any thing which appears to our thoughts with greater light and evidence, or of which we have more undeniably an intuitive perception, than that it is *right* to promote and pursue it.—So important a part of virtue is this, and so universally acknowledged, that it is become a considerable subject of debate, whether it be not the *whole* of virtue.

As, under the preceding head, it has been observed, that it would be strange that the good of another should make an action fit to be performed, but our own good not; the contrary observation may be here made; namely, that it cannot be consistently supposed that our own good should make an action fit to be performed, but that of others not.

All[1] rational beings ought to have a share in our kind wishes and affections: But we are surrounded with *fellow-men*, beings of the same nature, in the same circumstances, and having the same wants with ourselves; to whom therefore we are in a peculiar manner linked and related, and whose

[1 Ed. 1 adds 'sensitive and'.]

happiness and misery depend very much on our behaviour to them. These considerations ought to engage us to labour to be useful to mankind, and to cultivate to the utmost the principle of benevolence to them. And how amiable does the man appear in whose breast this divine principle reigns; who studies to make all with whom he has any connexion easy and happy; who loves others as he desires others to love him; whose joy is their joy, and misery their misery; who is humane, patient, humble, and generous; never gives the least indulgence to any harsh or unfriendly dispositions, and comprehends in what he counts *himself* his relations, friends, neighbours, country, and species?

Fourthly, The next head of virtue proper to be mentioned is GRATITUDE. The consideration that we have received benefits, lays us under *peculiar* obligations to the persons who have conferred them; and renders that behaviour, which to others may be innocent, to them criminal. That this is not to be looked upon as the effect merely of the utility of gratitude, appears, I think, sufficiently from the citation at the beginning of this chapter.

With respect to this part of virtue, it is proper to observe, that it is but one out of a great variety of instances, wherein particular facts and circumstances constitute a fitness of a different behaviour to different persons, independently of its consequences. The different moral qualifications of different persons; their different degrees of nearness to us in various respects; and numberless circumstances in their situations, and characters, have the like effect, and give just reason, in innumerable instances, for a preference of some of them to others. Some of these circumstances may be of so little moment in themselves, that almost any appearance or possibility of greater good may suspend their influence; although when there is no such appearance, they have a full effect in determining what is *right*. A fact of the same kind with this, I shall have occasion to mention under the head of *justice*.

What will be most beneficial, or productive of the greatest publick good, I acknowledge to be the most general and leading consideration in all our enquiries concerning *right*; and so important is it, when the publick interest depending is very considerable, that it may set aside every obligation which would otherwise arise from the common rules of justice, from promises, private interest, friendship, gratitude, and all particular attachments and connexions.

Fifthly, VERACITY is a most important part of virtue. Of this a good deal has been already said. As it has some dependence upon *different sentiments* and *affections* with respect to *truth* and *falshood*, it will not be improper to be a little particular in giving an account of the foundation of these.

The difference between truth and falshood is the same with the difference between something and nothing, and infinitely greater, than the difference between realities and chimeras or fictions; because the latter have a real existence *in the mind*, and so far, also a *possible, external* existence.— There is indeed an imaginary reality, with which we are obliged always to cloath falshood, in order at all to write or speak about it; but this is derived entirely from the reality of its contrary. We commonly speak of *disorder, silence* and *darkness*, as if they denoted somewhat positive; whereas, whatever positive ideas we can have when we mention them, must be ideas of the things themselves, of which they are negations.— Now, it cannot be conceived, that what is *real*, and what is not so, should be alike regarded by the mind. Truth must be pleasing and desireable to an intelligent nature; nor can it be otherwise than disagreeable to it, to find itself in a state of deception, and mocked with error.—As much error as there is in any mind, so much darkness is there in it; so much, if I may so express myself, is it less distant from non-existence.

As much truth as it is in possession of, so much has it of perception and knowledge. To disaffect truth or to love error, is to desire to see nothing as it is. We often indeed are pleased with finding that we have been mistaken; but it is never the having been mistaken that pleases, but some advantage it was the occasion of to us. In the same sense, an act of villainy may please us; that is, some of its consequences or circumstances may please us, not the villainy itself. We frequently delight in our errors, but not *as* errors. As soon as we discover in any instance that we err, so far in that instance we no longer err; and this discovery is always in itself grateful to us, for the same reason that truth is so.—In short, we shall, I believe, find, in whatever light we consider this subject, that the notion of the arbitrariness of the relish we have for truth, or of the distinction we make in our inward regards between it and falshood, implies what is impossible.

Truth then, necessarily recommends itself to our preference. And the essence of *lying* consisting in using established signs in order to *deceive*, it must be disapproved by all rational beings upon the same grounds with those on which truth and knowledge are desired by them, and right judgment preferred to mistake and ignorance.—No beings, supposed alike indifferent to truth and falshood and careless which they embrace, can be conceived to take offence at any imposition upon themselves or others; and he who will not say, that, consequences apart, (which is all along supposed) to *know* is not better than to *err*, or that there is nothing to determine any being *as rational*, to chuse wisdom rather than folly, just apprehensions rather than wrong, to be awake and actually to see rather than to be in a continual delirium: He, I say, who will not maintain this, will scarcely be unwilling to acknowledge an *immediate rectitude* in *veracity*.

Under this head, I would comprehend impartiality and honesty of mind in our enquiries after truth, as well as a sacred regard to it in all we say; fair and ingenuous dealing;

such an openness and simplicity of temper as exclude guile
and prevarication, and all the contemptible arts of craft,
equivocation and hypocrisy; fidelity to our engagements;
sincerity and uprightness in our transactions with ourselves
as well as others; and the careful avoiding of all secret
attempts to deceive ourselves, and to evade or disguise the
truth in examining our own characters.

Some of these particulars, though they belong to the
division of rectitude I have now in view, and which has truth
for its object; yet are not properly included in the signification of *veracity*.—But it requires our notice, that fidelity to
promises is *properly* a branch or instance of *veracity*.—*The
nature and obligation of *promises* have been said to be
attended with great difficulties; which makes it necessary to
desire this observation may be particularly considered.

By a *promise* some declaration is made, or assurance given
to another, which brings us under an obligation to act or not
to act, from which we should have been otherwise free. Such
an obligation never flows merely from declaring a *resolution* or
intention; and therefore a promise must mean more than this;
and the whole difference is, that the one relates to the *present*,
the other to *future* time.—When I say I *intend* to do an action,
I affirm only a present fact.—But to *promise*, is to declare that
such a thing *shall* be done, or that such and such events *shall*
happen. In this case, it is not enough to acquit me from the
charge of falsehood, that I *intend* to do what I promise, but it
must be actually done, agreeably to the assurances given.
After declaring a *resolution* to do an action, a man is under no
obligation actually to do it, because he did not say he would;
his word and veracity are not engaged; and the non-
performance cannot infer the guilt of violating truth. On the
contrary, when a person declares he *will* do any action, he
becomes obliged to do it, and cannot afterwards omit it,
without incurring the imputation of declaring falsehood, as

* See Treatise of Human Nature. Vol. III. Book III. part II. Sect. V.

really as if he had declared what he knew to be a false past or present fact; and in much the same manner as he would have done, if he had pretended to know, and had accordingly asserted, that a certain event would happen at a certain time which yet did not then happen. There is, however, a considerable difference between this last case, and the falshood implied in breaking promises and engagements; for the object of these is something, the existence of which depends on ourselves, and which we have in our power to bring to pass; and therefore here the falshood must be known and wilful, and entirely imputable to our own neglect and guilt. But in the case of events predicted which are not subject to our dominion, the blame, as far as there may be any, must arise from pretending to knowledge which we really want, and asserting absolutely what we are not sure of.

To *promise* then, being to assert a fact dependent on ourselves, with an intention to produce faith in it and reliance upon it, as certainly to happen; the obligation to keep a promise is the same with the obligation to regard truth; and the intention of it cannot be, in the sense some have asserted, to will or create a new obligation; unless it can be pretended that the obligation to veracity is *created* by the mere breath of men every time they speak, or make any professions. If indeed we mean by creating a new obligation, that the producing a particular effect or performance of an external action becomes fit, in consequence of some new situation of a person (or some preceding acts of his own) which was not fit before; it may be very well acknowledged; nor is there any thing in the least mysterious in it. Thus, performance becomes our duty after a promise, in the same sense that repentance becomes our duty in consequence of doing wrong, reparation of an injury, in consequence of committing it, or a particular manner of conduct, in consequence of placing ourselves in particular circumstances and relations of life.

As a confirmation of this account, if any confirmation was

necessary, it might be observed, that false declarations in general, and violations of engagements admit of the same extenuations or aggravations according to the different degrees of solemnity with which they are made, and the different importance of the subjects of them.

The last part of virtue, I shall mention, is JUSTICE: [1]Meaning by this word, that part of virtue which regards *property* and *commerce*.[1]

The origin of the idea of *property* is the same with that of right and wrong in general. It denotes such a relation of a particular object to a particular person, as infers or implies, that it is fit he should have the disposal of it rather than others, and wrong to deprive him of it. This is what every one means by calling a thing his *right*, or saying that it is *his own*.

Upon this there are two questions that may be asked. *First*, How an object obtains this relation to a person?— *Secondly*, Into what we are to resolve, and how we are to account for, the right and wrong we perceive in these instances?

The writers of *Ethicks* are very well agreed in their answers to the first of these questions. An object, it is obvious, will acquire the relation to a person which has been mentioned, in consequence of first possession; in consequence of its being the fruit of his labour; by donation, succession, and many other ways not necessary to be here enumerated.

It is far from being so generally agreed, what account ought to be given of this: But I cannot find any particular difficulties attending it. Numberless are the facts and circumstances, which vary and modify the general law of right, and

[1 Ed. I reads: 'This word is sometimes used to signify the whole of virtue and righteousness; but, most commonly, it is more confined in its signification, and means, either that part of universal righteousness which concerns our behaviour to mankind, or, yet more restrictively, that part of righteousness which regards *property* and *commerce*. In this last sense it is now used.']

alter the relations of particular effects to it. Taking possession of an object, and disposing of it as I please, abstracted from all particular circumstances attending such conduct, is innocent; but suppose the object was before possessed by another, the fruit of whose labour it was, and who consents not to be deprived of it, and then this conduct becomes wrong; not merely upon the account of its consequences, but *immediately*[1] wrong.—Taking to ourselves any of the means of enjoyment, when quite loose from our fellow-creatures, or not related to them in any of the ways which determine property, cannot be the same with doing this, when the contrary is true; nor is it possible to frame the same moral judgment concerning an action in these different circumstances.—That *first possession, prescription, donation, succession,* &c. should be circumstances which alter the *nature of a case,* determine right and wrong, and induce obligation, where otherwise we should have been free, is not less conceivable than that benefits received, private or publick interest, the will of certain beings, or any of the other considerations before insisted on, should have this effect. There is no other account to be given of this, than that 'such is truth, such the nature of things.' And this account, wherever it distinctly appears, is ultimate and satisfactory, and leaves nothing further for the mind to desire.

The limbs, the faculties, and lives of persons are *theirs,* or to be reckoned amongst their *properties,* in much the same sense and upon the same grounds with their external goods and acquisitions. The former differ from the latter, no more than the latter differ among themselves. The right to them is obtained in different ways, but is equally real and certain. And if, antecedently to society and conventions entered into for common convenience, there is no property of the latter kind, and it is naturally indifferent in what manner what we take and detain is related to another; it will be hard to shew

[¹ Ed. 1 adds '*and self-evidently*'.]

that the same is not true of the other kind of property, or that in reality there can be any right to any thing.

Were nothing meant, when we speak of the *rights* of beings, but that it is for the general utility, that they should have the exclusive enjoyment of such and such things; then, where this is not concerned, a man has no more right to his liberty or his life, than to objects the most foreign to him; and having no property, can be no object of injurious or unjust treatment. Supposing two men to live together, without being at all connected with or known to the rest of the world; one of them could possess nothing that did not in reason lie quite open to the seizure of the other, nothing that was *his*, or that he could properly *give* away: There would be nothing wrong in the most wanton and unprovoked invasion or destruction of the enjoyments of the one by the other, supposing this in the other's power, and that in any circumstances he knew he should gain as much by it as the other would lose. What little reason then have we, upon these principles, for rejecting the opinion that a state of nature is a state of war?

These observations may be more clearly applied to independent societies of men, who are to be looked upon as in a state of nature with respect to one another, and amongst whom it is very strange (as whatever one of them can take from the other may be equally useful to both) that the notions of *property* and *injustice* should prevail almost as much as amongst private persons, if these notions are not natural, or if derived wholly from the consideration of publick good. But besides, if publick good be the sole measure and foundation of *property* and of the *rights* of beings, it would be absurd to say *innocent* beings have a right to exemption from misery, or that they may not be made in any degree miserable, if but the smallest degree of *prepollent* good can arise from it. Nay, any number of innocent beings might be placed in a state of absolute and eternal misery, provided amends is made for their misery by producing at the same time a greater number of beings in a greater degree happy. For wherein would this be worse than producing a less rather than a greater degree of good, or than producing the excess only of the happiness above the misery, without any degree of the latter? What makes the difference between communicating happiness to a *single being* in such a manner, as that it shall be only the excess of his enjoyments above his sufferings; and communicating happiness to a *system of beings* in such a manner that a *great* number of them shall be totally miserable, but a *greater* number happy? Would there be nothing in such a procedure that was not right and just; especially could we conceive the sufferings of the unhappy part to be, in any way, the occasion or means of greater happiness to the rest? Is a man, be his relations or kindnesses to another what they will, capable of receiving no injury from him by any actions not detrimental to the publick? Might a man innocently ruin any number of his fellow-creatures, provided he causes in a greater degree the good of others? Such consequences are plainly shocking to our natural sentiments; but I know not how to avoid them on the principles I am examining.— It is indeed far from easy to determine what degree of superior good would compensate the irreparable and undeserved ruin of *one* person; or what overbalance of happiness would be great enough to justify the absolute misery of one innocent being.* Be these things however as they will;

* There are some actions, says *Cicero*, so foul, that a good man would not do them to save his country. *De Officiis*, Lib. I. Chap. XLV.—He praises *Fabius*, the Roman general, for sending back to *Pyrrhus* a deserter, who had offered privately to poison him for a proper reward from the *Romans*: And also *Aristides* for rejecting, because not just, a proposal very profitable to his country, made to him by *Themistocles*. Ib. Lib. III. Chap. XXII.—To the question: Would not a good man, when starving with hunger, force food from another man who is worthless? he answers, by no means; and gives this reason for it: *Non enim mihi est vita mea utilior, quam animi talis affectio, neminem ut violem commodi mei gratia.*—The like answer he gives to the question, Whether a virtuous man would, in order to save his life in a shipwreck, thrust a worthless man from a plank he had seized. Ibid. Chap. XXIII.—His decision also in the case of the famine at *Rhodes* is well known.

there is at least enough in the considerations now proposed to shew that publick happiness cannot be the sole standard and measure of justice and injustice. But without having recourse to them, the decision of this question might perhaps be rested entirely on the determination any impartial person shall find himself obliged to give in the following case.—Imagine any object which cannot be divided or enjoyed in common by two persons, and which also would be of equal advantage to both: Is it not fit, setting aside all distant consequences, that the *first possessor*, or he whose skill and labour had procured it, should have the use and enjoyment of it rather than the other? The affirmative in this case is very obvious;* and he who admits it, cannot think that there is no such origin of property as I have assigned.

What may have contributed towards deceiving some here, is the connexion observable in general between cruelty and injustice; but were these more inseparable than they are, we should have no reason for confounding them. A little reflexion may shew an unbiassed person, that the notion of an action's being *unjust* is different from that of its being *cruel, inhuman,* or *unkind.* How else could the guilt of a *cruel* action appear always highly aggravated by its being likewise *unjust?* I am sensible it may be replied to this, that the injus-

---

* There is now less occasion for saying much on this point, since Dr. Hutcheson, in his *System of Moral Philosophy,* not long since published, Book II. p. 253, &c. Ch. III. has acknowledged that we *immediately* approve of private justice as well as of veracity, without referring them to a system or to publick interest. But I know not well how to reconcile with this his general method of treating the subject of justice and rights, and particularly his saying, in the same chapter, that the ultimate notion of a *right*, is that which *tends to the universal good,* p. 266.—His chapter on the *rights of necessity,* Vol. II. may be particularly worth consulting on this occasion; in which he seems to allow, that some laws may be so *sacred* (such as those forbidding perjury, abjuring the true God, and particular kinds of treachery and injustice) that scarce any pleas of necessity to prevent impending evils, or obtain superior good, will justify a departure from them. One cannot help considering here, what it is he means by the *sacredness* of a law. Surely, not its importance as a means of private or publick good; for this would make even a doubt on this point ridiculous.

tice attending an act of cruelty, adding to the private damage done by it a damage also to the publick, makes it appear more cruel, and therefore more vicious. But how can it be imagined that remote considerations of ill effects to the publick (many of which are not immediately discovered by those who *search* for them) are always adverted to by the bulk of men, so as to make the simple and illiterate in some cases even better judges of what is just and unjust, than the learned and studious? Or how can any one think that the guilt of actions producing on the whole damages strictly equal, would not appear aggravated, if accompanied with injury and injustice?

An observation already made, is no where more obvious and remarkable, than on the subject we are now examining. When all things are alike, and no one can pretend that an object belongs to him rather than another, the most minute circumstance is sufficient to turn the balance, and to confer a true and full right. Thus, a remote relation to what is my property, contiguity, first sight, and innumerable other particulars in themselves frivolous, will give ground for a claim, which when nothing equivalent can be opposed to them, shall be valid.

The power a person has to transfer his property, is part of the idea of property, and equally intelligible with the power he has to dispose of his labour or advice, and to employ them in whatever way and for whatever purposes he thinks proper.

It may tend to remove some further difficulties which may occur to one who considers this subject, to remark, that amongst near relations and intimate friends, and also with respect to useful objects of which there is no scarcity, the ideas of property are always relaxed in proportion to the intimacy of the relation or friendship, and the degree of plenty. The reason in the first case may be chiefly the consent of the proprietors, which, where known or reasonably presumed, always removes the unlawfulness of taking and employing what belongs to them. Between married persons here has been a formal surrender of their respective possessions to one another: and between intimate friends, though no professions may have passed directly expressing such a surrender, there is always understood to prevail such an union as implies it. In the latter case, there is also a tacit and presumed surrender; for it cannot be conceived that any one should be unwilling to resign, or that he should at all attach himself to any thing, the loss of which he can immediately and with perfect ease repair.—Besides; enquiries concerning rights are only proper, as far as an object is of some value real or imaginary, mediate or immediate. To ask to whom belongs the property of what is of no value, is trifling and absurd: It is the same as to ask who ought to have the use of what is of no use. Now any *particular portion* of natural supplies which are so common as to bear no price, as water or air, is to be deemed really worthless, and so far no object of property. It is not certainly in the least wonderful, that objects procurable without any trouble; which can be the produce of no one's labour; which when taken from persons are always replaced immediately by others of the same value; and a sufficient quantity of which none can want: It is not, I say, in the least wonderful that objects of this kind should be incapable of acquiring the relation of property to particular persons, and that no injustice should be possible to be committed by any seizure of them. No objections then can, with any reason, be derived from hence against the account that has been given of property.

The particular rules of *justice* are various, and there are many instances in which it is difficult to determine what it requires. Of these it is not requisite that I should take any notice: But it is very proper to observe, that, though I cannot allow public good to be the *sole* original of justice, yet, undoubtedly, it has great influence upon it, and is *one* important

ground of many of its maxims. It gives a very considerabl
additional force to the *rights* of men, and, in some cases
entirely creates them.—Nothing is more evident than that
in order to the happiness of the world and the being of society
possessions should be stable, and property sacred, and no
liable, except upon very extraordinary occasions, to b
violated. In considering what common interest requires, w
are, besides the immediate effects of actions, to consider wha
their general tendencies are, what they open the way to, and
what would actually be the consequences if all were to ac
alike. If under the pretence of greater indigence, superfluity
to the owner, or intention to give to a worthier person, I may
take away a man's property, or adjudge it from him in a
court of justice; another or all, in the same circumstances
may do so; and thus the boundaries of property would be
overthrown, and general anarchy, distrust and savageness be
introduced.—Men in general, however, as before observed,
do not consider this; much less is it, by some views of this
kind and these only, that their sentiments on this subject are
always regulated.

The motives to the practice of justice are the same with
those to virtuous practice in general, and will be the subject
of the next chapter.

I omit taking any particular notice here of *justice*, as it
signifies the due treatment of beings according to their different moral characters, or the equitable distribution of rewards
and punishments; because it has been particularly considered
elsewhere.*

These then are the main and leading branches of Virtue.
It may not be possible properly to comprehend all the particular instances of it under any number of heads. It is by
attending to the different relations, circumstances, and quali-

* See Chap. IV.

ications of beings, and the natures and tendencies of objects, and by examining into the whole truth of every case, that we judge what *is* or *is not to be* done. And as there is an endless variety of cases, and the situations of agents and objects are ever changing; the universal law of rectitude, though in the abstract idea of it always invariably the same, must be continually varying in its *particular* demands and obligations.

This leads me to observe, that however different from one another the heads which have been enumerated are, yet, from the very notion of them, as *heads of virtue*, it is plain, that they all run up to one general idea, and should be considered as only different modifications and views of one original, all-governing law.* It is the same authority that enjoins, the same truth and right that oblige, the same eternal reason that commands in them all. Virtue thus considered, is necessarily *one* thing. No part of it can be separated from another.

From hence we may learn, by the way, how defective and inconsistent a thing *partial virtue* is. The same law that requires piety, requires also benevolence, veracity, temperance, justice, gratitude, &c. All these rest on the same foundation, and are alike our indispensable duty. He, therefore, who *lives* in the neglect of any one of them, is as really a rebel against reason, and an apostate from righteousness and order, as if he neglected them all. The authority of the law in one point is not different from its authority in another, and in all points. To transgress therefore in one point (I mean habitually and wilfully) is to throw off effectually our allegiance, and to trample on the whole authority of the law. True and genuine virtue must be uniform and universal. Nothing short of an *entire* good character can avail to our

---

* Οὗτω δὴ καὶ περὶ τῶν ἀρετῶν, κᾶν εἰ πολλαὶ καὶ παντοδαπαί εἰσιν, ἕν γέ τι εἶδος ταὐτὸν ἅπασαι ἔχουσι δι᾽ ὃ εἰσὶν ἀρεταί. *Plat.* in Men: 'So likewise concerning the virtues; though they are many and various, there is one common idea belonging to them all, by which they *are* virtues.'

acceptance. As long as any evil habit is retained, we cannot be denominated the loyal subjects of the divine government; we continue under the curse of guilt; slaves to vice, and unqualified for bliss.—It will come in my way to observe more to this purpose hereafter.

There is another coincidence between the foregoing heads of virtue worth our notice. I mean, their agreeing very often in requiring the same actions. An act of *justice* may be also an act of *gratitude* and *beneficence*; and whatever any of these oblige us to, that also *piety* to God requires. Were *injustice*, *fraud*, *falshood*, and a *neglect* of *private* good universally prevalent, what a dreadful state would the world be in? and how would the ends of *benevolence* be defeated?—No one of the several virtues can be annihilated without the most pernicious consequences to all the rest. This, in a good measure, appears from what happens in the present state of things; but, in the final issue of things, the harmony between them will be found much more strict. Whatever exceptions may now happen, if we will look forwards to the whole of our existence, the three great principles of the love of God, the love of man, and true self-love, will always draw us the same way; and we have the utmost reason to assure ourselves, that at last no one will be able to say he has bettered himself by *any* unjust action, or that, though *less scrupulous* than others, he has been *more successful and happy*.

But though the heads of virtue before-mentioned agree thus far in requiring the same course of action, yet they often also interfere. Though upon the whole, or when considered as making one *general system or plan of conduct*, there is a strict coincidence between them, yet in examining *single acts* and *particular cases*, we find that they lead us contrary ways.— This perhaps has not been enough attended to, and therefore I shall particularly insist upon it.

What creates the difficulty in morals of determining what is right or wrong, in many particular cases, is chiefly the interference now mentioned in such cases between the different general principles of virtue.—Thus, the pursuit of the happiness of others is a duty, and so is the pursuit of private happiness; and though, on the whole, these are inseparably connected, in many particular instances, one of them cannot be pursued without giving up the other. When the publick happiness is very great, and the private very inconsiderable, no difficulties appear. We pronounce as confidently, that the one ought to give way to the other, as we do, that either alone ought to be pursued. But when the former is diminished, and the latter increased to a certain degree, doubt arises; and we may thus be rendered entirely incapable of determining what we ought to chuse. We have the most satisfactory perception, that we ought to study our own good, and, within certain limits, prefer it to that of another; but who can say how far, mark precisely these limits, and inform us in all cases of opposition between them, where right and wrong and indifference take place?—In like manner; the nearer attachments of nature or friendship, the obligations to veracity, fidelity, gratitude, or justice, may interfere with private and publick good, and it is not possible for us to judge always and accurately, what degrees or circumstances of any one of these compared with the others, will or will not cancel its obligation, and justify the violation of it.—It is thus likewise, that the different foundations of property give rise to contrary claims, and that sometimes it becomes very hard to say which of different titles to an object is the best.—If we examine the various intricate and disputed cases in morality, we shall, I believe, find that it is always some interference of this kind that produces the obscurity. Truth and right in all circumstances, require one determinate way of acting; but so variously may different obligations combine with or oppose each other in particular cases, and so imperfect are our discerning faculties, that it cannot but happen, that we should be frequently in the dark, and that different persons should judge differently, according to the different views they have of the several moral principles. Nor is this less unavoidable, or more to be wondered at, than that in matters of mere speculation, we should be at a loss to know what is true, when the arguments for and against a proposition appear nearly equal.

The principles themselves, it should be remembered, are self-evident; and to conclude the contrary, or to assert that there are no moral distinctions, because of the obscurity attending several cases wherein a competition arises between the several principles of morality, is very unreasonable. It is not unlike concluding, that, because in some circumstances we cannot, by their appearance to the eye, judge of the distances and magnitude of bodies, therefore we never can; because undeniable principles may be used in proving and opposing particular doctrines, therefore these principles are not undeniable; or because it may not in some instances be easy to determine what will be the effect of different forces, variously compounded and acting contrary to each other; therefore we can have no assurance what any of them acting separately will produce, or so much as know that there is any such thing as force.*

These observations may be of some use in helping us to determine, how far and in what sense, morality is capable of demonstration. There are undoubtedly a variety of moral

---

* How unreasonable would it be to conclude from the difficulty there often is to determine the bounds of *equality* and *inequality* between quantities, or from its appearing doubtful to us in some instances, whether quantities are the *same* or *different*, that such quantities are in reality neither equal nor unequal, neither the same nor different, or that in such instances *equality* and *inequality*, *sameness* and *difference* run into one another? Just as unreasonable would it be to conclude, from its being often difficult to define the bounds of right and wrong, or from its appearing doubtful to us in some nice cases what way of acting is *right* or *wrong*, that in such cases, there is no particular way of acting truly and certainly right or wrong, or that *right* and *wrong* in these cases lose their distinction. The weakness of our discerning faculties cannot in any case affect truth. Things themselves continue invariably the same, however different our opinions of them may be, or whatever doubts or difficulties may perplex us.

principles and maxims, which, to gain assent, need only to be understood: And I see not why such propositions as these, 'gratitude is due to benefactors; reverence is due to our Creator; it is right to study our own happiness; an innocent being ought not to be absolutely miserable; it is wrong to take from another the fruit of his labour,' and others of the like kind, may not be laid down and used as axioms, the truth of which appears as irresistibly as the truth of those which are the foundation of Geometry. But the case is very different when we come to consider *particular* effects. What is meant by demonstrating morality, can only be reducing these under the general self-evident principles of morality, or making out with certainty their relation to them. It would be happy for us were this always possible. We should then be eased of many painful doubts, know universally and infallibly what we should do and avoid, and have nothing to attend to besides conforming our practice to our knowledge. How impracticable this is every one must see.—Were benevolence the only virtuous principle, we could by no means apply it always without any danger of mistake to action; because we cannot be more sure, a particular external action is an instance of beneficence, than we are of the tendencies and consequences of that action. The same holds true upon the supposition that self-love is the only principle of virtue. Until we can in every particular know what is good or bad for ourselves and others, and discover the powers and qualities of objects, and what will result from any application of them to one another, we cannot always demonstrate what either of these principles requires, but must continue liable to frequent and unavoidable errors in our moral judgment.—In like manner, what our duty to God, the regard due to the properties and rights of others, and gratitude require, we must be at a loss about, as far as in any circumstances we cannot be sure what the will of God is, where property is lodged, or who our benefactors are and what are our obligations to them.—Thus, if we consider the several moral principles singly (or as liable to no limitations from one another) we find that we must frequently be very uncertain how it is best to act.

But if we further recollect, that in order to discover what is right in a case, we ought to extend our views to all the different *heads* of virtue, to examine how far each is concerned, and compare their respective influence and demands; and that at the same time (as just now explained) they often interfere; a second source of insuperable difficulties will appear. It is not alone sufficient to satisfy us that an action is to be done, that we know it will be the means of good to others: we are also to consider how it affects ourselves, what it is in regard to justice, and all the other circumstances the case may involve must be taken in, and weighed, if we would form a true judgment concerning it. In reality, before we can be capable of deducing demonstrably, accurately and particularly, the whole rule of *right* in every instance, we must possess universal and unerring knowledge. It must be above the power of any finite understanding to do this. He only who knows all truth, is acquainted with the whole law of truth in all its importance, perfection and extent.

Once more; we may, by considerations of this kind, be helped in forming a judgment of the different sentiments and practices in several points of morality, which have obtained in different countries and ages. The foregoing general principles all men at all times have agreed in. It cannot be shewn that there have ever been any human beings who have had no ideas of property and justice, of the rectitude of veracity, gratitude, benevolence, prudence, and religious worship. All the difference has been about particular usages and practices, of which it is impossible but different persons must have different ideas, according to the various opinions they entertain of their relation to the universally acknowledged moral principles, or of their ends, connexions, and tendencies.—Those who plead for passive obedience and non-resistance, think that to be required by divine command, or publick good; which others, with more reason, think to be reproachful to human nature, and destructive of the very end of magistracy and government.—Those nations amongst whom the customs of exposing children and aged persons have prevailed, approved of these customs upon the opinion of their being conducive to the general advantage, and friendly to the sufferers themselves.—Self-murder amongst some of the antients was justified and applauded, because considered as a method of extricating themselves from misery, which none but men of superior bravery could use; and not as, what it truly is, an act of very criminal discontent and impatience, a desertion of the station assigned us by Providence, and a cowardly flight from the duties and difficulties of life.—As far as any persons have ever approved persecution, it could only be under the notion of its doing God service; its being an execution of his wrath upon his enemies; a just punishment of obstinacy and impiety; and the necessary means of discountenancing pernicious errors, and preventing the propagation of what tends to subvert true religion, and ruin the souls of men.—The most superstitious practices, and ridiculous rites of worship, have gained credit and support, merely because apprehended to be pleasing to God, means of procuring his favour, and proper expressions of homage and adoration.

In these, and innumerable other instances of the like kind, the *practical* errors of men have arisen plainly from their *speculative* errors; from their mistaking facts, or not seeing the whole of a case; whence it cannot but often happen, that they will think those practices right, which, if they had juster opinions of facts and cases, they would unavoidably condemn. The rules of judging are universally the same. Those who approve, and those who disapprove, go upon the same principles. The disagreement is produced by the different application of them. The error lies in imagining that to fall under a particular species of virtue, which does not. And it is just as reasonable to expect disagreement here, as in the application of the received principles of knowledge and assent in general. Nor would it be more extravagant to conclude that men have not speculative reason, because of the diversity in their speculative opinions, than it is to conclude, they have no powers of moral perception, or that there is no fixed standard of morality, because of the diversity in men's opinions, concerning the fitness or unfitness, lawfulness or unlawfulness, of *particular practices*. Until men can be raised above defective knowledge, and secured against partial and inadequate views, they must continue liable to believe cases and facts and the tendencies of actions, to be otherwise than they are; and, consequently, to form false judgments concerning right and wrong. And, till the bulk of mankind can be secured from the most gross delusions and taking up the wildest opinions, they must continue liable to judgments of this kind the most grossly wrong.

It should be also remembered, that it is not easy to determine how far our natural sentiments may be altered by custom, education, and example; or to say, what degree of undue attachment to some qualities, and vivacity to some ideas above others, they may give, or how much depravity and blindness they may introduce into our moral and intellectual powers. Notions the most stupid may, through their influence, come to be rooted in the mind beyond the possibility of being eradicated, antipathies given to objects naturally the most agreeable, and sensation itself perverted.

It would be unreasonable to conclude from hence, as some are disposed to do, that all we are is derived from education and habit; that we can never tell, when we are free from their influence, and believe on just evidence; or that there are no natural sensations and desires at all, and no principles of truth in themselves certain and invariable, and forcing universal assent.—Education and habit can give us no new ideas. The power they have supposes somewhat natural as their foundation. Were it not for the natural powers by which we perceive pleasure and pain, good and evil, beauty and deformity, the ideas of them could never be excited in us, any more than the ideas of colour in persons born blind; and no prejudices could be communicated to us for or against particular objects, under any notions of this kind.—Were there no ideas of proportion, similitude, existence, identity, &c. essential to our understandings, we should lose all capacity of knowledge and judgment, and there would be no possibility of being misled, or of being in any way influenced by wrong biasses. Neither, had we no natural ideas of virtue and vice, could we be capable of any approbation or disapprobation, any love or hatred of actions and characters otherwise than as advantageous or disadvantageous to us. All that custom and education can do, is to alter the direction of natural sentiments and ideas, and to connect them with wrong objects.—It is that part of our moral constitution which depends on instinct, that is chiefly liable to the corruption produced by these causes. The *sensible horror* at vice, and *attachment* to virtue, may be impaired, the conscience seared, the nature of particular practices mistaken, the sense of shame weakened, the judgment darkened, the voice of reason stifled, and self-deception practised, to the most lamentable and fatal degree. Yet the grand lines and primary principles of morality are so deeply wrought into our hearts, and one with our minds, that they will be for ever legible. The general approbation of certain virtues, and dislike of their contraries, must always remain, and cannot be erased but with the destruction of all intellectual perception. The most depraved never sink so low, as to lose all moral discernment, all ideas of right and wrong, justice and injustice, honour and dishonour. This appears sufficiently from the judgments they pass on the actions of others; from the resentment they discover whenever they are *themselves* th objects of ill treatment; and from the inward uneasiness an remorse, which they cannot avoid feeling, and by which, o some occasions, they are severely tormented. All the satis faction and peace within themselves, which they are capabl of enjoying, proceeds, in a great measure, from a studie neglect of reflexion, and from their having learned to dis guise their vices under the appearance of some virtuous o innocent qualities; which shews, that still vice is an objec so foul and frightful, that they cannot bear the direct view o it in themselves, or embrace it in its naked form. But, afte all, were every observation of this kind wrong, little regar would be due, in these enquiries, to what takes place amongs those whom we know to be the corrupt and perverted part o the species. Such, most certainly, cannot be the proper per sons by whom to judge of truth, or from whom to take ou estimate of human nature.

The sources of error and disagreement now insisted on would produce very considerable effects, though all the par ticulars of duty and rectitude were, in themselves, plain and easy to be determined; for that ought to be very plain indeed, about which great differences would not be occasioned by educations, tempers, views, and degrees of sagacity, so different as those of mankind; and inattention, prejudices, and corruptions so great as those which prevail amongst them.—But, if we will recollect the observations which have been made concerning the interference between the prin ciples of morality, and the impossibility of a complete and scientifick deduction of what we ought to do and avoid in particular circumstances, we shall own, that the subject itself is often involved in real darkness, and attended with insurmountable difficulties, which, therefore, must be a further ground of much greater and more unavoidable dis agreements.

Of the Subject-matter of Virtue

Upon the whole; what has been said seems sufficiently to account for the diversity of men's sentiments concerning moral matters; and it appears to be reasonable to expect, that, in the sense and manner I have explained, they should be no less various, than their sentiments concerning any other matters.

I shall only add, that though all men, in all cases, judged rightly what is virtue and right behaviour, there would still prevail a very considerable variety in their moral practices in different ages and countries. The reason is obvious: In different ages and circumstances of the world, the same practices often have not the same connexions, tendencies, and effects. The state of human affairs is perpetually changing, and, in the same period of time, it is very different in different nations. Amidst this variety, it is impossible that the subject-matter of virtue should continue precisely the same. New obligations must arise, and the proprieties of conduct must vary, as new connexions take place, and new customs, laws, and political constitutions are introduced. Many practices, very warrantable and proper under one form of government, or in the first establishment of a community, or amongst people of a particular genius, and where particular regulations and opinions prevail, may be quite wrong in another state of things, or amongst people of other characters and customs. Amongst the antient *Spartans*, we are told, theft was countenanced. The little value they had for wealth, and many circumstances in the state of their affairs, might justly relax their ideas of property, and render every instance of taking from another what he possessed, not the same that it is now amongst us. Some virtues or accomplishments may be more useful and more difficult, in some circumstances of countries and governments, than in others; and this may give just occasion for their being more applauded. Other instances, more obvious and unexceptionable of what is now meant, may easily offer themselves to the reader; and in considering the diversity of sentiments amongs mankind concerning any particular practices, it will b right, amongst other things, not to overlook the differenc in the real state of the case, which the differences of times an places make, and how far they alter the relation of suc practices to the general principles of morality.

CHAP. VIII.

Of the Nature and Essentials of Virtue *in* Practice, *as distinguished from* absolute Virtue; *and, the Principle of Action in a virtuous Agent.*

BEFORE I enter on the discussion of the principal point to be considered in this chapter, it is necessary a distinction on which what will be said is founded, and to which I have before had occasion to refer, should be distinctly explained: I mean, the distinction of virtue into ABSTRACT or ABSOLUTE virtue, and PRACTICAL or RELATIVE virtue.

It will, I think, plainly appear, that there is a just ground for this distinction: And we cannot, without attending to it, have an accurate view of the nature of virtue, or avoid a good deal of embarrassment in our enquiries into it.

ABSTRACT virtue is, most properly, a quality of the external action or event. It denotes what an action is, considered independently of the *sense* of the agent; or what, *in itself* and *absolutely*, it is right *such* an agent, in *such* circumstances, should do; and what, if he judged truly, he would judge he ought to do.—PRACTICAL *virtue*, on the contrary, has a necessary relation to, and dependence upon, the opinion of the agent concerning his actions. It signifies what he ought to do, *upon supposition* of his having such and such sentiments.—In a sense, not entirely different from this, good actions have been by some divided into such as are *materially* good, and such as are *formally* so.—Moral agents are liable to mistake the circumstances they are in, and, consequently, to form erroneous judgments concerning their own obligations. This supposes, that these obligations have a real existence, independent of their judgments. But, when they are in any manner mistaken, it is not to be imagined, that then nothing remains obligatory; for there is a sense in which it may be said, that what any being, in the sincerity of his heart *thinks* he ought to do, he *indeed* ought to do, and would b justly blameable if he omitted to do, though contradictor to what, in the former sense, is his duty.—It would b trifling to object to this, that it implies, that an action may at the same time, be both right and wrong; for it implies thi only, as the rightness and wrongness of actions are considered in different views. A magistrate who should adjudge ar estate to the person whose right it *appears* to be, upon a grea overbalance of evidence, would certainly do right in *on* sense; though, should the opposite claimant, after all, prove to be the true proprietor, he would as certainly do wrong ir *another* sense.

This distinction indeed cannot be rejected, without asserting, that whatever we *think* things to be, that they *are*; that we can, in *no sense*, ever do wrong, without incurring guilt and blame; that while we follow our judgments, we cannot *err* in our conduct; that though, through involuntary mistake, a man breaks the most important engagements, hurts his best friends, or bestows his bounty on the most worthless objects; though, through religious zeal and a blind superstition, he commits the most shocking barbarities, imagining he hereby does God service, and, from an apprehension of their lawfulness, practises violence and deceit; there is yet no sense in which he contradicts rectitude, or in which it can be truly affirmed he acts amiss. Thus the difference between an *enlightened* and an *erroneous* conscience would vanish entirely; no mistake of right would be possible; all the fancies of men concerning their duty would be alike just, and the most ignorant as well acquainted with the subject-matter of virtue, as the most knowing.—But to what purpose is it to multiply words on this occasion, when it is so apparent, that all enquiries after our duty, all instructions in it, all deliberations how it becomes us to act in the various circumstances into which we are cast, and the very expressions, *doing right*, and *perceiving right*, imply *objective rectitude*, or something separate from, and independent of the mind and its perceptions, to be enquired after and perceived?

It may be worth our notice here, that from knowing the nature and capacities of a being, his relations, connexions, and dependencies, and the consequences of his actions, the whole of what he ought to do, in the *first* sense, may be determined, without once attending to his private judgment. But, in order to determine this in the *latter* sense, the single point necessary to be considered is this judgment; or the real apprehensions of the being concerning what he does, at the time of doing it.—The former requires the greatest variety of circumstances to be taken into consideration, and is no more possible to be by us universally and unerringly determined, than the whole truth on any other subject. The latter, on the contrary, has few difficulties attending it. The greatest degree of doubt about the former, may leave us in no suspence about this. Our rule is to follow our consciences steadily and faithfully, after we have taken care to inform them in the best manner we can; and, where we doubt, to take the *safest* side, and not to venture to *do* any thing concerning which we have doubts, when we know there can be nothing amiss in *omitting* it; and, on the contrary, not to *omit* any thing about which we doubt, when we know there can be no harm in *doing* it. But, if we doubt whether the performance, and also whether the omission is right; in these circumstances, when the doubts on both sides are equal, and we cannot get better information, it becomes *practically* indifferent which way we act. When there is any preponderancy, it is evident we ought to take that way, in which there seems to us the least danger of going a-stray.—It is happy for us, that our title to the character of virtuous beings depends not upon the justness of our opinions, or the constant *objective* rectitude of all we do; but upon the conformity of our actions to the sincere conviction of our minds. A suspicion of the contrary, were it to prevail, would prove of very bad consequence, by causing us to distrust our only guide, and throwing us into a state of endless and inextricable perplexity. In this state it would be no relief to us to resolve upon total inaction, as not knowing but that, when acting with the most upright views, we may be the most blame-worthy; for such a resolution might itself prove the greatest crime, and fix upon us the greatest guilt.

I have applied the epithets *real* and *absolute* to the first kind of virtue, for an obvious reason; but care should be taken not to imagine, that the latter is not also, in a different sense and view, *real* virtue. It is truly and absolutely right, that a being should do what the reason of his mind, though perhaps unhappily misinformed, requires of him; or what, according to his best judgment, he is persuaded to be the will of God. If he neglects this, he becomes necessarily and justly the object of his own dislike, and forfeits all pretensions to integrity.*

* How absurd then are all claims to dominion over conscience? Such a dominion is little to the purpose of those who have pleaded for it, if it does not mean a power or right to oblige persons to act against their private judgment, that is, a *right* to oblige persons to *do wrong*. Every man ought to be left to follow his conscience because then only he acts virtuously. Where the plea of conscience is real, (and who but the searcher of hearts can judge how far in general it is or is not so?) it is wicked to lay restraints upon it. For it is violating the rights of what is above all things sacred, attempting to make hypocrites and knaves of men, and establishing *human* authority on the ruins of *divine*.—All that can ever be right, is necessary *self-defence*, when the consciences of men lead them to hurt others, to take away their liberty, or to subvert the publick.—It is no less a *contradiction to common sense*, than it is *impiety*, for any men to pretend to a power to oblige their fellow men to worship God in any manner different from that which is most agreeable to their consciences; that is, in any way but that in which alone it is acceptable and right in *them* to do it.—The civil magistrate goes out of his province, when he interposes in religious differences. His office is only to secure the liberties and properties of those under his jurisdiction; to protect *all* good subjects; to preserve the peace amongst contending sects, and to hinder them from encroaching on one another.

I hope I shall be excused, if I take this opportunity to add, that we have not much less than demonstration, that God will not and cannot grant, to any particular men or set of men, a power to direct the faith and practices of others in religious matters, without making them, at the same time, *infallible* and

These different kinds of rectitude have such an affinity that we are very prone to confound them in our thoughts and discourses; and a particular attention is necessary, in order to know when we speak of the one or the other. It is hardly possible, in writing on morality, to avoid blending them in our language, and frequently including both, even in the same sentence. But enough has been said to enable an attentive person to see when and how this is done, and to prepare the way for that explanation of the nature and essentials of PRACTICAL Virtue, to which I shall now proceed.

What first of all offers itself here, is, that *practical* virtue supposes LIBERTY.—Whether all will acknowledge this or not, it cannot be omitted.

The *liberty* I here mean is the same with the power of *acting* and *determining*: And it is self-evident, that where such a power is wanting, there can be no moral capacities. As far as it is true of a being that he *acts*, so far he must *himself* be the cause of the action, and therefore not necessarily determined to act. Let any one try to put a sense on the expressions; *I will*; *I act*; which is consistent with supposing, that the volition or action does not proceed from myself. Virtue supposes determination, and determination supposes a determiner; and a determiner that determines not himself, is a palpable contradiction. Determination requires an efficient cause. If this cause is the being himself, I plead for no more.

impeccable. For in what, otherwise, must such a grant issue? What would it be, but a grant of power to mislead and deceive? What errors, what corruptions, what desolation do we know have been actually produced by the pretence to it without these qualifications?—It is a part of the peculiar happiness of this nation, that principles of this kind have been so well explained, and are now so much received in it. May they be still more received, and better understood; and our constitution and laws, already the best in the world, grow to a perfect conformity to them. May the number of those who are for giving up their liberty and independency, and submitting to human authority in religious matters, be continually decreasing; and the joyful time soon come, when all slavish principles shall be universally contemned and detested.

Of the Principle of Action

If not, then it is no longer *his* determination; that is, *he is n* longer the determiner, but the motive, or whatever else an one will say to be the cause of the determination. To asl what effects *our* determinations, is the very same with askin who did an action, after being informed that such a one di it. In short; who must not *feel* the absurdity of saying, *m* volitions are produced by a *foreign* cause, that is, are no *mine*; I determine *voluntarily*, and yet *necessarily*?—We have in truth, the same constant and necessary consciousness o liberty, that we have that we think, chuse, will, or even exist; and whatever to the contrary any persons may say, i is impossible for them in earnest to think they have no active self-moving powers, and are not the causes of *their own* voli tions, or not to ascribe to *themselves*, what they must be conscious *they* think and do.

But, not to enter much further into a question which ha been strangely darkened by fallacious reasonings, and wher there is so much danger of falling into a confusion of ideas, I would only observe, that it is hard to say what virtue and vice, commendation and blame, mean, if they do not suppose *agency*, free choice, and an absolute dominion over our resolu tions.*—It has always been the *general*, and it is evidently the *natural* sense of mankind, that they cannot be accountable for what they have no power to avoid. Nothing can be more glaringly absurd, than applauding or reproaching ourselves for what we were no more the causes of, than our own beings, and what it was no more possible for us to prevent, than the returns of the seasons, or the revolutions of the planets. The whole language of men, all their practical sentiments and schemes, and the whole frame and order of human affairs, are founded upon the notion of liberty, and are utterly in consistent with the supposition, that nothing is made to de pend on ourselves, or that our purposes and determinations

* *Motus enim voluntarius eam naturam in seipso continet, ut sit in nostra potestate, nobisque pareat.* Cic. de fato.

are not subjected to our own command, but the result of physical laws, not possible to be resisted.

If, upon examination, any of the advocates of the doctrine of necessity should find, that what they mean by necessity is not inconsistent with the ideas of *agency* and *self-determination,* there will be little room for farther disputes; and that liberty, which I insist upon as essential to morality, will be acknowledged; nor will it be at all necessary to take into consideration, or to pay much regard to any difficulties relating* to the nature of that influence we commonly ascribe to motives.

Secondly, Intelligence is another requisite of practical morality. Some degree of this is necessary to the perception of moral good and evil; and without this perception, there can be no moral agency. It must not be imagined, that liberty comprehends or infers intelligence; for all the inferior orders of beings possess true liberty. Self-motion and activity, of some kind, are essential to every conscious, living being. There seems no difference between wanting all spontaneity, and being quite inanimate.—But though liberty does not suppose intelligence, yet intelligence plainly supposes liberty. For what has been now affirmed of all sensitive natures, is much more unexceptionably true of intelligent natures. A

* With respect to this, however, one may observe, that there seems to be very little mysterious in a man's chusing to follow his judgment and desires, or in his actually doing what he is *inclined* to do; which is what we mean when we say, motives determine him: Though, at the same time it be very plain, that motives can have no concern in *effecting* his determination, or that there is no *physical connexion* between his judgment and views, and the actions consequent upon them. What would be more absurd than to say, that our inclinations act upon us, or compel us; that our desires and fears *put* us into motion, or *produce* our volitions; that is, are *agents*? And yet, what is more conceivable, than that they may be the *occasions* of our putting *ourselves* into motion?—That there is an essential and total difference between the ideas of an *efficient cause* and an *account* or *occasion*, it would be trifling to go about to prove. What sense would there be in saying, that the *situation* of a body, which may properly be the occasion or account of its being struck by another body, is the *efficient* of its motion or its *impeller*?—A particular discussion of this question may be found in the CORRESPONDENCE between Dr. Priestley and Dr. Price, on the Subjects of MATERIALISM and NECESSITY. 8vo. printed for Mr. Johnson in St. Paul's Church-yard.

thinking, designing, reasoning being, without liberty, without any inward, spontaneous, active, self-directing principle, is what no one can frame any idea of. So unreasonable are all objections to the making of free creatures; and so absurd to ask, why men were made so. But,

Thirdly, The main point now to be insisted on is, 'that an agent cannot be justly denominated *virtuous*, except he acts from a consciousness of rectitude, and with a regard to it as his *rule* and *end*.' Though this observation appears to me undoubtedly true, and of the greatest importance on this subject; yet I know there are many, whose assent to it will not be easily gained; and, therefore, it will be proper that I should endeavour particularly to explain and prove it.

Liberty and *Reason* constitute the *capacity* of virtue. It is the *intention* that gives it *actual being* in a character.—The reader must not here forget the distinction before explained. To mere theoretical virtue, or (if I may so speak) the abstract reasons and fitnesses of things, praise-worthiness is not applicable. It is the actual conformity of the wills of moral agents to what they see or believe to be the fitnesses of things, that is the object of our praise and esteem. One of these may, perhaps, very properly be called the *virtue of the action*, in contradistinction from the other, which may be called the *virtue of the agent*. To the former, no particular intention is requisite; for what is *objectively* right, may be done from any motive good or bad; and, therefore, from hence alone, no merit is communicated to the agent; nay, it is consistent with the greatest guilt. On the contrary, to the other the particular intention is what is most essential. When this is good, there is so far virtue, whatever is true of the *matter* of the action; for an agent, who does what is *objectively wrong*, may often be entitled to commendation.

It may possibly be of some advantage towards elucidating this matter, to conceive that only as, in strict propriety, *done* by a moral agent, which he *intends* to do. What arises beyond ɔr contrary to his intention, however it may eventually happen, or be derived, by the connexion of natural causes, from his determination, should not be imputed to him. Our own determinations alone are, most properly, our actions. These alone we have absolute power over, and are responsible for. It is at least worth considering, in what different senses, we are said to do what we did, and what we did not *design* to do. The causality or efficiency implied in these cases, is certainly far from being the same.—There seems indeed scarcely any thing more evident, than that there are two views or senses, in which we commonly speak of actions. Sometimes we mean by them, the determinations or volitions themselves of a being, of which the intention is an essential part: And sometimes we mean the real event, or external effect produced. With respect to a being possessed of infinite knowledge and power, these are always coincident. What such a being designs and determines to do, is always the same with the actual event produced. But we have no reason to think this true of any inferior beings.

In further explaining and proving what I have now in view, it will be proper to shew, 'that the perception of right and wrong does *excite* to action, and is alone a sufficient *principle* of action;' after which we shall be better prepared for judging, 'how far, without it, there can be *practical virtue*.'

Experience, and the reason of the thing, will, if we attentively consult them, soon satisfy us about the first of these points. All men continually feel, that the perception of right and wrong excites to action; and it is so much their natural and unavoidable sense that this is true, that there are few or none, who, upon having it at first proposed to them, would not wonder at its being questioned. There are many supposable cases and circumstances, in which it is impossible to assign any other reason of action. Why would we, all circumstances on both sides being the same, help a *benefactor* rather than a *stranger*; or one to whom we had given promises, and made professions of kindness, rather than one to whom we were under no engagements? Why would any good being chuse such methods to accomplish his end as were consistent with *faithfulness* and *veracity*, rather than such as implied *deceit* and *falshood*; though he knew the latter to be equally safe, or, in a great degree, even more safe, more easy and expeditious?—Is it only for our own sakes, or out of a view to public utility, that we obey and honour the Deity?—How are we to account for a man's refraining from secret fraud, or his practising truth, sincerity, equity, justice, and honour, in many particular instances of their interfering, or seeming to interfere, with private and publick good, as well as with his strongest natural desires?—Let any one, for example, try what reasons he can find from benevolence or self-interest, why an honest man, though in want, though sure of being never suspected, would not secure a good estate, ease and plenty to himself, and relief and aid to his neighbours, by secreting or interpolating a will by which it of right devolved on a worthless person, already sufficiently provided for, and who, in all likelihood, would use it only to make himself and others miserable? What could influence, in such and many other like circumstances, besides a *sense of duty and honesty*? Or what other universal motive can there be to the practice of justice?

But further, it seems extremely evident, that excitement belongs to the very ideas of moral right and wrong, and is essentially inseparable from the apprehension of them. The account in a former chapter of *obligation*, is enough to shew this.—When we are conscious that an action is *fit* to be done, or that it *ought* to be done, it is not conceivable that we can remain *uninfluenced*, or want a *motive* to action.* It would be to little purpose to argue much with a person, who would deny this; or who would maintain, that the *becomingness* or

* *Optimi quique permulta, ob eam unam causam, faciunt, quia decet, quia rectum, quia honestum est.* Cic. *de finibus.* Lib. ii.

186

easonableness of an action is no reason *for* doing it; and the *immorality* or *unreasonableness* of an action, no reason *against* doing it. An affection or inclination to rectitude cannot be separated from the view of it.* The knowledge of what is right, without any approbation of it, or concern to practise it, is not conceivable or possible. And this knowledge will certainly be attended with *correspondent, actual practice*, whenever there is nothing to oppose it. Why a *reasonable* being acts *reasonably*; why he has a disposition to follow reason, and is not without aversion to wrong; why he chuses to do what he knows he *should* do, and cannot be wholly indifferent, whether he abstains from that which he knows is evil and criminal, and *not to be done*, are questions which need not, and which deserve not to be answered.

Instincts, therefore, as before observed in other instances, are not necessary to the choice of ends. The intellectual nature is its own law. It has, within itself, a spring and guide of action which it cannot suppress or reject. Rectitude is itself an end, an ultimate end, an end superior to all other ends, governing, directing and limiting them, and whose existence and influence depend on nothing arbitrary. It presides over all. Every appetite and faculty, every instinct and will, and all nature are subjected to it. To act from

---

* Those who own, that an action may not be less right, though certain to produce no overbalance of private pleasure; and yet assert that nothing, but the prospect of this to be obtained, can influence the will, must also maintain, that the mere rightness of an action, or the consideration that it is fit to be done, apart from the consideration of the pleasure attending or following it, would leave us quite uninclined, and indifferent to the performance or omission of it. This is so inconceivable, that those whose principles oblige them to admit it, cannot, one would think, really mean by right and wrong the same with the rest of mankind. That, supposing virtue to denote any thing distinct from pleasure and independent of it, it is possible to *conceive*, that a virtuous action may not produce an overbalance of private pleasure; or, which answers the purpose as well, that an agent may *believe* this of an action to be done by him, which yet he does not the less consider as virtuous, it would be trifling to say any thing to prove: But this it is necessary those, whose opinion I have now in view, should deny.

affection to it, is to act with light, and conviction, and knowledge. But acting from instinct is so far acting in the dark, and following a blind guide. Instinct *drives* and *precipitates*; but reason *commands*. The impulses of *instinct* we may resist, without doing any violence to ourselves. Our highest merit and perfection often consist in this. The dictates of *reason* we can, *in no instance*, contradict, without a sense of shame, and giving our beings a wound in their most essential and sensible part. The experience we have of the operations of the former, is an argument of our imperfection, and meanness, and low rank. The other prevails most in the higher ranks of beings. It is the chief glory of God, that he is removed infinitely from the possibility of any other principle of action.

It being therefore apparent that the determination of our minds concerning the nature of actions as morally good or bad, suggests a motive to do or avoid them; it being also plain that this determination or judgment, though often not the prevailing, yet is always the first, the proper, and most natural and intimate spring and guide of the actions of reasonable beings: Let us now enquire, whether it be not further the *only* spring of action in a reasonable being, as far as he can be deemed morally good and worthy; whether it be not the *only* principle from which all actions flow which engage our esteem of the agents; or, in other words, whether virtue be not itself the end of a virtuous agent as such.

If we consider that alone as most properly *done* by an agent, which he *designs* to do, and that what was no way an object of his design is not strictly imputable to him, or at least cannot give him any claim to merit or praise, it will follow that he cannot be properly said to practise virtue who does not *design* to practise it, to whom it is no object of regard, or who has it not at all in his view. It seems indeed as evident as we can wish any thing to be, that an action which is under no influence or direction from a *moral judgment*, cannot be in the practical sense *moral*; that when virtue is not pursued or intended, there is no virtue in the agent. Morally good intention, without any idea of moral good, is a contradiction. To act virtuously is to obey or follow reason: But can this be done without knowing and designing it?

I know, indeed, that according to the account some have given of virtue, it presupposes an intention in the agent different from that to itself, because, according to this account, it denotes only the emotion arising in us upon observing actions flowing from certain motives and affections, and, in the original constitution of our natures, is applicable alike to actions flowing from *any* motives. Were this account true, it would be a gross fallacy to suppose that a sense of virtue and duty, or any regard to moral good, can ever influence to action. But this consequence cannot be regarded by one who believes not the opinion which implies it; nor is it with me a small objection to this opinion, that such a consequence arises from it.

If a person can justly be styled *virtuous* and *praise worthy*, when he never reflects upon virtue, and the reason of his acting is not taken from any consideration of it, intelligence certainly is not necessary to moral agency, and brutes are full as capable of virtue and moral merit as we are.—Besides, might not a person with equal reason be reckoned *publick spirited*, who without any view to publick good, should accidentally make a discovery that enriches his country? May not that course of behaviour be as well styled *ambitious*, to which the love of honour and power did not excite; or that *selfish*, which did not aim at private interest; or that *friendly*, which was attended with no friendly intention?*

I have the pleasure to find the author of the *Characteristicks* agreeing with me in these sentiments. 'In this case alone,

---

* Ἔστι γὰρ αὐτὴ ἡ εὐπραξία τέλος. *Arist.* Ethic. Lib. vi. Chap. v.—αἱ δὲ κατ' ἀρετὴν πράξεις καλαί, καὶ τοῦ καλοῦ ἕνεκα.—ὁ δὲ διδοὺς οἷς μὴ δεῖ, ἢ μὴ τοῦ καλοῦ ἕνεκα, ἀλλὰ διά τινα ἄλλην αἰτίαν, οὐκ ἐλευθέριος, ἀλλὰ ἄλλος τις ῥηθήσεται. Ibid. Lib. iv. Chap. i. And to the same purpose in many other places.

says he, it is we call any creature worthy or virtuous, when it can have the notion of a publick interest, and can attain to the speculation or sense of what is morally good or ill, admirable or blameable, right or wrong. For though we may vulgarly call an ill horse vicious, yet we never say of a good one, nor of any mere ideot or changeling, though ever so good natured, that he is worthy or virtuous. So that if a creature be generous, kind, constant, and compassionate, yet if he cannot reflect on what he himself does or sees others do, so as to take notice of what is worthy and honest, and to make that notice or conception of worth and honesty to be an object of his affection, he has not the character of being virtuous; for thus and no otherwise he is capable of having a sense of right or wrong, &c.' See the *Enquiry*, Part II. Sect. III. And elsewhere he observes that, 'if that which restrains a person and holds him to a virtuous-like behaviour be no affection towards virtue or goodness itself, but towards private good merely, he is not in reality the more virtuous.' Ibid. Sect. IV.*

But it may be asked, 'is not *Benevolence* a virtuous prin-

---

* 'Others may pursue different forms and fix their eyes on different species, as all men do on one or other; the real honest man, however plain he appears, has that highest species, honesty itself in view.' *Charact.* Vol. III. page 34. *See also* page 66. 'But as soon as he comes to have affection towards what is morally good, and can like or affect such good for its own sake, as good and amiable in itself, then is he in some degree good and virtuous, and not till then.'—This truly noble author has no where expressed clearly and distinctly his sentiments concerning the original of our ideas of virtue; but from some expressions he has used, it seems probable that he was for a surer and deeper foundation of morals, than either arbitrary will or implanted senses. *See* Vol. II. pages 36, 43, 49, 50, 53, 257.—Vol. III. page 33.—His account of virtue in his *Enquiry*, is, indeed, on several accounts extremely deficient, particularly on account of his limiting virtue so much as in general he seems to do, to the cultivation of natural affection and benevolence; and overlooking entirely, as Dr. *Butler* observes, the *authority* belonging to virtue and the principle of reflexion. Yet he has, I think, made many excellent observations on virtue and providence, on life and manners; nor can it be enough lamented, that his prejudices against Christianity have contributed so much towards defeating the good effects of them, and staining his works.

ciple? And do we not approve all actions proceeding from it?'—I answer, Benevolence, it has been shewn, is of two kinds, *rational* and *instinctive*. *Rational benevolence* entirely coincides with rectitude, and the actions proceeding from it, with the actions proceeding from a regard to rectitude. And the same is to be said of all those affections and desires, which would arise in a nature as intelligent. It is not possible that endeavours to obtain an end which, as reasonable, we cannot but love and chuse, should not be by reason approved; or that what is *necessarily desirable* to all beings, should not be also *necessarily right to be pursued*.

But *instinctive benevolence* is no principle of virtue, nor are any actions flowing merely from it virtuous. As far as this influences, so far something else than reason and goodness influences, and so much I think is to be subtracted from the moral worth of any action or character. This observation agrees perfectly with the common sentiments and determinations of mankind. Wherever the influence of mere natural temper or inclination appears, and a particular conduct is known to proceed from hence, we may, it is true, love the person, as we commonly do the inferior creatures when they discover mildness and tractableness of disposition; but no regard to him as a *virtuous* agent will arise within us. A soft and silly man, let him be ever so complying, liberal, and good-tempered, never stands high in our esteem; because we always apprehend him to be what he is, not so much from any influence of reason and moral good, as from a happy instinct and bent of nature born with him: And, in the same manner, the tenderness of parents for their offspring, a fond mother's exposing her life to save her child, and all actions proceeding from the nearer attachments of nature appear to have as much less moral value, as they are derived more from natural instinct, and less attended with reflexion on their reasonableness and fitness. As long as this reflexion is wanting, it is in a moral account indifferent, whether the action

proceeds from kind affection or any other affection.—But i
must not be forgot, that such reflexion will, in general
accompany friendly and benevolent actions, and cannot but
have some concern in producing them. Approbation is inseparable from the view of them, and some ideas of right and
wrong are present always with all men, and must more or
less influence almost all they do. We have an unavoidable
consciousness of *rectitude* in relieving misery, in promoting
happiness, and in every office of love and good-will to others.
It is this *consecrates* kindness and humanity, and exalts them
into virtues.

Actions proceeding from universal, calm, and dispassionate benevolence, are by all esteemed more virtuous and
amiable than actions producing equal or greater moments of
good, directed to those to whom nature has more particularly
linked us, and arising from kind determinations in our minds
which are more confined and urgent. The reason is, that in
the former case the operations of instinct have less effect, and
are less sensible, and the attention to what is morally good
and right is more explicit and prevalent. Were we prompted
to the acts of universal benevolence in the same manner that
parents are to the care of their children, we should not conceive of them as more virtuous. These facts cannot be explained consistently with the notion, that virtue consists in
acting from kind affections which cannot be derived from
intelligence, and are incapable, in their immediate exercise,
of being attended with any influence from it. For why then
should not the virtue be greatest where the kind impulse is
strongest? Why should it, on the contrary, in such a case,
be least of all, and entirely vanish, when all use of reason is
precluded, and nothing but the force of instinct appears?
Why, in particular, should resisting our strongest instincts,
and following steadily in contradiction to them,* the deter-

* More to this purpose has been said by Mr. *Balguy*, in his *Tract on the Foundation of Moral Goodness*.

minations of cool unbiassed reason, be considered as the very highest virtue? Probably, those who plead for this opinion would give it up, and acknowledge what is now asserted, could they be convinced that benevolence is essential to intelligence, and not merely an implanted principle or instinct.

All these observations may very justly be applied to self-love. *Reasonable and calm* self-love, as well as the *love of mankind*, is entirely a virtuous principle. They are both parts of the idea of virtue. Where this is greatest, there will be the most ardent and active benevolence, and likewise the greatest degree of true prudence, the highest concern about bettering ourselves to the utmost, and the most effectual and constant pursuit of private happiness and perfection, in opposition to whatever hindrances and temptations to neglect them may be thrown in our way.

Our natural desires carrying us to private good are very strong, and the pursuit of it is more likely to arise from these desires without any rational reflexion, or interposition of moral judgment, than the pursuit of publick good; which is one reason why it is less considered as virtue. Avoiding a *present* danger or securing a *present* good to ourselves, is not often looked upon as in any degree virtuous: but the same cannot be said of endeavouring to prevent a *future* danger, or to secure a *future* good: The reason of which is, that we are drawn towards what is *present* with a greater degree of instinctive desire.* It makes more sensible impressions upon

* This is a very wise and necessary disposition of our natures. Had we the same sensible determination to *distant* good that we have to *present*, how distracted should we be in our pursuits? How regardless of what is present, how impatient, how miserable would it render us?—The consequence, on the other hand, of giving us a greater propensity to present than future good, must be the danger of chusing and resting in the one to the neglect of the other. This inconvenience, however, (which it is the business of reason and a principal part of virtue to prevent) is far from being equal to the contrary inconveniencies which would have attended a different constitution of our natures.—It may seem upon a general reflexion very strange, that persons, when acting solely from

us, and strikes our minds more forcibly. Yet, in some circumstances of opposition from particular passions and competition between different pleasures, acting from a regard even to *present* good may be really virtuous. And, always, the more remote a good is, and the more temptations we have to forego our own interest, the greater is our virtue in maintaining a proper regard to it. In these cases, reason is necessarily more called forth to interpose and decide; our passions concur less with its dictates; and our determinations are more derived from its authority. Some kinds of future good there are, the pursuit of which *always* proves virtue. Others are so agreeable to the lower parts of our natures, and so connected with strong instinctive desires, that actions produced by the view of them can argue little or no virtue, though reason should approve the choice of them. But when reason condemns any particular gratifications; when pleasures of a baser nature stand in competition with those of a higher nature; or when, upon any account, pleasures in themselves innocent are proper to be resigned; in these cases, guilt and blame become the consequences of pursuing them.

From hence we may see plainly, how far hope and fear may be virtuous principles; and why, for instance, though a regard to private good, should be capable of knowingly chusing a less rather than a greater, a present rather than a future much more important good. If we were on such occasions determined by nothing but the simple and calm view of good as such, this fact would indeed be entirely unaccountable. But when we attend to the observation now made, and consider that we have a stronger instinctive determination to present than to future good, the difficulty in a great measure vanishes. The fact I have mentioned will not be more unaccountable than a man's following his passions and instincts in any other instances, in opposition to his own happiness, and all the reasons that can be proposed to him.—In other words; we have a *particular tendency or appetite* to *present good*, from whence it happens, that good is far from always affecting and influencing us, in proportion to the apprehended degree of its absolute worth. The view of *present good*, therefore, getting the better of the calm and dispassionate views of our *greatest interest upon the whole*, is only one instance of what happens continually in the world, namely, 'blind desire, unintelligent inclination or brute impulse, getting the better of motives and considerations, known by the mind to be of incomparably greater weight.'

doing an action to escape an ignominious death, or to obtain a profitable place, be not virtue; yet it is virtue, in many instances, to refrain from gratifications which we know are hurtful to us, or to quit a course of debauchery to which passion and habit strongly urge us, from an apprehension of its bad effects on our healths and fortunes.

These observations (to which might be added many more of the same kind) are all very evident proofs of the truth of the conclusion I would establish; namely, 'that the virtue of an agent is always *less* in proportion to the degree in which natural temper and propensities fall in with his actions, instinctive principles operate, and rational reflexion on what is right to be done, is wanting.'

It is further worth our particular notice, that the observations which have been now made on self-love, and the actions flowing from it, shew us plainly how far a conduct founded on religious principles, and influenced by the consideration of the rewards and punishment to follow virtue and vice in another state, can be justly represented as destitute of moral goodness. It is indeed surprizing, that extending our care to the *whole* of our existence, acting with a view to the final welfare of our natures, and elevating our minds above temporal objects out of a regard to a blessed immortality; it is, I say, surprising, that such conduct should have been ever in any degree depreciated. If any thing gives dignity of character, and raises one man above another, this does. If any thing is virtue, this is. Especially; as the very reward expected is itself virtue; the highest degrees of moral improvement; a near resemblance to God; opportunities for the most extensive beneficence, and admission into a state into which nothing that defileth can enter, and the love and hope of which imply the love of goodness.—In a word; if in all cases, a reasonable and steady pursuit of private happiness amidst temptations to forego it from passion and present gratifications, be virtuous; how easy is it to determine what opinion we ought to entertain of the pursuit of *such* a happiness as virtuous men are taught to expect in another world?

Let me add, on this occasion, that the firm belief of future rewards is in the greatest degree advantageous to virtue, as it raises our ideas of its dignity by shewing us the Deity engaged in its favour, and as it takes off every obstacle to the practice of it arising from self-love, sets us at liberty to follow the good inclinations of our hearts, gives all good affections within us room to exert themselves, and engages us, by an additional motive of the greatest weight, to cultivate them as much as possible; and thus, by occasioning a course of external actions flowing from them, gradually strengthens and exalts them, and fixes, confirms, and cherishes the habit and love of virtue in the mind.

But to return to the main purpose of this chapter.—What has been said of virtuous actions may easily be applied to vicious actions. These can be no farther *in the agent* vicious, than he knew or might have known them to be so. The wrong can be no farther chargeable upon *him*, than he *saw* it, and acted in opposition to his *sense* of it. Or, to speak agreeably to a foregoing observation, and perhaps more properly, the *viciousness* in an action is no farther the agent's, than the *vicious* action is his; and no more of the vicious action is his, than was included in his intention.

When it appears, that a person had no suspicion of wrong in an action performed by him, and that he would certainly not have done it, had he entertained such a suspicion, nothing can be more unjust than to charge him, in this particular, with guilt and ill-desert. His being thus unsuspicious, it is true, may be the effect of criminal error and carelessness; but then in *these* lies the guilt, and not in the consequent actions themselves which are performed with the apprehension that they are innocent. Every single action of a being has in it some precise and fixed degree of guilt, innocence or virtue, which is entirely determined by his perceptions, views, and state of mind at the time of doing it, and cannot be rendered greater or less by what went before it, or what comes after it. What has been once true of an event, must always remain true of it. What is at the time of performance, the real determinate character of an action, in respect of commendableness or blameableness, must for ever remain its character without increase or diminution.—The pernicious consequences arising from an action aggravate its guilt, only so far as the agent, when he did it, foresaw or suspected them, or had some consciousness that he ought to have taken greater care, and considered better, what might prove the effects of his conduct. A series of evil actions may also be the occasion of other evil actions, which when only *materially* evil, may indeed often be a very severe punishment of former wickedness, but cannot increase the agent's guilt, or subject to further punishment. This can be the consequence only, when such actions are themselves criminal, or instances of the violation of conscience and repetitions of former wickedness. If we are to lay it down for true, that one faulty step may taint all the actions to which it may unhappily have been the introduction, whatever our *present* sense of them may be; or, that consequences arising from actions which we did not foresee, render them criminal; how deplorable is our condition? For who can ever know all the effects that will result from his actions? or be sure, in many instances, when acting upon particular opinions, that throughout the whole progress of his thoughts in forming them, he was under no influence from any undue biass?*

* It might have been further worth remarking here, that *true* opinions are often the effects of guilt as well as *false* ones, and that when they are so, they are no less culpable, and must have the same effects on the imputable nature of the actions occasioned by them.—This, by the way, should be more considered by us, when we justify our censures of others for their errors, by saying, they

Of the Principle of Action

Let it not be imagined that what has been now asserted, has a tendency to render men negligent in their enquiries. Though a crazy or drunken man may not be *immediately* blameable in doing many actions in themselves very evil, yet for a man to put himself into a state in which he knows he shall be liable to do such actions, is extremely wicked. The difference is not great, between doing what we foresee may cause us to do an evil blindly and unknowingly, and doing the evil deliberately.

This shews us, how inexcusable all *voluntary* ignorance is, and of how great importance it is, that we avoid all unfairness in forming our sentiments. No upright person can be indifferent about this. We have not indeed on any occasion more scope for virtue, or better opportunities for exercising some of the noblest dispositions of mind, than when employed in enquiring after truth and duty: and, considering the dismal evils which may arise from dishonesty here; how sad it is to have the light that is in us darkness, and to what mazes of error, superstition and destructive conduct, a misguided judgment may lead us; we cannot be too diligent in labouring rightly to inform our consciences; or too anxious about obtaining just apprehensions, and freeing ourselves from the power of whatever prejudices or passions tend to warp our minds, and are inconsistent with that coolness, candour, and impartiality which are indispensibly necessary qualifications in one who would discover what is *true* and *right*.

Thus have I given what I think the true account of the nature and requisites of *practical virtue*. I observed first of all, that it requires liberty and intelligence. But what I have chiefly insisted on, is, that we characterize as *virtuous* no actions flowing merely from instinctive desires, or from any

proceed from criminal dispositions and prejudices. For we ourselves, however right our opinions may be, are equally blameable on their account, as far as they are owing to the like criminal dispositions, or proceed from pride, implicitness, negligence, or any other wrong causes.

principle except a regard to *virtue itself*. This, I have endeavoured to prove, to be the object of the supreme affection and the ultimate end of a *virtuous** agent *as such*.—Virtue, if I have argued right, must be desired, loved, and practised on its own account.† Nothing is any exercise of it, but what proceeds from an inward relish for it and regard to it, for its own sake.—It has also, I hope, been sufficiently explained, how benevolence and self-love, and the actions to which they excite us, as far as morally good and praise-worthy, are derived from this source. Nothing would be more unreasonable than for any one further to urge, that a regard to the divine will is a principle of virtuous conduct, not reducible to that I have insisted on. Is it not from a sense of duty that virtuous agents obey the will of God? What merit would there be in obeying it, out of a blind awe or servile dread, unaccompanied with any knowledge of it as *fit* and *becoming*? The true ground then of moral merit in this case, is evidently the influence of moral discernment. Here, as in all other instances, 'the ultimate spring of virtuous practice in reasonable beings, is the reasonable faculty itself, the *consideration of duty*, or the *perception of right*.'

---

* This, in reality, is but little more than maintaining what cannot possibly be denied, that it ought to be the first care of every reasonable being to do all that he thinks to be right, and to abstain from all that he thinks to be wrong; or, that reason, as it is the *principal*, ought to be the *leading* and *governing faculty*, in every reasonable being.

† 'From the distinction between self-love, and the several particular principles or affections in our nature, we may see how good ground there was for the assertion maintained by the several ancient schools of philosophy, against the *Epicureans*, namely, that virtue is to be pursued as an end eligible in and for itself. For if there be any principles or affections in the mind of man distinct from self-love; that the things the principles tend towards, or that the objects of these affections are each of them in themselves eligible, to be pursued on its own account, and to be rested in as an end, is implied in the very idea of such principle or affection. They, indeed, asserted much higher things of virtue, and with very good reason; but to say thus much of it, that it is to be pursued for itself, is to say no more of it than may be truly said of the object of every natural affection whatsoever.' Preface to Dr. *Butler*'s Sermons, p. 32.

CHAP. IX.

Of the different Degrees of Virtue and Vice, and the Methods of estimating them. Of difficulties attending the Practice of Virtue, the Use of Trial in forming reasonable Beings to Virtue, and the Essentials of a good and bad Character.

THROUGHOUT the whole of this Treatise, until the last chapter, I had considered virtue more generally and abstractly; its nature, foundation, obligation, and principal divisions. I have, in that chapter, considered it more particularly in its reference to actual practice, and the capacities and wills of moral agents; and I am now to proceed in thus considering it, and to explain the various *degrees* of it in different actions and characters, and to shew how we compute them; how far the temper should be formed by it; and what relation the faculty that perceives it bears to our other powers.

It is, as shewn in the last chapter, the reflexion on the *fitness* of an action and the *right of the case*, that constitutes us *virtuous* and *rewardable*. It is the intention to practise virtue, and the influence which a regard to it has upon our resolutions, that renders us objects of moral praise and esteem. And the greater this influence is, the greater must we account the virtue, and the more must we admire the action. Hence then, 'the *degree* of regard or disregard, of attachment or the want of attachment to truth and rectitude evidenced by actions, is what determines the judgment we make of the *degree* of moral good and evil in them.' *External actions* are to be considered as signs[1] of the motives and views of agents. We can, in general, infer the latter from the former with sufficient certainty. But when this happens to be impracti-

[1 Ed. 1 adds 'of *internal actions*, or'.]

cable, we are rendered incapable of forming any judgment of the merit or demerit of actions.

The rule I have now laid down, will be sufficiently proved, by attending to the following facts.

Doing a good action which we have few or small temptations to omit, has little virtue in it; for the regard to virtue must indeed be very low in that being, who will not be engaged by it to do a good action, which will cost him but little trouble and expence, and thwarts not sensibly any of his natural desires.—When secular interest, love of fame, curiosity, resentment, or any of our particular propensions conspire with virtue in exciting to an action, it is in the same proportion virtuous as the apprehension of its rectitude influenced to it, which can never be accounted much, when the action is known to fall in with the bent and humour of our minds and the current of our passions.—When difficulties occur, and secular interest, humour, vanity, or any of our inferior powers clash with virtue, the degree of it is in proportion to the difficulties surmounted, or the number and violence of the passions it overcomes.—When all or several of the different species of virtue unite in engaging to one and the same action, doing it, in these circumstances, argues less virtue than if it had been done from the consideration of one of them singly. Thus; any given right action attended with given difficulties, and performed with equal effect, and flowing merely from gratitude, is more virtuous, than if also a regard to publick and private interest, to justice and to veracity had required it, and concurred in producing it. Hence, therefore, the virtue must be *greatest* when any single species of it, when every view of what is decent and fit, every decision of our practical judgments, is sufficient to determine us in opposition to *all* temptations; when we are ready to follow *where-ever* virtue leads us, and possess such a moral sensibility as to shrink from every *appearance* of wrong, and such a horror at guilt as to dread all the *approaches* to it.

With respect to vicious actions, we may observe in general, that the same circumstances which *diminish* the virtue of any action, *increase* the vice in omitting it, and *vice versa*. The commission of an evil to which we have little temptation, though there can be but little virtue in abstaining from it, is yet always very criminal; for it shews very great weakness of the moral principle.—When an action is not at all reflected upon as evil, there can be no disregard to virtue shewn, and therefore no guilt contracted.—When an action is reflected upon as evil, but the motives to commit it are very strong and urgent, the guilt attending the commission of it is diminished, and all that can be inferred is, not the *absolute*, but the *comparative* weakness of the virtuous principle, or its inferiority in strength to some other principles.—The more deliberately any wrong action is done, the more wicked it appears to us; because, in this case, reason and conscience have time to gather their whole force, and exert their utmost strength; but nevertheless are conquered. For this reason, a single act of vice, when thus deliberate and wilful, may be the strongest proof of a bad moral state, and a sufficient indication of the whole moral character; which cannot be said of any faults of surprize, to which the violence of sudden passions may sometimes hurry men.—In a word; the greater the evil itself is that a man commits; the more it contradicts, not only his ideas of rectitude, but his instinctive desires; the greater number of the different kinds of moral obligation it violates; the clearer his perception is of wrong in it; the longer his time for reflexion is, and the less the number and strength of his temptations are; the greater vice is he chargeable with, and the more flagrant is his guilt. On the other hand, it is evident, that by increasing the number and strength of temptations, and lessening the time for reflexion and the sense of wrong, the degree of guilt in an evil action will be diminished; and it may by such causes be reduced so low, that all disapprobation of the agent shall vanish.

From these observations we may draw the following inferences.

First, The difficulties surmounted enhancing the virtue of the character, no otherwise than as they evidence a stricter attachment to righteousness and more influence of the virtuous principle; it is plain, that they can by no means be *essential* to virtue. As long as the degree of virtuous attachment is the same, it matters not whether or no any opposition is subdued: The character remains equally worthy. The man who, in a course of goodness, meets with less hindrance than another from his passions and temper, may be equally virtuous, if he has in him that affection to goodness, which would engage him, if he had the same opportunities and trials with another, equally to master the same hindrances. Difficulties and inconveniencies attending virtue are the means of shewing to others, who cannot see immediately into our hearts, what is in us, and what our moral temper is. And they have also the following effects upon ourselves. They awaken our attention to righteousness and goodness; they call forth the moral principle to exert itself in a manner not otherwise possible, and thus become the means of producing stronger virtuous efforts, and of encreasing the force and dominion of reason within us, and of improving and confirming virtuous habits.*—These are the uses of the difficulties and temptations attending virtuous practice; but then it must be acknowledged that, in some respects, they are likewise the causes of very great evils. If they are the means of *improving* virtue, they are also the means of *overwhelming* and *ruining* it. If they give rise to moral discipline, they likewise obstruct it; they produce moral depravity, and occasion all the corruptions and vices of the world. It would

---

* If surmounting of difficulties, or subduing opposition, is not what properly *constitutes* the virtue of an agent, it follows, that neither is it what constitutes his *merit* or *rewardableness*; any further than as it may be the means of *improving* his virtue, and, at the same time, of diminishing the *present* happiness attending it.

be foreign to my present purpose to enter into an explanation of this fact. I cannot however omit digressing so far as to observe, that we cannot certainly say, how far the evils I have mentioned, might have been prevented among beings like ourselves, growing up gradually to the use of reason, and, in the mean time, under a necessity of acquiring some habits or other, and of being guided by instinctive principles. Can virtue be *disciplined* and *tried* without being *endangered*? or *endangered* without being sometimes *lost*? Can we acquire any security or confirmation in virtue, till we are habituated to it? And before the habit is acquired, and in the dawn of reason, must there not be the hazard of degenerating?

It may, indeed, be said, that an order of beings may be so made, and, in the beginning of their beings, so circumstanced, that, while they are advancing towards maturity of reason, and acquiring sufficient views of the nature and excellence of virtue to keep them steady in the practice of it, their inclinations and desires shall always coincide with their duty, and no habits be liable to be contracted which are unfavourable to it. And this, for aught I know, may be possible; and, for this reason and many others, it must be owned, that the present state of mankind has a great deal in it, which we are not capable of accounting for. It would in truth be very strange if it had not, or if any object in nature had not, considering our station and standing in the universe and the shortness of our views.—But, be this as it will, it cannot be improper to observe, that, as the natures and circumstances of men now are, had their desires and their duty always coincided, we might, after much time spent in a practice *objectively* virtuous, been so little established in *true* virtue, and the moral principle might, all the while, have lain so dormant, that, upon a change in our situation, the slightest temptation might have led us astray. But difficulties attending the discharge of our duty, and particular desires drawing us contrary to it, have a tendency, by obliging us to a more anxious, attentive, and constant exercise of virtue, in a peculiar manner, to accelerate our progress in it and establish our regard to it. And though, at first, the virtuous principle may be scarcely able to turn the balance in its own favour, or but just prevail; yet every repeated instance, in which the inward spring of virtue thus exerts its utmost force, and overcomes opposition, gives new power to it:* And it has often actually happened, that virtuous men by a course of virtuous struggles and long practice of self-denial, by being accustomed to repel temptations, to restrain appetite and to contemn sufferings, when not to be avoided with innocence, have gradually so strengthened the virtuous principle and established the sovereignty of conscience in themselves, that difficulties have in a manner vanished; and virtue has become easy and delightful. And let it be well minded, that though this is the period in which the difficulties of such persons are *least*, yet it is also the period in which their virtue is *greatest*. The truth therefore is, that the difficulties a virtuous agent meets with prove, in general, only the *defects* of his virtue. Had he a sufficient degree of virtue, he could meet with *no* difficulties; and the more of it he possesses, the less effect has any given degree of temptation in turning him aside from it, or disturbing his resolutions; the more master he is of every inclination within him; the less reluctance he feels in the discharge of his duty, and with the more pleasure and ardor he adheres to it.

How unreasonable then is it to affirm, that human virtue exceeds that of angels, because of the opposition it encounters; or to regard it as a question of difficulty, whether the excellence of the moral character of the Deity would not be encreased, if he had within him some dispositions contrary to goodness?—Can the very circumstances which argue *imperfection in virtue*, add to the *merit*[1] of it? As much superior

* See the Chapter on *Moral Government* in Butler's *Analogy*.
[[1] Ed. 1 reads 'perfection'; ed. 2 'merit'.]

as is the virtue of angels, so much the less capable must it be
of being endangered by any difficulties, or at all affected by
causes which would put an entire end to ours. As much
higher as their reason is and more perfect their natures, so
much the less must every thing weigh with them, when set
in opposition to virtue; so much the more sensible they must
be, that nothing is of consequence, nothing worth wishing
for, when compared with virtue, or when not to be obtained
without violating it.—With respect to the Deity particularly
such is the perfection of his nature, and such his discernment
of the nature, glory and obligation of the eternal laws of
righteousness,* that nothing whatsoever can come in competition with them, or have any tendency to draw him aside
from them. His moral excellence consists in such a degree of
purity or holiness, as renders him incapable of being *tempted*
to evil, and raises him infinitely above all possibility of a
biass to deviate from what is right. To suppose such a biass
in him, is to suppose him of finite and derived wisdom and
goodness. If he prevails over it, but only in a limited degree,
or so that some backwardness is left, it will follow, that he is
not *completely* good.† If he prevails over it infinitely or perfectly, so that no reluctance remains and no proportion
exists between its influence and the influence of moral recti-

* The manner of speaking here used concerning the Deity is suitable to our
common ways of conceiving of his perfections; but it is by no means strictly
proper. It is generally indeed scarce possible to speak otherwise than improperly
of him. He that approves the sentiments on this subject, which have been
delivered in the fifth chapter, (and which will be more fully explained in the
Dissertation at the end of this Treatise) may easily correct by them all such
forms of expression, whenever they occur.

† What is here said, may be illustrated by substituting *power* in the room of
virtue, and comparing the opposition the latter may meet with, to that which the
former may meet with, in producing any particular effects. The *power* of a
being is the same, whether it meets with any opposition or not. The difficulties
it finds, in overcoming opposition, prove in general only its weakness: The
greater the power is, the less difficulty it must find in producing any given
effect; and, when supposed infinite, as in the Deity, the very notion of difficulty
and opposition becomes a contradiction.

ude; this will be the same as to have no such biass, or to meet with no opposition. So apparent is it, that the supposition of difficulties attending the perfect goodness of the Deity (or of dispositions in him contrary to rectitude) by which it may at first sight seem, that his moral perfection would be increased, overthrows it.—But, in truth, we know not what we say, when we talk in this manner, or make suppositions of this sort. In a necessary and simple nature there can be no jarring principles. It is supposing a contradiction to suppose, that a being, who is *pure, original, infinite reason*, can possess any tendencies *repugnant to reason*, or any that do not coincide with it, and resolve themselves into it.

From these observations also it appears, that what has been said of the extenuation of guilt by the strength of temptations, must be understood with some restrictions. For that temptations are *strong*, may argue nothing more, than that our power of resistance is *weak*; that the spring of virtue (the contrary force in our minds which should repel them) is relaxed or broken. How wretched an excuse then for vice is this, as it is frequently pleaded? To what do temptations commonly owe their strength, but to strong evil habits the guilty person has contracted, and the low and languishing state of his moral powers? And how absurd is it to make the want of virtue a plea for the want of virtue, and to justify guilt by guilt?—However; though the idea affixed to the term *great*, when applied to temptations, like the same idea when applied to bodies, be wholly relative, or the result of a comparison between our moral and our other principles; yet there are undoubtedly different degrees of temptation, and some conceivable by us, for which no human virtue could be a match. And though our liableness to be overcome by *any* temptations, arises from the imperfection of human virtue; yet, as all temptations are far from equal, being overcome by some of them may argue far less defect of virtue, than being overcome by others; which is all that is meant by their extenuating guilt. No one, for instance, will say, that a crime committed through fear of immediate tortures and death, implies equal guilt with the same crime committed to avoid a slight inconvenience.

Secondly, We may remark, that what has been said on the subject of the present enquiry, has little or no relation to the question, whether there are any different degrees of *objective* right and wrong in actions, and determines nothing concerning it. Though there were no different degrees of right and wrong in this sense; though these characters were supposed to be absolute and complete, or not at all, in every single object to which they are applied; there would still be the same room left for an infinite variety of degrees of virtue and vice, of merit and guilt *in agents*; and also in *actions*, considered, not in their *absolute* and *abstract* sense, but *relatively* to the intentions and views of reasonable beings, or as *signs* and *effects* of their regard to *absolute virtue*.* It is thus most commonly we consider actions, and this is the true source and meaning of the different degrees of commendation and blame, of praise and censure we bestow upon them, and of the various appellations and phrases by which these are signified. And though, sometimes, we speak of actions as being, in the former sense, more or less right or wrong; this, perhaps, is to be understood in much the same manner with the greater or less *ratio's* of mathematicians, or with the different degrees of equality and inequality in quantities.

Thirdly, It may be worth observing, how very deficient Dr. *Hutcheson*'s manner of computing the morality of actions

---

* This distinction has, I believe, been greatly overlooked in the dispute I have here in view. An ingenious writer, in proving the inequality of good and bad actions, in opposition to the *Stoicks*, plainly means their inequality in this last sense; and, one would think, the *Stoicks* could never mean seriously to assert their equality in any other, than the former of these senses. See Mr. *Grove's System of Moral Philosophy*, p. 262, &c. Vol. I. See also *Cic.* Parad.

s.* For this purpose he gives us this general Canon. 'The virtue is as the moment of good produced, diminished or increased, by the private interest concurring with or opposing it, divided by the ability.' This plainly takes for granted, as all his subsequent rules likewise do, that benevolence is the whole of virtue; and that no action directed merely to private happiness, or by which any thing is intended, besides some overbalance of public good, can be, in any degree, virtuous. How very maimed such an idea of virtue is, I have endeavoured to shew. Some of the noblest acts of virtue and worst acts of wickedness, may be those which have only ourselves, or the Deity, for their objects; and many relating to our fellow-creatures, which, not being viewed as the means of any moment of good or of misery, must, according to the foregoing canon, be wholly indifferent.—If, instead of *benevolence*, we substitute, in the rules he has given, *regard to right*, or *attachment to virtue and duty*, they will, I think, be in the main just.

Fourthly, We may further observe, that the reason, which has been sometimes given for the greater amiableness of some good actions than others, namely, their being more free, cannot be just. It is very improper to speak of degrees of *natural* liberty and necessity. Between being the efficient of an effect, and not the efficient; between determining ourselves, and not determining ourselves; between *agency* and its contrary, there seems no conceivable medium. Every act of volition I am conscious of, if *my* act, must be entirely *mine*, and cannot be more or less *mine*. It is no objection to this, that two or three or any number of causes may concur in producing one and the same effect: For then each cause has its own proper share of the effect to produce, which this cause alone produces, and which it would be absurd to say,

* Vid. *Enquiry concerning Moral Good and Evil*, Sect. 3. Art. II. and Sect. 7. Art. 9.

he was helped to produce.—Besides, voluntary determination is not a complex and compounded, but simple effect, which admits not of more than one cause or principle, it being a contradiction to suppose, that the determination of a being may be partly *his*, and partly *another's*.

But waving this; let us turn our thoughts to what will be more easily understood, and consider, that, by the necessity which is said to diminish the merit of good actions, must be meant, not a *natural* (which would take away the whole idea of action and will) but a *moral* necessity, or such as arises from the influence of motives and affections on the mind; or that certainty of determining one way, which may take place upon supposition of certain views, circumstances, and principles of an agent. Now, it is undeniable, that the very greatest necessity of this sort is consistent with, nay, is implied in, the idea of the most perfect and meritorious virtue; and, consequently, can by no means lessen it.* The more confidently we may depend on a being's doing an action, when convinced of its propriety, whatever obstacles may lie in his way; that is, the more efficacious and unconquerable the influence of conscience is within him, the more amiable we must think him.—In like manner, the most abandoned and detestable state of wickedness implies the greatest necessity of sinning, and the greatest degree of moral impotence. He is the most vicious man, who is most enslaved by evil habits, or in whom appetite has gained so far the ascendant, and the regard to virtue and duty is so far weakened, that we can, at any time, with certainty foretel, that he will do evil when tempted to it. Let me therefore, by the way, remark, that

---

* If, when it is said, that a virtuous action is more amiable the less necessary it is, the meaning be, that it will be more amiable the less the agent is urged to it by instinctive desires, or any motives distinct from virtuous ones; this will be very true. But then, what increases the virtue of the action in this case, is not the mere circumstance of its being less necessary, but its proceeding more from the influence of love to virtue; agreeably to what has been observed in the beginning of this chapter.

very idea of liberty must be very erroneous, which makes it inconsistent with the most absolute and complete certainty or necessity of the kind I have now taken notice of, or which supposes it to overthrow all steadiness of character and conduct. The greatest influence of motives that can rationally be conceived, or which it is possible for any one to maintain, without running into the palpable and intolerable absurdity of making them *physical efficients and agents*, can no way affect liberty. And it is, surely, very surprising, that our *most willing* determinations should be imagined to have most of the appearance of not proceeding from *ourselves*; or, that what a man does with the fullest consent of his will, with the least reluctance, and the greatest desire and resolution, he should, for this very reason, be suspected not to do *freely*, that is, not *to do at all*.

Again; from the account which has been given of the various degrees of virtue and merit in actions, and of the manner in which we estimate them, we may see why, 'when we judge calmly and impartially,' we form much the same judgment of good actions affecting strangers, that we do of those affecting ourselves or friends; and also, why our esteem of an agent is never the less, though he has no opportunities for exerting his virtue, or though his good endeavours may produce effects contrary to those he designed. There is no account to be given of these facts, if virtue be (what it must be if we owe our ideas of it to an implanted sense) no more than a particular kind of agreeable feeling or sensation: For it seems plain upon this supposition, that the sensible pleasure or impression being, in the case I have mentioned, so much magnified or lessened, our conceptions of the degree of virtue must also be proportionably varied: Whereas the account here given, affords us a stable and fixed rule of judgment, and shews us the object concerning which we judge to be real and determinate in itself, and unchangeably the same, whatever our apprehensions of it may be, and in whatever point of view we contemplate it.* But the notion of virtue I have mentioned, makes it plainly no object of any rational estimate, leaves no fixed standard of it, and implies that all apprehensions of it are equally just; no man, while he expresses truly what he feels, or the emotion accompanying his observation of a particular action or character, being capable of pronouncing any thing wrong concerning the morality or immorality of it.† He may, it is true, err with respect to the quantity of good produced, or the degrees of kind affection influencing the agent; but these are properly, by this scheme itself, as different from *virtue*, as the cause is different from the effect, or as certain tastes are different from the motion and textures of the substances producing them.

I have added the restriction, 'when we judge calmly and impartially,' because it is too evident to be denied, that the causes I have mentioned, do frequently pervert and mislead our judgments. The partiality of persons to ourselves is always apt to biass our judgments in their favour, and to enhance our good opinion of them; while a stranger, a competitor, an adversary, or a person of a different religious persuasion, can often be hardly allowed to have any thing good in him. In like manner, to an enterprise which has proved unsuccessful, or issued in harm instead of good, we cannot easily give those commendations which it may really deserve; as, on the contrary, the happy consequences of an undertaking, especially if we ourselves or those related to us share in them, have a tendency, by interesting our affections, to engage us to ascribe much greater merit to it than it may

---

* See Chap. I. Sect. 3.

† 'The distinction of moral good and evil is founded on the pleasure or pain, which results from the view of any sentiment, or character; and as that pleasure or pain cannot be unknown to the person who feels it, it follows, that there is just so much vice or virtue in any character, as every one places in it, and that it is impossible, in this particular, we can ever be mistaken.' See Mr. *Hume*'s *Treatise of Human Nature*, Vol. III. page 154.

truly have. Against these and the like sources of false judgment, by which we are so very liable to be insensibly led astray, we ought carefully to guard ourselves, if we would keep clear of the inconceivable mischiefs arising from party attachments; escape the sad effects of following a blind guide, and see characters and men just as they are. We should attend to the situation in which we are placed, and the state and temper of mind in which we view objects, study to make proper allowances for them, and remember that the degree of approbation or blame due to an action, is determined by somewhat more stedfast than private passion, variable impressions, or casual consequences; and that the true desert of a character is never altered by the mere circumstances of our interest in it, or relation to it.

Having thus explained the general foundation of the different degrees of virtue and vice in actions, and stated the principles and rules by which we judge of them; it will be useful next distinctly to consider what is requisite to constitute an agent properly a *virtuous* agent, or to give his *character* this denomination rather than the contrary.

All beings, who have any idea of moral good, must have an affection to it, which cannot fail, more or less, to influence their actions and temper.—It is not conceivable that a *reasonable* creature should be void of *all* regard to *reason* and its dictates; that he should want all notion of the distinction which we express when we say, '*this* is to be done, or *that* is not to be done;' or that, having such a perception essential to his nature, and always present with him, it should ever become *wholly* inefficacious.—Nor, strictly speaking, can a reasonable being have any tendencies within him *contrary* to rectitude. I mean, he can have no aversion to rectitude as such, or tendency to wrong *as* wrong.—The former cannot be supposed without supposing the entire destruction of the intelligent powers of the being; and the very idea of the latter is self-repugnant and contradictory. In other words; there can be no being so corrupt as that the unreasonableness of an action, that is, his seeing reason *against* it, shall be to him a reason *for* or not a reason *against* doing it: Or, whose regard to truth and right shall not at least have weight enough to turn the scale when even, and be sufficient to render it certain, that he will determine agreeably to them, when he has no temptation to violate them; nothing to divert or mislead him; nothing to incline or biass him any other way.

These things then not being possible, and making no part of the idea of an evil character, it should be remembered, that the sources of all vice are our inferior propensities and appetites, which, though in themselves natural, innocent, and useful, cannot but, in our present state, on many occasions, interfere with reason, and remain to influence us, as well when they *cannot* be lawfully gratified, as when they *can*. Hence it comes to pass, that we often actually deviate; and that the reflecting principle is found in men in all degrees of proportion to their instinctive powers and desires. Its rightful place in the mind is that of superiority to all these powers and desires, and of absolute dominion over them. In the nature of it is implied (to speak after Dr. *Butler*) that it belongs to it, in all cases, to examine, judge, decide, direct, command, and forbid; that it should yield to nothing whatsoever; that it ought to model and superintend our whole lives; and that every motion and thought, every affection and desire, should be subjected constantly and wholly to its inspection and influence. So intimate to men is reason, that a deliberate resolution not to be governed by it, is scarcely possible; and that, even when urged by passion and appetite, they can seldom avowedly contradict it, or in any instance break loose from its guidance, without the help of dishonest art and sophistry; without many painful winkings at the ight, and hard struggles to evade the force of conviction; without studiously searching for excuses and palliatives, and thus making some shift to throw a cloud before their eyes, to reconcile themselves to the guilty practice, hide its deformity, and deceive themselves into an opinion of its warrantableness or innocence in *their* circumstances. How plainly may we hence learn how great the force of reason is; how sovereign and unsurmountable it is in its nature; how it adheres to us when we are endeavouring to cast it off; and what sway it will, in some manner or other, have in our minds, do what we will to obscure, abuse, or subvert it.

The essential *pre-eminence* now observed to belong to the reasonable faculty, is what ought chiefly to be considered, in settling the true idea of human nature.* It proves to us,

* The human mind would appear to have little order or consistency in it, were we to consider it as only a system of passions and affections, which are continually drawing us different ways, without any thing at the head of them to govern them, and the strongest of which for the time necessarily determines the conduct. But this is far from being its real state. It has a faculty essential to it, to which every power within it is subjected, the proper office of which is to reconcile the differences between all our particular affections, to point out to us when and how far every one of them shall or shall not be gratified, and to determine which, in all cases of competition, shall give way. This faculty is our *Moral faculty*, and it is therefore the reference of all within us to this faculty, that gives us the true idea of human nature. This supremacy of the moral faculty, I have observed, is implied in the idea of it; but we have also a demonstration of it from fact: For whereas the *least* violation of this faculty, in compliance with *all our other powers* in conjunction, would give us pain and shame; the *greatest* violation, on the contrary, of our other powers, in compliance with *this*, is approved by us; nay, the more we contradict our other powers in compliance with it, and the greater sacrifice we make of their enjoyments and gratifications to it, the more we are pleased with ourselves, and the higher inward satisfaction and triumph we feel.—See Dr. *Butler*'s Sermons on *Human Nature*, and the *Preface*. I find also Dr. *Hutcheson*, in his *System of Moral Philosophy*, asserting to the same purpose that our moral faculty, or, as he calls it, the *Moral sense*, is the 'directing principle within us, destined to command all our other powers; and that the desire of moral excellence is the supreme determination or affection of our minds, and *different from all our kind affections*.' See p. 61, 67, 68, 70, 77, &c. Vol. I.

Though I entirely approve these sentiments, I cannot help detaining the reader while I make a few remarks, in order to shew him how difficult it is to

beyond contradiction, that the original, proper, and sound
state of our natures, is that in which this faculty, this *thei*

reconcile them with this writer's other sentiments of virtue. It is much to be
wished that he had been more explicit on this subject, and explained himseli
more particularly. Had he done this, he would, I fancy, either not have wri
in this manner, or given a different account of the nature of moral approbation
and of our moral faculty.

If *Moral approbation* be only a kind of *sublimer sensation*, or a *species of menta*
taste, it can surely have no influence on our purposes and actions; much less can
it have such influence, as to be the supreme and commanding principle within
us. The *Moral sense* is properly the determination in our natures to be pleased
or displeased with actions proceeding from certain motives. It therefore always
supposes some distinct motives, and can never be itself a spring of action. Is it
not then wonderful to find this very ingenious and able writer, contrary to what
he had done in his **Illustrations on the Moral Sense*, confounding *senses* with
instincts; and, contrary to what the very idea of *the Moral sense*, as he seems to
have explained it, admits of, representing it as a distinct spring of conduct in
the mind, talking of its *force and efforts within us, its recommending, enjoining, con-*
trouling, and governing,† nay, setting it up as the *sovereign director of our affections and*
actions, superior even to Benevolence? This can be consistent and proper on no
other supposition, than that our Moral faculty is the Understanding, and that
moral approbation implies in it the perception of truth, or the discernment of a
real character of actions.

Again; what is *Moral excellence?* On the principles I am considering, it must
mean, either those affections and actions themselves to which we give the
denomination of *excellent*, or that *grateful sensation*, of which, when observed,
they are the occasions.—If it means the former, or, in other words, the having
and exercising an extensive and ardent benevolence; how can the desire of it
be different from benevolence? How can it be, as Dr. *Hutcheson* says it is,‡ in
another order of affections?—If it means the latter, how can it be proper to speak
of the desire and love of it? Can the desire of the *relish* we have for particular
objects, as distinct from the desire of the objects themselves, mean any thing,
besides the desire of enjoying the pleasures attending it; and can it therefore
influence our actions any otherwise than by means of self-love? In short, it
must appear, I should think, to every one, very absurd to speak of the desire of
Moral excellence, to suppose a calm, immediate determination to *Moral good*
itself, and to ascribe a commanding power to the faculty which perceives it, if
Moral good, or *Moral excellence*, signifies nothing distinct from a *feeling of the*
heart, or nothing absolute and immutable and independent of the mind. It is
however some indication of the truth on this subject, that those, with whose
sentiments it is inconsistent, find themselves led insensibly to write and think of
our moral faculty, (or the sense of duty and moral excellence) as the ultimate
and supreme guide of our actions. Nor can it be easy for any one who will

---

* See Chap. I.   † See his *Moral Philosophy*.
‡ Ibid. p. 70.—See also *the Preface* by the excellent Dr. *Leechman*, p. 44, &c

distinguishing and pre-eminent part, is indeed, (or as to its effect on the life and temper) *pre-eminent*, and all the other powers and principles are obedient to it.—Now *Goodness* in mankind is this state restored and established. It is the power of reflexion raised to its due seat of direction and sovereignty in the mind; conscience fixed and kept in the throne, and holding under its sway all our passions. The least it implies

examine this matter, not to feel that it is unavoidable to conceive this to be indeed the case, and that therefore every account of morality must be false that implies the contrary.

Once more. Our moral faculty, Dr. *Hutcheson*, we find, acknowledges to be the supreme commanding power within us. But can there be a higher power in a reasonable being than reason? and is this power a *sense*? How strange would this seem?—I do not find that *Plato*, and others of the antient moralists, had any notion that the τὸ ἡγεμονικόν in man, which they insist so much upon, was any thing else than *reason*. τὸ φύσει δεσποτικόν, τουτέστι τὸ λογιστικόν, says *Alcinous de Doctrina Platonis*, Chap. xxviii.

Let me add, that the very question which has been asked, and which naturally arises when we are settling a scheme of life and conduct; 'what *ought* to be the end of our deliberate pursuit, *private* or *public* happiness;' or, 'which *ought* to give way, (that is, which is it *right* should give way) in case of opposition, the calm selfish, or the calm benevolent affection?' See the *Preface* just quoted, page 45, &c. This question, I say, plainly implies, that the idea of *right* in actions is something different from and independent of the idea of their flowing from kind affections, or having a tendency to universal happiness; for certainly, the meaning of it cannot be, which will proceed from kind affection, or which has a tendency to promote universal happiness, following our desires of private or of universal happiness.—It also supposes, that the perception of *right* influences our choice; for otherwise such a question could never be asked with any view to the determination of our choice, nor could an answer to it have any effect this way.—It supposes finally, that the appeal in all cases is to our moral faculty, as the ultimate judge and determiner of our conduct; and, that the *regard* to *right*, to *duty*, or to *moral excellence*, is a superior affection within us to *benevolence*; for it comes in, in cases of interference between self-love and benevolence, to turn the scale in favour of benevolence, to recommend and order the generous part, or, as Dr. *Hutcheson* speaks,* to make the determination to public happiness the supreme one in the soul.

Thus then, here, as in other parts of this work, we find an object, '*Moral Good*, of unrivalled worth; of supreme influence; eternal, divine, all-governing; perceived by reason; necessarily loved and desired as soon as perceived; and the affection to which (including benevolence, but not the same with it) is the chief affection in every good being, and the highest dignity and excellence of every mind.'

* Ibid. p. 77.

is some *predominancy* of good affections, and superiority o
virtuous principles above all others.—*Wickedness*, on the con
trary, is the *subversion* of this original and natural state of the
mind, or the prevalency of the lower powers in opposition to
the authority of reason. It implies the *inferiority* of good principles to others within us, a greater attachment to some
particular objects than to truth and righteousness, or such a
defective regard to virtue as is consistent with indulging, *in
any instance*, known guilt. It is the violent and unnatural state
of the mind; the deposition of reason, and the exaltation of
appetite; the death of the man, and the triumph of the brute;
slavery in opposition to liberty; sickness in opposition to
health; and uproar and anarchy in opposition to order and
peace.

If then we would know our own characters, and determine
to which class of men we belong, the good or the bad; we
must compare our regard to everlasting truth and righteousness with our regard to friends, credit, pleasure, and life; our
love of God and moral excellence with our love of inferior
objects; the dominion of reason with the force of appetite;
and find which *prevail*. Until the rational part gets the victory over the animal part, and the main bent of the heart is
turned towards virtue; until the principles of piety and goodness obtain in some degree the supremacy, and the passions
have been made to resign their usurped power, we are
within the confines of vice and misery.—There is reason to
believe that many deceive themselves by concluding, that
since they possess many valuable qualities and feel the workings of good principles, since they love virtue and hate vice,
and do perhaps good in their stations, they can have little
reason to distrust their characters; not duly considering the
point here insisted upon; or that what they ought chiefly to
attend to is the place and degree of these principles in comparison with others; and that it is not those who hate vice,
but those who hate it above pain, dishonour, or any thing

whatever; not those who love virtue, but those who love it above all that can come in competition with it and possess a *supreme* regard to it, who are truly the virtuous and worthy. It is a common observation, that it is the *ruling passion* that denominates the character. The ruling love of power, fame, and distinction, denominates a man *ambitious*; the ruling love of pleasure, a *man of pleasure*; of money, a *covetous* man. And, in like manner, the ruling love of God, of our fellow-creatures, and of rectitude and truth, denominates a man *virtuous*.

It is natural to enquire here, how in particular we may know, that the love of virtue is thus predominant in us; or what are the marks and effects of that superiority of good affections which has been represented as essential to a good character. In answer to this enquiry, it will be proper to observe,

First, That the predominant passion always draws after it the thoughts, furnishes them with their principal employment, and gives a tincture of itself to all our studies and deliberations. What we most love, is that which we oftenest think of, and which engages most of our attention. If then we would know whether virtue and conscience *rule* within us, we must examine which way the main current of our thoughts runs; what objects present themselves to them most frequently and unavoidably; what lies upon them with the greatest weight; and what, in settling all our schemes and resolutions, we dwell most upon and take most into consideration.

Particularly; when deliberating about any undertaking, do you consider, not so much how it will affect your credit, fortune, or ease, as what, all things considered, reason and right require of you; what you would expect that another should do in the same circumstances; what good it may produce; how it will appear to you hereafter; what effect it will have on the divine favour to you; how it consists with your interest on the whole, and suits the dignity of a being endowed with your faculties, standing in your relations, and having your expectations? But,

Secondly, This predominancy will principally shew itself in *actual practice*, or in *the course of the life and conversation.* What stands foremost in our thoughts and hearts, our actions never fail to express. The strength of *inward affections* is always in proportion to their effects on the *external conduct.* When the intellectual and moral principle, therefore, is the *reigning* principle, it excludes every thing irregular and immoral from the behaviour; all unreasonable courses are forsaken; the whole of duty is faithfully attended to and discharged; no ill habits are spared; no wrong dispositions indulged; no known obligation wilfully and statedly neglected.

It is above all things necessary to constitute our characters good, that our virtue be not *partial*; that we conform ourselves to every relation in which we stand, however made known to us; attend, not to one duty or part of right conduct to the neglect of others, but regard with equal zeal every species of duty, and the whole of moral rectitude. He that is just, kind, meek, and humble, but at the same time an habitual drunkard, can have no pretence to genuine virtue. The same is true of him who is sober and temperate, but will deceive and cheat; of him who prays and fasts, is exact in all the external parts of religion, and zealous for truth and piety, but wants candour, gentleness, meekness, veracity, and charity; of him who is chaste, generous, friendly, and faithful, but wants *piety*, or *neglects any relations higher than those to men,* in which he may have reason to think he stands. The reason of this has been in part already given in the seventh chapter; and we may here add, that an habitual breach of *one* divine law, or retention of *one* bosom-vice, demonstrates that had the person equal temptations to transgress in all other instances, he would do it, and become totally abandoned. As long as any passion preserves an ascendency over us, and remains rebellious and lawless, there is plainly something within us *stronger* than virtue, something that masters and subdues it; God and conscience have not the throne; the due balance continues wanting in the mind, and its order and health are not recovered. Until we possess an *equal* and *entire affection* to goodness, we possess none that is *truly acceptable*, or that can be of much account and value. However unblameable a person of the character I am now considering may in several respects be; and with whatever ardour he may apply himself to the practice of some branches of virtue which happen not to lie very cross to his inclinations and temper; it is obvious, that he is not to be reckoned her faithful votary, and that his heart is at the bottom false to her interests and authority. Were not this the case, he would not in *any* instance desert her: He would not prefer to her the indulgence of *any* desire, or resign her for *any* enjoyments. Such is her dignity and amiableness, that every thing is sordid and contemptible compared with her: Such her nature, that she can admit of no rival. He then loves her not at all, who loves her not *first*.—A partial regard to rectitude is inconsistent and absurd. That attachment to it alone is genuine, which has itself merely, its own native obligation and excellence for its object and end, and is unadulterated by the mixture of any foreign and indirect motives. And such an attachment will necessarily be directed alike to all the parts and instances of it. What comes short of this is incomplete, unsatisfactory, variable, and capricious.—Be then *consistently* and *thoroughly* good, if you would be so *effectually*. Yield yourself *entirely* and *universally* to the government of conscience, and conquer every adverse inclination, or lay no claim to true virtue, and give up all hope of the happiness in reserve for it.

Every one will see, I do not mean that we must be *perfect*. Of this we are indeed quite incapable. A work of any kind may have all its essentials, and be complete in all its parts, when yet it may be unfinished, and require much more of the hand and labour of its cause. There may be *real* life, at the same time that it admits of great improvement, and is very weak and languishing. Some infirmities will cleave to the best, and it is impossible at present always to hold our passions under such strict discipline, as that they shall *never* surprize or hurry us into any thing which our hearts shall disapprove. But whenever this happens, it is essential to the character of a good man, that it is his *greatest* trouble, and that he is put by it upon more future vigilance. His settled *prevailing* regard in heart and life is to truth, piety, and goodness; though unhappily he may be sometimes misled. Conscience has the ascendant; the sovereignty of reason is established; and ill habits are extirpated, though not to that degree, that he shall be in no danger of deviating, and the enemies of his virtue never find him off his guard.

Thirdly, In order to determine whether the love of virtue is predominant in us, it is proper further to enquire, what degree of *delight* we have in it. That which gives the soul its prevailing cast and bent, and engages its chief pursuit, will be *agreeable* to it. All acts arising from established habits are free, unconstrained and chearful. What our hearts are most set upon will make the principal part of our happiness. What we love most, or have the greatest esteem and relish for, must be the source of our greatest pleasures.—Well therefore may *he* suspect his character, who finds that virtuous exercises, the duties of piety, and the various offices of love and goodness to which he may be called, are distasteful and irksome to him. Virtue is the object of the chief complacency of every virtuous man; the exercise of it is his chief delight; and the consciousness of it gives him his highest joy. He ought to be always ready to undertake whatever it requires from him, never reluctant when convinced in any case of his duty, and never more satisfied or happy than when engaged in performing it.

Some may probably be apt to enquire here, whether the pleasures inseparable from virtue, especially those attending the higher degrees of it, have not a tendency to render it so much the less disinterested, and consequently to sink its value.—I answer; this may indeed be the consequence, as far as it is possible that the pleasure itself merely attending virtue, can be the motive to the practice of it: But it is scarcely in our power (whatever we may think) to be thus refined in our pursuits, or really to deceive ourselves in this manner. For that only being *the virtue* which any one can justly applaud himself for, and derive pleasure from, which proceeds from a regard to *right* and *duty*; it is evidently contradictory to suppose, that the desire of this pleasure itself, can in any instance be the motive to the practice of it. For a person to propose acting thus, is exactly the same as for him to propose acting from *one motive*, in order to have the pleasure of reflecting that he has acted from *another*.—The truth therefore is, that the pleasure attending virtue, instead of *debasing*, necessarily *supposes* it, and always increases or lessens in proportion to the degree of virtue presupposed. The more benevolent and worthy a man is, the more he must be pleased with himself; the more satisfaction of mind he must feel. As much greater as his affection and attachment to virtue are, so much the more must he rejoice in it, and so much the happier it must render him.—How absurd would it be to assert, that the more pleasure a man takes in beneficence, the less disinterested it must be, and the less merit it must have? Whereas just the reverse is the truth; for the pleasure being grounded upon and derived from the gratification of the affection of benevolence, the greater degree of it plainly argues only a proportionably greater degree of benevolence.—Such difficulties as these would never have been much regarded, had an observation already made been more considered, namely, 'That pleasure is founded in desire, and not desire in pleasure; or that, in all cases, *enjoyment* and *happiness* are the *effects*, not the *causes* and *ends* of our affections.'

There remains another criterion of a good character, which must not be overlooked; I mean, a constant endeavour to *improve*. True goodness must be a *growing* thing. All habits by time and exercise gain strength. It is not to be imagined, that he has sound principle of virtue in him, who is not concerned about confirming them to the utmost, and obtaining a total victory over all the enemies of his happiness and perfection. Whoever has tasted of the joys of benevolence and righteousness, aspires after *more* of them, and grieves under the remains of moral imperfection in his character. He cannot possess so little zeal, as only to desire to keep within the bounds of what is innocent or lawful. A person who thinks himself *good enough*, may be sure that he is not *good at all*. When the *love of virtue* becomes the *reigning affection*, it will not be possible for us to satisfy ourselves with any degrees of it we can acquire.—What is analogous to this, we find to take place, whenever any of our *lower affections* obtain the ascendency. Every passion, when it becomes uppermost, is always putting us upon providing new gratifications for it. A man whose *prevailing passion* is the love of *power*, or of *money*, or of *fame*, seldom thinks (be his acquisitions what they will) that he has acquired enough; but is continually grasping at more, and labouring to add to his glory and treasures.—This insatiableness which attends the passions, when they pass their natural boundaries, is a sad perversion of a disposition which is truly noble, and becomes often the occasion of the most insupportable misery. To virtue it ought to be directed. This alone is true gain and true glory. The more aspiring and insatiable we are here, the more amiable and blessed we are rendered. One of the most pitiable spectacles in nature, is a covetous, an ambitious or voluptuous person, who not contented with what he has, loses the whole enjoyment it might afford him, and is tortured perpetually on the rack of wild and restless desire. But how desirable and happy is the state of a man, who, in goodness, cannot content himself with present acquisitions; who anxiously cherishes in himself the high and sacred ambition to grow wiser and better, to become liker to the Deity, and advance continually nearer and nearer to perfection?

It would perhaps in some respects be a needless work, as well as not much to my present purpose, to point out particularly what occasion and what room the best have for improvement. It may, however, be worth observing in this place, that, as what renders men more or less virtuous, is the greater or less degree of the superiority of the moral principle within them above others; so this principle is capable of increase and advancement without end.

The understanding may be very properly considered, as either *moral* or *speculative*. Our *speculative understanding* is evidently capable of infinite improvement; and therefore our *moral understanding* must be so likewise; for these being only different views of the same faculty, must be inseparably connected, and cannot be conceived not to influence each other. Every improvement of the speculative knowledge of a good being; every advance in the discovery of truth, and addition to the strength of his reason, and the extent and clearness of its perceptions, must be attended with views of moral good proportionably more enlarged and extensive; with a more clear and perfect acquaintance with its nature, importance and excellence; and consequently with more scope for practising it, and a more invariable direction of the will to it. This, joined with the growing effects of habit and constant exercise, may by degrees so strengthen and exalt the practical principle of rectitude, as to cause it to absorb every other principle, and annihilate every contrary tendency.

There is therefore no point of *moral* as well as *intellectual* improvement, beyond which we may not go by industry, attention, a due cultivation of our minds, and the help of proper advantages and opportunities.—The contrary may perhaps, with good reason, be said of vice. It is not very easy to conceive of any degree of this, beyond which beings may not also go through a careless neglect of themselves, through voluntary depravation, sophistical reasonings, and an obstinate perseverance in evil practices. The *least wickedness* of character supposes something which conquers conscience, and leads a being *habitually* astray; and the *greatest*, consequently, would imply, that conscience is so far overpowered as to be wholly extirpated, and *all* regard to right and wrong and *all* influence from it destroyed; which is a pitch of corruption at which, as I have before observed, no being can arrive while he remains, in any degree, reasonable and accountable. Within this limit, the force of the higher moral and reflecting powers admits of endlessly various degrees of weakness, compared with the other powers, and an agent may be, in any degree, more or less corrupt, his nature more or less perverted, and his mind more or less a *Chaos* and a *Hell*.

I might, on this head, further take notice of the extent of our duty; the various hindrances of our improvement; the degeneracy into which we are sunk, and the numerous enemies which beset our frail natures. Such is the present condition of man; so great is the disorder vice and folly have introduced into our frame; and so many are the surprizes to which we are liable; that to preserve in any degree the integrity of our characters and peace within ourselves, is difficult. But, to find out and correct the various disorders of our minds; to preserve an unspotted purity of life and manners; to destroy all the seeds of envy, pride, ill-will, and impatience; to listen to nothing but reason in the midst of the clamour of the passions, and continue always faithful to our duty, however courted by the world, allured by pleasure, or deterred by fear; to cultivate all good dispositions, guard against all snares, and clear our breasts of all defilements.—What an arduous work is this?—What unwearied diligence does it call for?—And how much of it, after our utmost care and labour, must remain undone?

But what a deeper sense of imperfection must possess us, to view ourselves in the light of God's perfect and eternal rectitude? How low must this sink us in our esteem; and what a boundless prospect does it set before us, of higher moral excellence to which we should aspire?

We have then infinite scope for improvement, and an everlasting progress before us. With what zeal should we set ourselves to that work now, which we must be pursuing for ever, apply ourselves to the practice of true righteousness, and resolve to make it our whole ambition to subject all our powers to the *reasonable* and *divine* part of our natures, to weaken the force of rebellious appetites as much as possible, and cause goodness and love and resignation to be so effectually wrought into our tempers, as to possess themselves of the whole frame and bent of our souls?

One question more on this subject may be proper to be attended to.—It may be asked, 'whether a due order of the several inferior powers of our natures amongst themselves, ought not to be taken into our idea of a good character, as well as their common subordination to the faculty of reason?' —It will be a sufficient answer to such an enquiry, to observe, that this subordination of the lower powers implies likewise their due state, measure, and proportion in respect of one another. Tho' some of them should be stronger than of right they ought to be in comparison with others; yet, if reason governs, the irregularity which would otherwise follow will be prevented, and the right balance will by degrees be restored; the defect on the one side will be *supplied* by a higher principle, and the excess on the other, will, by the same principle, be *restrained*; so that no harm shall ensue to the character, and nothing criminal discover itself in the life and temper.—It has been elsewhere observed, that, as far as we increase the force of reason, we diminish the occasion for appetite and instinct. By consequence, then, no inconvenience could possibly arise from any depression of instinct, if reason is proportionably exalted. But in men it is in fact impossible so far to improve this faculty, as that the greatest evils shall not arise from taking away our instincts and passions. They were very wisely and kindly given us to answer the purposes of our present state; to be the sources of many pleasures to us; to be our sole guides till reason becomes capable of taking the direction of us, and, after this, to enforce its dictates, and aid us in the execution of them; to give vigour and spirit to our pursuits, and be, as it were, sail and wind to the vessel of life. What we are to study then is, not to eradicate our passions, (which, were it possible, would be pernicious and wicked) but to keep reason vigilant and immoveable at the helm, and to render them more easily governable by it and more absolutely ministerial to it. When they happen to be in any way unfavourable and perverse, they will indeed throw difficulties in our way and expose us to great danger; but it is the office of reason, at all times, to direct and controul them; to supply the needed force when they are too languid; to moderate their effects when too impetuous, and to guard against every threatening danger.

The character and temper of a man who has naturally the passion of *resentment* strong, and but little compassion to balance it, will certainly degenerate into *malice* and *cruelty*, if he is guided solely by instinctive principles. But, if he is guided by reason and virtue, the exorbitancy of resentment will be checked; all that is hard, unequal, injurious, revengeful, or unkind will be excluded from his conduct; his temper will be softened and humanized; the miseries of others will be duly regarded, and all that is proper will be done to ease their burdens and encrease their joys. The like may be said of a person whose *self-love* and desire *of distinction* are naturally too high in proportion to his *benevolence*; and who, therefore, unless governed by reason, would become *proud, selfish,* and *ambitious*; and in all other cases of the undue adjustment of the passions to one another.—A virtuous man as such cannot allow any exorbitancy in his affections, or any internal disorder which he is sensible of, or which he can possibly discover and rectify. Neither anger, nor self-love, nor the desire of fame, can be so powerful, or so deficient, as to render him envious, morose, covetous, luxurious, cowardly, self-neglectful, mean-spirited, or slothful. Piety and virtue consist in the just regulation of the passions. No better definition can be given of them. They signify nothing any farther than they exclude whatever is inconsistent with true worth and integrity; make those who pretend to them *better* in every capacity of life; and render the peevish, good-natured; the fierce and overbearing, gentle; the obstinate, complying; the haughty, humble; the narrow and selfish, open and generous; the voluptuous, temperate; and the false and deceitful, faithful and sincere. Reason is repugnant to all kinds of unreasonableness and irregularity. It is essential to it to direct, as far as its dominion extends, the passions to their proper objects; to confine them to their proper functions; to prevent them from disturbing our own peace, or that of the world; and, in short, to correct whatever is amiss in the inward man, and inconsistent with its sound and healthful state.

It is scarcely possible to avoid reflecting here, on the happy state of the person whose temper and life are governed by reason in the manner I have now described. What tranquility and bliss must that mind possess whose oppressors and tyrants lie vanquished; which has regained its health and liberty; is independent of the world, and conscious of the peculiar care of the Almighty; where no seditious desire shews itself, and the inferior powers are all harmonious and obedient; where hope and love, candour, sincerity, fortitude, temperance, benignity, piety, and the whole train of heavenly virtues and graces, shed their influences, and have taken up their residence? What *beauty*, or what *glory* like that of such a mind? How well has it been compared* to a well regulated and flourishing state, victorious over every enemy; secure from every invasion and insult; the seat of liberty, righteousness, and peace; where every member keeps his proper station, and faithfully performs his proper duty; where faction and discord never appear; order, harmony, and love prevail, and all unite in chearful submission to one wise and good legislature?—Is there any thing that deserves ambition, besides acquiring *such* a mind? In what else can the true blessedness and perfection of man consist? With what *contempt*, as well as *pity*, must we think of those who prefer *shadows and tinsel* to this *first and highest good*; who take great care of the order of their *dress*, their *houses* and *lands*, while they suffer their *minds* to lie waste; and anxiously pursue *external* elegance, but study not to make *themselves* amiable, to cultivate *inward* order, and to establish a regular and happy state of the heart and affections?

And now, to conclude this chapter; let me observe, that the account it contains of what is necessary to constitute a good character, gives us a melancholy prospect of the condition of mankind. True goodness, if this account is just, is by no means so common as we could wish; and that indifference and carelessness which we see in a great part of mankind, must be utterly inconsistent with it.—Many of even those who bear fair characters, and whose behaviour is in the main decent and regular, are perhaps what they appear to be, more on account of the peculiar favourableness

---

* This comparison is finely drawn in *Plato*'s Dialogues on a Republick. See particularly the conclusion of the fourth and ninth Dialogues.

of their natural temper and circumstances; or, because they have never happened to be much in the way of being otherwise; than from any genuine and sound principles of virtue established within them and governing their hearts. The bulk of mankind is not composed of the grosly wicked, or of the eminently good; for, perhaps, both these are almost equally scarce; but of those who are as far from being *truly good*, as they are from being *very bad*; of the indolent and unthinking; the neglecters of God and immortality; the wearers of the *form* without the *reality* of piety; of those, in short, who may be blame-worthy and guilty, not so much on account of what they *do*, as what they *do not do*.

We have, therefore, all of us the greatest reason for being careful of ourselves, and for narrowly watching and examining our hearts and lives.—It is, I doubt, much too common for men to think, that less is incumbent on them than is really so; and to expect (however unreasonable such an expectation must be in beings, who find it contradicted by all they observe of the course of the world) that they may rise to bliss under the divine government of course, without much solicitude or labour.—There is not, indeed, any thing more necessary, than to call upon men to consider seriously the nature of the present state, the precariousness of their situation, and the danger they are in of remaining destitute of that virtuous character and temper, which are the necessary qualifications for bliss. There is nothing they want more, than to be warned to save themselves from the evil of the world; and to be admonished, frequently, 'that if they would escape future condemnation, they must exercise vigilance, attention and zeal, and endeavour to be better than mankind in general are.'

CHAP. X.

The Account of Morality given in this Treatise, applied to the Explication and proof of some of the principal Doctrines of Natural Religion; particularly, the moral Attributes of God, his moral Government, and a future State of Rewards and Punishments.

BEFORE I enter on the subjects to be considered in this *chapter*, I shall beg the reader's patience and attention while I recapitulate part of what has been hitherto said in this treatise; and, at the same time, endeavour to set before him in one view, and the distinctest manner, the whole state of the controversy about the *foundation of virtue*.

'Tis discouraging to think of the confusion which is occasioned in most debates and enquiries, by the ambiguous senses of words. Were it possible for us to understand precisely one another's meaning, to observe accurately our different views, and to communicate our naked and genuine sentiments to one another, without being under the necessity of having them more or less mistaken, through the imperfections of language; we should find, that there are few or no points on which we differ so much as we seem to do. Many questions there are which have been, for many ages, controverted with great zeal, though the disputants on both sides have, in reality, all along meant much the same, and been nearly agreed, as far as they had ideas. I say, *as far as they had ideas*; for it is certain, that there is nothing that the generality of men want more; and that a controversy may become very tedious and voluminous, while neither party have any determinate *opinions* about the subject of it; but their zeal and contention are entirely for or against a set of phrases. This evil will never be cured, till men learn to *think* as well as *talk*, and resolve to proceed from *words* to *things*, to give up their attachment to particular phrases, and study more, in all cases, what is *meant* than what is *said*.

A great deal of this perplexity, arising from the ambiguity of words, has attended the subject now before us; and particularly it seems that the word, *foundation*, admits of various senses, which, if not attended to, cannot but produce endless disputes. For how is it possible, that we should agree in determining what the *foundation* of virtue is, when we annex different meanings to the term *foundation*, and therefore have different ideas of the nature and design of the question?

Let us then consider accurately what we mean, when we enquire what is the 'FOUNDATION of virtue.' And let it be premised, that by VIRTUE is now meant ABSOLUTE VIRTUE, or that RIGHTNESS, PROPRIETY, or FITNESS of certain actions, which all own in some instances or other, and which can be explained no other way, than by desiring every one to reflect on what, in such instances, he is conscious of. When now we ask, what the FOUNDATION *of virtue* thus understood, is, we may mean, 'what is the *true account or reason* that such and such actions are *right*, or appear to us under this notion?'— And *but two accounts* of this can possibly be assigned.—It may be said either, that *right* is a species of *sensation*, like taste or colour, and therefore denotes nothing absolutely true of the actions to which we apply it; which lays the foundation of it entirely in the will and good pleasure of the author of our natures. Or, on the other hand, it may be said, that it denotes *a real character of actions*, or something *true* of them; something necessary and immutable and independent of our perceptions, like *equality*, *difference*, *proportion*, or *connection*; and, therefore, that no other account is to be given, why such and such actions are right, than why the natures of things are what they are; why, for example, the opposite angles made by the intersection of two right lines are *equal*, or why it is *impossible*, that any thing should exist without a cause.—It would be extremely unreasonable for any person to pretend to want farther information here, and to ask, what is the foundation of TRUTH? When we have traced a subject to the natures of things, we are, in all cases, completely satisfied; and it is trifling and impertinent to desire any farther account. Would *he* deserve an answer, or could we think him quite in his senses, who should seriously ask, why the whole is *greater* than a part, or two *different* from twenty? It has been said, that the *will of God* is the foundation of truth. This is asserting what no one can understand. It is sacrificing to the single attribute of *will* all the divine perfections; and even, under the appearance of magnifying it, subverting it, and taking away the very possibility of it. For upon what is it founded itself? Can there be *power* without *possibles*, or *will* without *objects*, without any thing to be willed? Or can *these*, which *will supposes*, be *dependent* upon it, and *derived* from it?—Some perhaps there may be, who, with me, will further think, that *truth* having a reference to *mind*; *necessary truth*, and the *eternal natures of things*, imply a *necessary*, *eternal mind*; and *force* us upon the acknowledgment of the *Divine, unoriginated, incomprehensible wisdom and intelligence.*

Again; when we enquire what is the *foundation* of virtue, we may mean, 'what are the *primary principles and heads* of virtue; or, the considerations inferring obligation in particular cases and rendering particular actions *right*?' Thus, should I enquire why a person *ought* to act in such or such a particular manner, in certain circumstances: it would be proper to reply, because he has received benefits from others; because it conduces to his happiness; or because God commands it. And, in this sense, there will be as many *foundations* of virtue, as there are *first* principles of it. This, probably, is what those mean by *foundation*, who will allow no other *foundation* of virtue, than *private happiness*; that is, they mean that nothing *obliges*, nothing renders actions, in any circumstances, *fit* to be performed, but some prospect of obtaining private happiness, and avoiding private misery. Should we enquire farther of such persons, what it is that renders promoting our own good *right*, and how we are to account for its being the object of our desires and studies; they would not, probably, be against recurring to truth and the natures of things; and thus we should be agreed about the *foundation* of virtue, in the former sense, and differ only about what is discussed in the seventh chapter, or the *subject-matter* of virtue. —This also must necessarily be the meaning of those, who plead for the *will of God* as the only efficient of virtue and obligation, as far as they are not for making it likewise the efficient of *all* truth. If they will carefully consider, why we *ought* to do the will of God, or what they mean by the *obligation* to obey God, they will find, that they must either make this to be an *instance* of necessary self-evident truth and duty; or account for it from the power of God to make us happy or miserable, as we obey or disobey him; which would reduce this scheme into that of self-love, and make all the same observations applicable to it.*

We may once more observe, that by the *foundation* of virtue, may be meant, 'the *motives* and *reasons*, which lead us to it, and support the practice of it in the world.' This must be the meaning of those who are for uniting the several schemes; and represent *the will of God, self-interest*, the *reasons of things*, and the *moral sense*, as all distinct and coincident *foundations* of virtue. 'Tis indeed undeniable, that these, with their joint force, carry us to virtue. But, if we keep to the first sense of the term *foundation*, it will appear that only one or other of the two last can be the true foundation of virtue.

He that would obtain a yet more accurate view of this subject, and avoid, as much as possible, perplexity and confusion, should farther attend to the various acceptations of the words *action* and *virtue*. That which I have stiled the *virtue of the agent*, or *practical virtue*, is to be understood in a very different manner from *absolute virtue*. But of this dis-

* See Note F in the *Appendix*.

tinction I have already, in the eighth chapter, given an account which seems to me sufficient.

It remains that I now make some general remarks on the whole of what has been hitherto advanced in this treatise.

What is here of most consequence is, to point out the advantages attending the account I have given of morality in our enquiries into the nature and character of the first Cause, and in explaining and proving the facts of *Natural Religion.*

Were it certain, that the origin of our moral perceptions is an implanted sense, it could no more be inferred from our having such perceptions, that the Deity likewise has them, than the like inference could be drawn with respect to any of our other mental relishes, or even the sensations of sight and hearing. Were there nothing, in the natures and reasons of things, to be a ground of a moral and righteous disposition in the mind of the Deity, or by which we could account for his preferring happiness to misery, and approving goodness, truth, and equity, rather than their contraries, it would be far less easy than it is to ascertain his will and character; nay, I think, it would be utterly inconceiveable to us, how he could have any moral character at all.—This may appear, not only from the reasoning used in the latter part of the first chapter, but also from the following reasoning.

If, in respect of *intrinsick* worth and goodness, all rules and measures of conduct are alike; if no end can have more *in* it than another to recommend it to the choice of the Deity; if, in particular, there is nothing, in the natures of things, to be the ground of his preference of happiness to misery, or of his approbation of goodness rather than cruelty; then his nature must be essentially indifferent alike to all ends; it was always as possible that he should be *malevolent* as *benevolent*; there is no account to be given of his being one of these, rather than the other; and therefore he cannot possess any determinate character. For most certainly, whatever he is, he is *necessarily*. There can be nothing in his nature, which he might have wanted, or of which he can be conceived to be deprived, without a contradiction.

It will be of use, towards illustrating this reasoning, to apply it in the following case:—Suppose only one body to exist in nature, and let it be conceived to be in motion in any particular direction. Now, either we might certainly know concerning this body, that it could not have been moving from eternity in this direction without any cause, or we might not. If we might; it could be only on such principles as the following. Whatever has existed from eternity without an efficient cause, must have existed *necessarily*. But, in the case under consideration, it was from eternity equally possible, that the supposed body should have moved in any other direction; and, consequently, there being no account of its motion from necessity, or the nature of the thing, it must have been moved by some cause, and exclusive of all causality and efficiency, its motion and even existence are impossible.

The reasoning in the former case is the same with this. If, in the one case, among many directions of motion, in themselves alike possible, 'tis absurd to suppose any particular direction to take place without some *directing* cause; it must be equally absurd in the other, amongst many determinations of will and character in themselves indifferent and alike possible, to suppose any particular determination to take place without some *determining* cause.

I might go on to observe, that if, *from the natures of things and necessity*, there is no such thing as a rule of conduct to intelligent beings, then there is *necessarily* no such thing; the whole notion of it is contradictory.

The distinction between *necessary* and *contingent* existence, is the main foundation of all that we believe concerning the first cause. This distinction we perceive intuitively. The particular objects by the contemplation of which it is suggested

to us, force the idea of it upon our minds. Some thing
appear to us self-evidently to be *effects, precarious* and *arbitrar*
in their natures, indifferent to existence or non-existence
and possible alike to possess any one of an infinity of differen
manners of existence. These things then we know certainl
to be *derived, dependent,* and *produced.* Of this kind are matte
and motion; the form and order of the world; and all par
ticular sensible objects. We do not see more clearly, in an
case, that there is such a thing as *productive power,* or a *depen
dence* of one thing on another, than we do, that these objects
and, in general, all imperfect and limited existences, ar
effects, and require a *cause.*—In short; whatever we can con
ceive not to be, 'tis certain *may* not be; and whatever *may no*
be, must, if it exists, have had its existence produced by some
cause.—On the contrary, some things we see intuitively no
to be *effects,* to want no cause, to be underived, self-existent
and unchangeable. To suppose otherwise of them we see to
imply a contradiction. We cannot possibly conceive them
either not to be, or to be in any respect different from wha
they are. Of this kind are *space* and *duration,* and all *abstrac
truth* and *possibles.*

But waving these observations;* it will be more to the
present purpose to repeat an observation already made,
namely, that the account of morality I have opposed, seem
to imply that the Deity, if benevolent, must be so *contrary* to
his understanding. This seems to be as evident, as it is, that
to be conscious of doing what is indifferent, or of employing
power in pursuing an end which has nothing in it worthy of
pursuit, is to be conscious of trifling. There is at least sufficient weight in this observation to shew, that it is the grossest
disparagement to the perfections of the Deity, to suppose him
actuated entirely by unintelligent inclination; or to conceive
of him as proceeding invariably in a course of action, which

* See Chap. 5th, and the Dissertation on the Being and Attributes of the
Deity at the end of this Volume.

as nothing in it *right*, and which, consequently, he cannot really approve.*

Reasonings of this kind plainly tend to shew us, that if the distinctions of right and wrong, and moral good and evil, are nothing in the natures of things; the Deity can be of no character. This indeed is a conclusion which is contradicted by certain fact; for his creating at all, and much more final causes, and his acting with the uniformity and wisdom we see in the constitution of nature, imply some dispositions, some principle of action, or some character. But this is only saying, that the whole course of things proves the scheme upon which I have been arguing, and from whence such a conclusion follows, to be false.†

But though in opposition to the precedent reasonings, and the sentiments on which they are founded, *effects* thus prove the Deity·to be of some character; yet it may be doubted, whether, from these alone, we could obtain any undeniable proofs of his being of the particular character of goodness; for it seems not impossible to account for them on other suppositions. An unintelligent agent cannot produce order and regularity, and therefore wherever *these* appear, they *demonstrate* design and wisdom in the cause. But it cannot be said in like manner, that a selfish, a capricious, or even a malicious agent, may not produce happiness; nor consequently, that the appearance of this in an effect demonstrates the goodness of the cause. Let it be granted, as surely it must, that good is greatly prevalent in what we see of the works of God; that all that comes within our notice of the world, shews kind design; and that the primary direction of every law and

* See chap. I. sect. 3 and also chap. III. latter end.
† 'To suppose God to approve one course of action, or one end, preferably to another, which yet his acting at all from design, implies that he does, without supposing somewhat prior in that end, to be the ground of the preference, is as inconceiveable, as to suppose him to discern an abstract proposition to be true, without supposing somewhat prior in it to be the ground of the discernment. See *Butler's Analogy*, p. 170. 4th edit.

regulation of nature, is to happiness; 'yet who knows (ma~ some say) what different scenes may have heretofore existed or may *now* exist in other districts of the universe? An evi being may *sometimes* be the cause of good, just as a good being may of sufferings and pain. How little do we see of nature! From what we observe in a *point* and a *moment*, what certain conclusion can we draw with respect to what prevails *univer- sally* and *eternally*? Concerning a plan of boundless extent, and which was contrived and is carried on by an incompre- hensible being, what can be learned from such a superficial and imperfect observation as we can make of what is next to nothing of it? Can it be right to establish a general con- clusion on a single experiment, or to determine the character and views of a being, of whom independently of experience we can know nothing, from a few acts which will bear several different interpretations? If we had nothing distinct from effects to rely on, nothing in necessary truth and reason to argue from, would it not be natural to enquire with doubt and anxiety, whether great changes may not hereafter happen in the world; whether caprice or a love of variety, instead of goodness, may not be the principle of action in the first cause; or whether *the design of what we now see and feel, may not be to give a keener edge to future disappointment, and thus universal misery appear at last to be intended?*'*

What regard is due to these objections, every one may determine as he pleases. I am far from thinking them of weight enough to shew that effects, independently of all arguments from moral fitness, cannot furnish us with suffi- cient arguments for the goodness of God.

When we first reflect, that undoubtedly he is of some will and character, and that it is in itself as possible and as credible, that he should be of this particular character as any other; the consideration after this, that his works as far as we see them, have upon them obvious marks of benignity and

* *Wisdom the first spring of action in the Deity,* by Mr. Grove, chap. I. sect. 9.

ove, will necessarily incline us to think that he is good. When we have no more evidence for than against a proposition, any preponderating circumstance ought to determine our understandings and engage our assent, with an assurance proportionable to its apparent weight. And with respect to the objections and suspicions before-mentioned, it may be justly said, that we are to judge of what we do *not* see by what we *do* see, and not the contrary; and that consequently, as long as the appearance on the whole of what lies before us of God's works, though comparatively little, is clearly as if happiness was their end, the fair conclusion is, that this is indeed the truth. Besides; the more extensive we suppose the creation, the greater chance there was against our being cast into that part of it wherein goodness is so much exerted, if indeed any other principle influences the author of it, to which therefore, on the whole, it must be supposed to be conformable.—Some however, (particularly those who entertain dismal ideas of human life, as upon the whole unhappy) are likely, if they think consistently, not to be much influenced by this argument. What regard is in reality due to the appearances of evil in the world, and what reason arises from hence, and from the greater degrees of happiness which we imagine we see *might* have been communicated, to suspect that goodness may not be the spring of action in the Deity, are questions of considerable importance, which have been often well discussed.—It deserves particular regard, that the *natural* state of a being is always his *sound*, and *good*, and *happy* state; that all the corruptions and disorders we observe are plainly *unnatural deviations and excesses*; and that no instance can be produced wherein *ill* as such is the genuine tendency and result of the original constitution of things.*

* It might have been objected here, that from effects alone it can at best be only possible to gather the *present* disposition of the Deity; and that though they demonstrated this to be benevolent, yet we should still want evidences to prove the *stability* of his character, or that he always has been and will for ever continue to be good. The full reply to such objections may be learnt from the

If now, at the same time that the voice of all nature, as far as it comes within our notice, furnishes us with these arguments, it appears to us, that all ends are not the same to an intelligent regard; that there is something intrinsically *better* in goodness, veracity, and justice, than in their contraries, something morally different in their natures; our evidence of God's moral attributes, will be increased in the same degree, that we think we have reason to believe this. And if it appears to us clear and certain, that intelligence implies the approbation of beneficence; that the understanding is the power which judges of moral differences; and that from a necessity in the natures of things, goodness rather than malice must constitute the disposition and end of every mind in proportion to the degree of its knowledge and perfection; our evidence, on the present point, will become equally clear and certain.

But, how much inferior evidence on points the most interesting, shall we be forced to satisfy ourselves with, if we reject these principles, and embrace the opinion, that all our ideas of *worth* and *virtue*, of *morality* and *excellence*, have no foundation in truth and reality?—Our approbation of goodness, if derived from intellectual perception, infers *demonstrably* the goodness of God; but if derived entirely from an arbitrary structure of our minds, is at best, only one instance among many of kind design; and was necessary, supposing the universal plan, whatever it is, to be such as required that what is *here*, and in *this part of duration*, revealed of it, should carry the appearance of benevolence. A few facts, when we have antecedent evidence from the nature of the subject, may confirm a truth beyond the possibility of doubt; but can, by no means, give equal satisfaction when we have no such evidence, and experience is our only medium of information.

Indeed, upon the principles defended in this treatise,

observations on the nature of the *necessary* existence of the Deity which will be found at the end of this Treatise.

nothing can be more easy to be ascertained than the moral perfections of the Deity.—The *nature* of happiness is, without doubt, as shewn in the 3d chapter, the true account of the desire and preference of *private* happiness. This leads us unavoidably to conclude, that it is also the true account of the desire and preference of *publick* happiness. And if it is, it appears at once, that the Deity must be benevolent.—In short; if there is a rule of right, arising from the differences and relations of things, and extending as far as all the possible effects of power; which, to the degree it is known, forces the regard and affection of all reasonable beings, and which its own nature constitutes the proper, the supreme, and eternal guide and measure of all their determinations: If, I say, there is indeed such a rule or law, it follows *demonstrably*, that the *first intelligence*, that is, the Deity, must be under the direction of it more than any other nature; as much more, as his understanding is higher, and his knowledge more perfect. He is, in reality, the living independent spring of it. He cannot contradict it, without contradicting *himself.* 'Tis a part of the idea of reason, and therefore, in the *self-existent infinite reason*, must be of absolute and sovereign influence.

There can therefore be no difficulty in determining what the principle of action is in the Deity. As it is evident that the seat of *infinite power* must be the seat of *infinite knowledge*; so it appears from hence no less evident, that it must be also the seat of *absolute rectitude*: and these qualities, thus implying one another and *essentially one*, complete the idea of Deity, and exhibit him to us in the most awful and glorious light. Amongst the various possible schemes of creation, and ways of ordering the series of events, there is a *best*; and this is the rule and end of the divine conduct; nor is it possible, that seeing this, and all things being equally easy to him, he should deviate from it; or, that the being into whose nature, as the *necessary exemplar and original of all perfection*, every thing true, right, and good, is ultimately to be resolved, should ever chuse what is contrary to them. To understand perfectly what upon the whole is most fit, and to follow it invariably thro' all duration and the whole extent of the universe, is the highest notion we can frame of MORAL EXCELLENCE.

Here let us, by the way, consider what we can wish for beyond being under the care of this being; and with what joy we may reflect, that as certainly as God exists, all is well; a perfect order of administration prevails in nature, and all affairs are under the wisest and kindest direction.

But to go on; the independency and self-sufficiency of God raise him above the possibility of being tempted to what is wrong. 'Tis not conceivable that he should be subject to partial views, mistake, ignorance, passion, selfishness, or any of the causes of evil and depravity of which we have any notion. His nature admits of nothing arbitrary or instinctive; of no determinations that are independent of reason, or which cannot be accounted for by it. In an underived being of absolute simplicity, and all whose attributes must be essentially connected, there can be no interfering properties. The same necessity and reasons of things cannot be the ground of the approbation and love of rectitude, and of biasses contradictory to it.

Before we quit what we are now upon, it will be proper, lest I should be misunderstood, to observe particularly, that whenever I represent *necessity* as the account of the *rectitude* of the Deity, or speak of *goodness* as *essential* to him, it is the *principle* of rectitude I mean; and not the *actual exercise* of this principle. No absurdity can be greater than to suppose, that the divine being *acts* by the same kind of necessity by which he *exists*, or that the *exertions* of his power are in the same sense necessary with his *power itself*, or with the *principles* by which they are directed. All voluntary action is, *by the terms*, free, and implies the *physical possibility* of forbearing it. What is meant by this *possibility* is not in the least inconsistent with the utmost *certainty of event*, or with the *impossibility*, IN ANOTHER SENSE, that the action should be omitted.—It may be *infinitely* more depended upon, that God will never do wrong, than that the wisest created being will not do what is most destructive to him, without the least temptation. There is, in truth, *equal* impossibility, tho' not the *same kind* of impossibility, that he who is the abstract of all perfection should deviate into imperfection in his conduct, infinite reason act unreasonably, or eternal righteousness unrighteously; as that infinite knowledge should mistake, infinite power be conquered, or necessary existence cease to exist.—It may be as *really* impossible for a person in his senses, and without any motive urging him to it, to drink poison, as it is for him to prevent the effects of it after drinking it; but who sees not these impossibilities to be totally different in their meaning? or what good reason can there be against calling the one a *moral*, and the other a *natural* impossibility?

This distinction, which many are unwilling to acknowledge, and which yet, I think, of great importance, may perhaps be in some measure illustrated by what follows.

Suppose a die or solid, having a million of faces: It may be said to be *certain*, that an agent void of skill will not, the first trial, throw an assigned face of such a die; for the word *certain* is often used in a sense much lower. But that such an agent should throw an assigned face of such a die, a million of times together without failing, few would scruple to pronounce *impossible*. The *impossibility* however meant in this case, would plainly be very different from an absolute *physical* impossibility; for if it is possible to succeed the first trial, (as it undoubtedly is) it is equally possible to succeed the second, the third, and all the subsequent trials; and consequently, *in this sense of possibility*, 'tis as possible to throw the given face*

---

* There is in truth an infinity of numbers of trials, in which it is morally certain this would actually happen.

a million of times together, as the first time.—But farther that a million of dice, each having a million of faces, and thrown together for a million of times successively, should always turn the same faces, will be pronounced yet much more impossible. Nevertheless, it will appear, by the same reasoning with that just used, that there is the same *natural* possibility of this, as of any other event.—If any one thinks what is now said of no weight, and continues yet at a loss about the difference between these two sorts of impossibility, let him compare the impossibility that the last mentioned event should happen, with the impossibility of throwing any faces which there are not upon a die.

To pursue this exemplification yet farther, let us consider that the improbability of throwing any particular face of a die, is always in proportion to the number of faces which it has. When therefore the number of faces is *infinite*, the improbability of the event is *infinite*, or it becomes *certain* it will not happen, and *impossible* that it should happen, in a sense similar to that in which we say, it is *impossible* a wise man should knowingly and without temptation do what will be destructive to him. However, as one face must be thrown, and the given face has the same chance for being thrown with any other, it is *possible* this face may be thrown, and the assigned event happen; in the same manner as a wise man has it *in his power*, knowingly and without temptation, to do what will be destructive to him. The certainty that a particular face of an infinite die will not be thrown *twice together*, exceeds infinitely the certainty that it will not be thrown *the first time*; but the certainty that it will not be thrown *perpetually and invariably for an infinity of trials*, is greater than this last mentioned certainty in the same proportion that the *infiniteth power of infinite* is greater than *infinite*. Yet still the impossibility of event which all must be sensible of in these cases, is as far from a physical one, as in the simplest cases. Now, he that should in such cases, confound these different kinds of impossibility, (or necessity) would be much more excuseable, than he that confounds them, when considering the events depending on the determinations of free beings, and comparing them with those arising from the operation of blind and unintelligent causes. The one admits of endlessly various degrees; the other of none. That necessity by which twice two is not twenty, or a mass of matter does not continue at rest when impelled by another, is, wherever found, always the same, and incapable of the least increase or diminution.

I shall only add on this head, that the necessity of the eternal conformity of all the divine actions to the rules of wisdom and righteousness, may be exemplified by the certainty, that an infinite number of dice, each having an infinite number of faces, and thrown all together for an infinite number of trials, would not always turn precisely the same faces; which though infallibly true that it will not happen, yet *may* happen, in a sense not very unlike that in which the Deity has a power of deviating from rectitude; of creating, for instance, a miserable world, or of destroying the *world after a supposed promise not to destroy it.

But dismissing this subject; let us now apply the account which has been given in this treatise of the nature and subject-matter of morality, to another Question of considerable importance relating to the Deity; I mean, the Question 'whether all his moral attributes are reducible to benevolence; or whether this includes the *whole* of his character?'

It has been shewn, that the negative is true of inferior beings, and in general, that virtue is by no means reducible

* If any dislike the word *infinite* as used here, they may substitute the word *indefinite* in its room, which will answer my purpose as well.

The analogy I have here insisted on answers, I think, the end of an illustration with great exactness, and on this account, I hope, I shall be excused if it should appear to have any thing in it unsuitable to the dignity of the subject to which it is applied.

to benevolence. If the observations made to this purpose are just, the question now proposed is at once determined. Absolute and eternal rectitude, (or a regard to what is in all cases most fit and righteous) is properly the ultimate principle of the divine conduct, and the sole guide of his power. In this GOODNESS is first and principally included. But GOODNESS and RECTITUDE, how far soever they may coincide, are far from being identical. The former results from the latter, and is but a part of it. Which therefore stands first in the divine mind, and which should give way, supposing an interference ever possible, can (one would think) admit of no controversy. For will any person say, that it is not because it is *right*, that the Deity promotes the happiness of his creatures; or that he would promote it in any *instances* or in any *manner*, wherein it would be *wrong* to promote it?—Such reasonings and suppositions will, I know, appear very absurd to some: But it is certain they are not absurd, unless it must be taken for granted, that *right* signifies only conduciveness to happiness,* and that nothing but such conduciveness can at any time render one action morally better than another.

It must however be admitted, that the character of God is much more nearly reducible to goodness, than that of any inferior beings.—What I mean will be better understood, if we make the supposition of a *solitary being*† *not perfectly happy*, but capable of acquiring happiness for himself, and improving in it; and afterwards consider, into how narrow a compass

---

* 'The *righteousness* and goodness of actions is not the same notion with their *tendency to universal happiness*, or flowing from the desire of it. This latter is the highest species of the former. Our *moral sense* has also other immediate objects of approbation, &c.' Dr. *Hutcheson's System of Moral Philosophy*, book ii. chap. iii. sect. ii.

† The same supposition is made in a pamphlet, intitled, *Divine Benevolence; or an attempt to prove that the principal end of the Divine Providence and Government, is the Happiness of his Creatures*, printed for Noon, 1731.—I am sorry this pamphlet is out of print. The author was Mr. BAYES, one of the most ingenious men I ever knew, and for many years the minister of a dissenting congregation at TUNBRIDGE WELLS.

the obligations of such a being would be brought. Having by the supposition no connection with any other reasonable being, what could require his attention besides his own interest? What else could he calmly and deliberately propose to himself as the end at which it would be *right* for him constantly to aim? The exercise of gratitude, benevolence, justice, and veracity, would be impossible to him; and every duty would vanish, except that of prudence, or a wise and steady pursuit of his own highest good.

If now we change the supposition, and consider a being, such as the Deity, who is *perfectly happy in himself*, absolutely supreme and independent, and the creator of all things; will it not evidently appear, that he can have nothing to employ his power, and no end to carry on, different from the *good of his creatures*? As all the views, studies and endeavours of the *solitary being* I have supposed, necessarily terminate in *himself*; the contrary must be true of this being. To him *others* must be all; and the care of their interests, the *due adjustment* of their states among themselves, and the *right administration* of their affairs must comprehend the principles and views of all his actions. As he can have no superior, is self-sufficient, and incapable of having any *private end* to carry on, it is wholly inconceivable, what, besides a disposition to communicate bliss, could engage him *at first* to produce any being, or what *afterwards* can influence him to continue the exercise of his power in preserving and directing the beings he has made, besides some regard to their good, or some reasons taken from their circumstances and wants.

Happiness is an object of essential and eternal value. The fitness of communicating it gave birth to the creation. It was for this the world was produced, and for this it is continued and governed. Beauty and order, which have been strangely said to be of equal, nay superior value, are chiefly to be regarded as subservient to this, and seem incapable of being proposed as proper *ends* of action. How triflingly employed would that being appear to us, who should devote his time and studies to the making of regular forms, and ranging inanimate objects into the most perfect state of order and symmetry, without any further view? What would be the worth or importance of any system of mere matter, however beautifully disposed; or, of an universe in which were displayed the most exquisite workmanship and skill, and the most consummate harmony and proportion of parts, but which, at the same time, had not a single being in it that enjoyed pleasure, or that could perceive its beauty?—Such an universe would be equivalent to just nothing.*

But while we thus find it necessary to conclude, that *Goodness* is the principle from which the Deity created; we ought, in honour to it, never to forget, that it is a principle founded in *reason*, and guided by *reason*, and essentially *free* in all its operations. Were not this true of it, or were it a mere physical propensity in the divine nature which has no foundation in reason and wisdom, and which, from the same necessity by which the divine nature is eternal or omnipresent, produces all its effects, we could perceive no moral worth in it, nor reckon it at all an object of gratitude and praise.

Happiness is the *end*, and the *only* end conceivable by us, of God's providence and government: But he pursues this end in subordination to rectitude, and by those methods only which rectitude requires. *Justice* and *Veracity* are *right* as well as *goodness*, and must also be ascribed to the Deity.—By *justice* here I mean principally *distributive justice*, impartiality and equity in determining the state of beings, and a constant regard to their different moral qualifications in all the communications of happiness to them. 'Tis this attribute of the Deity we mean, when we speak of his spotless holiness and purity. From hence arises the everlasting repugnancy of his nature to all immorality, his loving and favouring virtue, and making it the unchangeable law of his creation, and the

* See *Wisdom the first Spring of Action in the Deity*, by Mr. Grove.

universal ground and condition of happiness under his government.—It would, I think, be a very dangerous error to consider goodness in God as undirected by justice in its exercise. *Divine benevolence* is a disposition, not to make all indiscriminately happy in any possible way, but to make the *faithful*, the *pious*, and *upright* happy.

That *justice* is not merely a mode of goodness, or an instance of its taking the most effectual method to accomplish its end; or that the *whole* reason why God favours virtue and punishes vice, is not their contrary effects on the welfare of the world, I have endeavoured particularly to shew in the fourth chapter, where I treated of good and ill desert.*

Again; *Veracity* is another principle of rectitude, not reducible to goodness, which directs the actions of the Deity, and by which all the exertions of his goodness are conducted and regulated.

There is nothing unreasonable in believing it possible, that falshood and deceit may frequently have equal aptitude to produce happiness with truth and faithfulness. Supposing then this should, in any circumstances of the world, happen, 'tis surely not to be doubted but that God would prefer the latter. If this is denied; if it is indeed true, that, exclusive of consequences, there is nothing right in the one, or wrong in the other, what can we depend on? How shall we know that God has not actually chosen the methods of falshood and general deception? Great must be our perplexity, if we are to wait for a satisfactory solution of such doubts, till we can make out, that such are the circumstances of our state

* 'Some men seem to think the only character of the author of nature to be that of simple absolute benevolence. This, considered as a principle of action and infinite, is a disposition to produce the greatest happiness without regard to persons' behaviour, otherwise than as such regard would produce higher degrees of it. And supposing this to be the only character of God, veracity and justice in him would be nothing but benevolence conducted by wisdom. Now surely this ought not to be asserted unless it can be proved, for we should speak with cautious reverence upon such a subject.' See *Butler's Analogy*, Part I. Chap. iii.

and of the world, that it can never be equally advantageous to us to deceive us; especially, as experience shews us in numberless instances, that an end may be obtained, and often most expeditiously and effectually, by deviating from truth.

But, though we are thus to conceive of God as *just* and *true*, as well as *good*; *justice* and *truth*, 'tis manifest, could never engage him to create. They suppose beings actually existing endowed with reason and moral capacities, and signify a certain manner of acting towards them, or the methods in which their happiness is to be pursued.

It is, besides, rather properer to say, that they *direct*, than that they *limit* God's goodness; for they are by no means inconsistent with unlimited communications of happiness, or the exercise of *everlasting*, and *infinite beneficence*.

It will not be amiss farther to observe, though there may be no great occasion for it, that, from the manner in which I have all along expressed myself, a careful reader may easily see, that I am not guilty of an inconsistency in denying that the moral attributes of God are resolvable into benevolence, at the same time that I affirm happiness to be the end, and, in all probability, the *only* end, for which he created and governs the world.—Happiness is the end of his government; but it is happiness, I have said, in subordination to rectitude: 'Tis the happiness of the *virtuous* and *worthy*, preferably to that of others: 'Tis happiness obtained, not in *any* way, but consistently with justice and veracity.—In a word; we may admit that goodness comprehends the whole divine moral character, provided we understand by it *a reasonable, sincere, holy, and just goodness.*

Finally; it is necessary for us, on this occasion, to recollect, that though it be proper, and often unavoidable, to speak of goodness, justice, and veracity, as *different* attributes of the Deity; yet they are different only as they are different views, effects, or manifestations of one supreme principle, which includes the whole of moral perfection; namely, *everlasting rectitude*, or *reason*. These reflexions shall suffice on the character of the Deity.

I shall now proceed, in the same manner, to examine the other principles and facts of Natural Religion; and to point out the peculiar evidences for them, arising from the account I have given of the nature and foundation of morals.

In the moral character of God, as it has been just explained and proved, is clearly implied his moral government; or that he requires all his reasonable creatures to practise virtue, and connects with it the effects of his benevolence.—Between the actions and characters of reasonable beings there is a real moral difference. This difference, he who knows all things, must know perfectly and completely. GOOD actions and GOOD characters he must regard as such. To regard them as such is to *approve* them; and to *approve* them is to be disposed to *favour* them.—Evil actions and evil characters, on the contrary, he must perceive to be evil; that is, he must *disapprove* them, and be disposed to discountenance them. 'Tis contradictory then to think, that the evil and the good are equally the objects of his benevolent regard; and most unreasonable to doubt, whether they will be differently treated by him.— As sure as it is that God knows what virtue and vice are; so sure is it that he delights in the one, and forbids the other; and that he will regulate all his distributions of good by the respective degrees of them in his creatures. What is *lovely* and of good desert, he cannot but *love* and distinguish. What is hateful and of ill desert, he cannot but be displeased with and punish. 'Tis self-evident that virtue *ought* to be happier than vice; and we may be very confident, that what *ought to be*, the universal, governing mind will take care *shall be*. If the state of the world, and of every individual in it, is determined invariably according to *right*, and it is one principle of rectitude, 'that all beings should receive according to their works;' we may be assured that no events or facts contradictory to this, can ever take place in the world.

All this will be confirmed and illustrated, if we consider how reasonable it is to think, that it must be acceptable to God, that his intelligent creatures should direct *their* actions by those rules of goodness, justice, and righteousness, by which he directs *his* actions. In truth it cannot be less necessary, that he should require his *subjects* and *children* to do what is right, than it is that he should *himself* do what is right. The *law of truth* must be the *law of the God of truth*. Those duties which arise from the relations in which he has placed us, it must be his will that we should discharge. Those moral differences and obligations, which have their foundation in his nature, cannot be counteracted without counteracting his nature. And so far as we have contracted habits of vice, so far have we established in our natures a contrariety to his nature, and alienated ourselves from the fountain of good.— What can be plainer than this? What may we not question, if we can question, whether God is pleased to see his creatures carrying on the same end which he carries on, acting by the same rule, and conforming themselves to the dictates of that reason of which he is himself the eternal source? Must he not have a particular complacency in those who bear his own image? And is it possible that he should not distinguish them from others? Or is it conceivable that he will permit any to be happy in a course of opposition to him; or to suffer by endeavouring, in the best manner they can, to obey and resemble him?

In short, if there is an intelligent Being at the head of all, who made things what they are; if moral good and evil are real and immutable differences, and not mere names and fancies; if there is a law of righteousness which the Deity regards, and according to which he always acts; if virtue deserves well, and is essentially *worthy* of encouragement, and vice deserves ill, and is a proper object of punishment; then, it may be depended on that the lots of the virtuous and vicious will be different; that God is *for* the one, and *against* the other; or, that the administration of the world is strictly moral and righteous.

This conclusion might be farther proved, from the consideration of the contrary effects virtue and vice necessarily have on the state of the world. Virtue, by the nature of it, tends to promote order and bliss; vice is directly subversive of these. *Goodness*, therefore, joins with *justice* in requiring, that the one should universally and for ever be encouraged under the divine government, and the other discouraged and punished.

Let it now be carefully considered here, that if it should appear, that, in the present world, virtue and vice are not distinguished in the manner which these observations require; the unavoidable consequence must be, that 'there is a future state.'—How this matter stands, and wherein the force of this inference lies, are points which deserve particular examination.

On the one hand, it must be granted, that, in general, virtue is the *present* good, and vice the *present* ill of men; and that we see enough in the present state, without having recourse to any abstract arguments, to satisfy us that the Deity favours the virtuous, and to point out to us the beginnings of a moral government.—But, on the other hand, it is no less evident, that we now perceive *but* the beginnings of such a government; that it is by no means carried so far as we have reason to expect.

Virtue *tends* to produce much greater happiness than it now actually produces, and vice to produce much greater misery. These contrary tendencies neither do nor can, during the short period of this life, in any instance, produce their full effects; and often they are prevented from taking the effect they *might*, and generally *do* take, by many obstacles arising from the wickedness of mankind, and other causes of a kind plainly temporary, and which cannot be reckoned natural or necessary. How reasonably may we presume, that tendencies thus interrupted and opposed, and yet so inseparable from virtue and vice, and so essential to the constitution of things, will, some time or other, issue in their genuine effects?—Do they not declare to us evidently the *purpose* of him who made the world what it is? And can we think, this purpose will be defeated?

Though virtue always tends to happiness, and though it is the nature of it to advance our happiness and to better our condition, in proportion to the degree in which we possess it; yet such is the state of things here below, that the event sometimes proves otherwise. 'Tis impossible to survey the world, or to recollect the history of it, without being convinced of this. There is not the least probability, that all men are constantly and invariably more or less happy, as they are more or less conscientious and upright. How often has virtue been oppressed and persecuted, while vice has prospered and flourished? Good men may have a disposition to an unreasonable and perplexing scrupulosity, or to lowness of spirits and melancholy, and in consequence of this may be rendered ignorant of their own characters, and live in perpetual distrust and terror: or they may entertain such false notions of religion and the Deity, as may give them great trouble, and take away from them many of the joys that would otherwise have attended their integrity. And are such men; or others, who, perhaps, through the faults of their parents or those of their education, carry about with them diseased bodies, and languish away life under pain and sickness; or who are harrassed and defamed for their virtue, driven away from all that is dear to them, and obliged to spend their days in poverty, or in an *inquisition*; are these persons, equally happy with many others, who, though not *more* virtuous, may nevertheless be exempted from all such trials? Or, indeed, are they equally happy with many vicious persons, who swim with the current of the world; comply with its customs; deny themselves nothing they can procure consistently with a good name; are cast into the most affluent circumstances; enjoy health and vigour of body, and tempers naturally easy and gay; live in a state of habitual thoughtlessness about what may happen to them hereafter, or entertain opinions that fill them with false hopes; and at last die without concern or remorse? Have there *never* been any instances of this kind? Does it *never* happen,[1] that the very honesty of persons subjects them to peculiar difficulties and inconveniencies, at the same time that prevarication and dishonesty make their way to ease, and honour, and plenty?

Indeed, all things considered, this world appears fitted more to be a school for the *education* of virtue, than a station of honour to it; and the course of human affairs is favourable to it more by *exercising* it, than by *rewarding* it. Though, in equal circumstances, it has always greatly the advantage over vice, and is alone sufficient to overbalance many and great inconveniences; yet it would be very extravagant to pretend, that it is at present completely, and without exception, its own[2] happiness; that it is alone sufficient to overbalance *all possible* evils of body, mind, and estate; or that, for example, a man who, by *base* but *private* methods, has secured a good estate, and afterwards enjoys it for many years with discretion and credit, has less pleasure than another, who, by his benevolence or integrity, has brought himself to a dungeon or stake, or who lives in perplexity, labour, self-denial, torture of body, and melancholy of mind. It may, 'tis true, be justly said, that virtue, though in the most distressed circumstances, is preferable to vice in the most prosperous, and that expiring in flames ought to be chosen, rather than the greatest wages

[1 Eds. 1 and 2 read 'Does it *never*, or does it *seldom* happen'.]
[2 Ed. 1 adds 'reward and'.]

of iniquity.* But the meaning of this is not, that virtue in such circumstances is more *profitable* than vice (or attended with more pleasure) but that it is of *intrinsick* excellence and obligation; that it is to be chosen for itself, independently of its utility; and remains desirable and amiable above all other objects, when stripped of every emolument, and in the greatest degree afflicted and oppressed.

What has been last said leads us to a farther observation on the state of virtue and vice in the present world, which deserves particular notice; and that is, that the most worthy characters are so far, in the present state of things, from *always* enjoying the highest happiness, that they are *sometimes* the greatest sufferers; and the *most* vicious the *least* unhappy. A person who sacrifices his life, rather than violate his conscience, or betray his country, gives up all possibility of any present reward, and loses the more in proportion as his virtue is more glorious.

But, in the *ordinary course* of life, there are circumstances which subject the best men to sufferings, to which all others must be strangers. The greater their virtue is, the higher ideas they have of virtue, and the more difficult 'tis for them to attain to that degree of it they wish for; the more anxiety they feel about the state of their own characters; the more concerned they must be for past miscarriages; the more sensible of their own imperfections; the more scrupulous and tender their consciences are, and the more susceptible of

* No one can think this assertion in any degree inconsistent or extravagant, who does not hold that virtue is good and eligible and obligatory, only as the means of private pleasure; and that nothing else can be an object of desire and preference. Upon this supposition, indeed, the very notion of parting with life, or of resigning an enjoyment to preserve innocence, and for the sake of virtue, would imply a contradiction. For being *obliged* to nothing, and therefore nothing being our *duty*, but that by which we shall obtain some over-balance of pleasure; what would otherwise have been *right* becomes *wrong*, when we are to be, in any measure, losers by it. So that, on these principles, it would be not *virtue* or *duty*, but *vice* and *guilt*, for a man to consent not to give up one hour's life, or the *least* degree of present enjoyment, to procure the greatest blessings for all mankind, supposing no future state. See chap. VI. page 107, &c.

distress from the smallest deviations. For this reason it may, I believe, be safely said, that the *infirmities* of some of the best men often give them more uneasiness, than the indulged *vices* of *some* wicked men. Be this however as it will, it can scarcely be denied with respect to wickedness, that it would very frequently be much better for a man, (I mean, more for his own present ease) to be *thoroughly* wicked than *partially* so. A man who loves virtue without uniformly practising it, who possesses many good dispositions, and is sufficiently convinced of the danger and malignity of all vice to cause him heartily to detest it, and, *in some instances*, to avoid it, but not enough to prevent his being, *in other instances*, driven by unconquered desires into the commission of it; such a person must doubtless be very miserable. He possesses neither virtue nor vice enough to give him any quiet. He is the seat of a constant intestine war, always full of vexation with himself, and torn and distracted between contending passions. 'Till reason is effectually subdued, it will be on all occasions endeavouring to regain its throne, and raising insurrections and tumults. The greater power it retains, where it is not suffered to govern, the greater disturbances it must produce, and the severer torments it must inflict.

'Tis worth adding, that in much the same condition with this now described is a vicious person, during the first period of his reformation. The pangs of remorse and self-reproach, the lashes of an awakened conscience, and the painful struggles with evil habits and passions yet craving and violent, cannot but for some time give him unspeakable trouble, and prevent his experiencing the peace and happiness naturally resulting from virtue: And if we suppose him taken away from life before he has completed what he has begun and attained a settled virtuous character, it will be true of him, that he has only been more miserable for his change: And yet, surely, for every thing good in a man, it is fit he should be a gainer rather than a sufferer.

Of the principal Doctrines

If now, on the other hand, we consider the condition of the obstinately and thoroughly vicious, we shall find it very different. The more the power of reason within them is weakened, the less troublesome it must prove. The nearer they are to being past feeling, the less they must feel. And, in general, we may observe, that the *most* wicked endure the *least* uneasiness from the checks of conscience, attend the least to moral and religious considerations, are least sensible of shame and infamy, practise most readily and effectually the arts of self-deceit, and thus may escape many of the sharpest miseries of vice, which, had they been less obdurate, they must have suffered.

Do not such observations point out to us a future state, and prove this life to be connected with another? Shall we, rather than receive this conclusion, retreat to *Atheism*, and deny that a being *perfectly reasonable* governs all things? Or must we maintain that it does not follow from his being himself righteous, that he approves and will support righteousness, and distinguish between those who do his will and imitate his goodness, and those who do not? If nothing is to be expected beyond this world, no suitable provision is made for many different cases amongst men; no remarkable manifestation is seen of the divine holiness; and the most noble and excellent of all objects, that on which the welfare of the creation depends, and which raises beings to the nearest resemblance of the Deity, seems to be left without any adequate support. Is this possible under the *Divine* government? Can it be conceived, that the wisdom and equity of providence should fail only in the instance of virtue? That here, where we should expect the exactest order, there should be the least?—But, acknowledge the reference of this scene to a future more important scene, and all is clear; every difficulty is removed, and every irregularity vanishes. A plain account offers itself of all the strange phænomena in human life. 'Tis of little consequence, how much at any time virtue suffers and vice triumphs *here*, if *hereafter* there is to be a just distinction between them, and every inequality is to be set right. Nay, it may be *sometimes* proper, that a vicious man should be permitted to enjoy the world; and also that a good man should be suffered to struggle with difficulties; which may very well happen, at the same time, that God leaves not himself without abundant witness to the reason of our minds and in the *general* course of events, and the frame of our natures, of his perfectly righteous disposition and character.

A moral plan of government must be carried into execution gradually and slowly through several successive steps and periods. Before retribution there must be probation and discipline. Rewards and punishments require, that, antecedently to them, sufficient opportunities should be given to beings to render themselves proper objects of them, and to form and display their characters; during which time it is necessary that one event should often happen to the good and the bad. Were every single action, as soon as performed, to be followed with its proper reward or punishment; were wickedness, in every instance of it, struck with *immediate* vengeance, and were goodness always at ease and prosperous; the characters of men could not be formed; virtue would be rendered interested and mercenary; some of the most important branches of it could not be practised; adversity, frequently its best friend, could never find access to it; and all those trials would be removed which are requisite to train it up to maturity and perfection. Thus, would the regular process of a moral government be disturbed, and its purposes defeated; and therefore, the very facts which are made objections to it, appear, as mankind are now constituted, to be required by it.—In a word; shall we, from present inequalities, draw conclusions subversive of the most evident principles of reason, though we see the constitution of the world and the natural tendencies of things to be such as will, if they are allowed time and scope for operating, necessarily exclude them? Is it reasonable to give up the wisdom and righteousness of the universal mind, to contradict our clearest notions of things, and to acknowledge errors in the administration of the Deity, notwithstanding innumerable appearances in the frame of the world of his infinite power and perfection, rather than receive a plain, easy, and natural supposition, which is suggested to us in innumerable ways, which mankind in all ages have received, and which is agreeable to all our best sentiments and wishes?

No one would doubt, whether a piece of workmanship or production of art, supposed to be accidentally discovered and entirely new to us, was made for a particular use, provided the plan and structure of it plainly answered to such a use, and the supposition of this use of it explained every thing in it that would otherwise be disproportioned and unaccountable, and made it appear throughout regular and beautiful. What would be more perverse than obstinately to deny that it was intended for such a use; and, in consequence of this, contrary to undeniable marks of the most masterly hand in various parts of it, to maintain it to be the work of some bungling artist, who either had not *knowledge*, or not *power* enough to make it more perfect?

Again, how unreasonable would it be to assert, that a particular passage in a book which seemed strange to us, was *nonsense* or *blasphemy*, when an obvious and natural sense of it offered itself to us, which the turn of the passage itself pointed out to us, and which rendered it of a piece with the wisdom apparent in other parts of the book, and agreeable to what previously we had the best reason to believe concerning the character and abilities of the author?

I have thought it necessary to make these observations, with a particular view to those who are fearful of allowing any thing *irregular in the present distribution of happiness

* I mean what *would be* irregular were this life unrelated to another. 'Tis an

and misery, from an apprehension that the consequence must be our wanting sufficient evidence for a perfect order in

obvious truth, which 'tis strange any should overlook, that what is perfectly right and just, when considered in its relations to *the whole* to which it belongs, may be quite otherwise, when considered by itself, and as a detached part.

It ought to be remembered, that the observations made above prove nothing concerning the *nature* of the future state, except that, in general, it will be a state in which the retribution begun in this life will be rendered adequate. But it is very plain this may happen, and yet all mankind perish at last. Reason, therefore, leaves us much in the dark on this subject. We are sure of no more than that it shall, on the whole, be *better* or *worse* for every person in proportion as he has been morally better or worse in his conduct and character. But what, *in particular*, will be the different lots of the virtuous and vicious hereafter, we cannot tell. The highest human virtue is very defective, and were we to receive no more on the account of it than we could claim from distributive justice, our expectations would be very low. A short period hereafter would settle our account, and completely vindicate the ways of Providence.—Many who are now virtuous may formerly have been great offenders; and it is by no means clear how far repentance must be available to break the connection established between sin and punishment, or what peculiar treatment the cases of *penitents*, as distinguished from *innocents*, may require under the divine government.— Every person, I fancy, who is truly contrite for the miscarriages of his past life is likely to feel the force of these observations. The consciousness which he must have of his own demerit, would scarcely suffer him to use any other prayer than that of the Prodigal in the parable, *I have sinned, O father, against heaven and in thy sight, and am no more worthy to be called* thy son. *Make me as one of thy* hired servants.—Here, I think, the information given us by the CHRISTIAN REVELA-TION comes in for our relief most seasonably and happily. It acquaints us that the return of every man to his duty shall restore him, not merely to some lower place in God's family, but to all those privileges of a *son* which he had forfeited, break the whole connection between sin and punishment, and issue in full favour and everlasting glory through that great MESSIAH *who loved us and gave himself for us.* To this *Messiah* the scriptures tell us the present state has, from the first, stood in a particular relation, and had it not been for this relation our state might perhaps have been so ordered, that adequate retribution should have taken place even here, and all mankind sink in death, without the hope or possibility of a resurrection.—That we are to be delivered at all from death to a new life of any kind may, therefore, be owing to JESUS CHRIST, consistently with the argument for a future state on which I have insisted. But that we are to be delivered from death to a new life that shall *never* end of *complete* happiness, this is unspeakably more than any arguments from distributive justice can teach us to expect; and we may well acquiesce in the scripture doctrine concerning it, and consider our whole future existence as derived under God's goodness, from the benevolent agency of that SAVIOUR, who came into the world that all the nature, and for the wisdom and equity of providence. It would, indeed, be scarcely possible to avoid Atheism were the assertions of some writers on this subject true.—Thus, should it be asked, why, from a view of what lies before us of the constitution and order of the divine government, we may not gather what will take place hereafter under it, as well as we may in many other cases collect what is unknown from what is known, (infer, for instance, the whole meaning of a person from hearing only a part of what he said) it would be replied, that in the last case our inference would be founded on a previous acquaintance with the speaker, with language, and the general manner in which men use it to express their sentiments; that, independent of such acquaintance, supposing we understood the meaning of the particular words we heard, we could not infer any thing from them beyond the ideas they immediately conveyed, or see the least reason to suspect any further intention in the speaker; and that, in like manner, having no previous acquaintance with the divine nature and government, we can know nothing more concerning them than is directly signified to us by the state of things about us; there can be no reason to think any order prevails in the creation greater than we at the present moment observe, or to conclude that the first cause possesses any powers and qualities in a higher degree than they are actually exhibited to us in what falls under our notice of his works. Nay, as antecedently to experience, we could not frame any notion, upon hearing particular articulate sounds, of a *speaker*, or of any ideas signified by them, or indeed know any thing further than that we were conscious of such and such particular impressions; so likewise with respect to this visible universe, it might be said, (and much the same* has

truly virtuous might *not only have life, but have it more abundantly.* John x. 10.— The best account I can give of this subject may be found in my Sermons on the Christian Doctrine.

* See the *Essay on a particular providence and future state*, in Mr. Hume's *Philosophical Essays*.

been said) that being an object *wholly singular* to us, we cannot draw any conclusions from it, or determine any thing concerning the nature, designs, and properties of its *cause*, or even know that it has a *cause*.

This is the upshot of the principles I have in view. But such objections can have no effect on one, who doubts not but that an account very different from that on which these difficulties are founded, is to be given of the operations of our minds; and that the human understanding, however it may be preceded by sensible impressions, and be supplied by them with the first *occasions* of exerting itself, is a faculty infinitely superior to all the powers of sense, and a most important source of our ideas, by means of which we can,* independently of experience, demonstrate innumerable truths concerning many objects, of which otherwise we must have been for ever ignorant.—'Tis the peculiar advantage of the principles I have maintained, that they furnish us with direct and demonstrative proofs of the *truths of natural religion*, and particularly of the *righteousness and goodness of God*; at the same time, that they aid and support all reasonings *a posteriori*.

I shall conclude this chapter, with mentioning one further use which may be made of the principles maintained in this treatise. We may learn from them, in the clearest manner, 'the great importance of virtue, and evil of vice.' Every part of the account I have given of morals has a tendency to teach us this.

I wish I could here obtain the reader's attention, and engage him to recollect carefully the nature of virtue and vice according to the account I have given of them, and to consider the following general and summary account of the *importance* of the one, and the *evil* of the other.

Virtue is of *intrinsick* value and good desert, and of indispensible obligation; not the *creature of will*, but *necessary* and

* See Chap. I. Sect. II.

immutable; not *local* or *temporary*, but of equal *extent* and *antiquity* with the DIVINE MIND; not a *mode of* SENSATION, but *everlasting* TRUTH; not *dependent on power*, but the *guide of all power*. It has been the principal design of this treatise to prove these assertions.—But farther; VIRTUE is the foundation of honour and esteem, and the source of all beauty, order, and happiness in nature. It is what confers value on all the other endowments and qualities of a reasonable being, to which they ought to be absolutely subservient, and without which the more eminent they are, the more hideous deformities and the greater curses they become. The use of it is not confined to any one stage of our existence, or to any particular situation we can be in, but reaches through all the periods and circumstances of our beings.—Many of the endowments and talents we now possess, and of which we are too apt to be proud, will cease entirely with the *present state*; but this will be our ornament and dignity in *every future state* to which we may be removed. *Beauty* and *wit* will die, *learning* will vanish away, and all the *arts of life* be soon forgot; but *virtue* will remain for ever. This unites us to the whole rational creation, and fits us for conversing with any order of superior natures, and for a place in any part of God's works. It procures us the approbation and love of all wise and good beings, and renders them our allies and friends.—But what is of unspeakably greater consequence is, that it makes God our friend, assimilates and unites our minds to his, and engages his almighty power in our defence.—Superior beings of all ranks are bound by it no less than ourselves. It has the same authority in all worlds that it has in this. The further any being is advanced in excellence and perfection, the greater is his attachment to it, and the more is he under its influence.— To say no more; 'tis the LAW of the whole universe; it stands first in the estimation of the Deity; its original is his nature; and it is the very object that makes him lovely.

Such is the importance of VIRTUE.—Of what consequence,

therefore, is it that we practise it?—There is no argument or motive which is at all fitted to influence a reasonable mind, which does not call us to this. One virtuous disposition of soul is preferable to the greatest natural accomplishments and abilities, and of more value than all the treasures of the world.—If you are wise then, study virtue, and contemn every thing that can come in competition with it. Remember, that nothing else deserves one anxious thought or wish. Remember, that this alone is honour, glory, wealth, and happiness. Secure this, and you secure *every thing*. Lose this, and *all* is lost.

But let us next consider *Vice*. To the same degree that *Virtue* is *important and amiable*, this is *evil and detestable*. 'Tis of essential malignity and ill-desert, the only real object of censure and blame, and the source of all evils. Other evils, such as diseases, poverty, losses, and calumny, affect only what is external and foreign to us; but they need not disturb our minds, or do the least injury to what is truly *ourselves*. But vice pierces and wounds, and lays waste *ourselves*. It hurts not the *body*, the *reputation*, or *fortune*, but the *man*; and plants anguish, uproar, and *death* in the soul itself.—Other evils may in the end prove to be benefits to us, but this is eternally and unchangeably evil; the bane of every heart into which it enters; the ruin of all who do not in time rescue themselves from its dominion; and the sting and misery in whatever else afflicts us.—'Tis impossible to conceive what it is to set up *our own wills* against *Reason* and the *Divine will*, to violate the order of the world, and depart from that law which governs all things, and by which the Deity acts. There is no object in nature so monstrous as a reasonable being defiled with guilt, living in contradiction to the remonstrances of his understanding, trampling on the authority of God, and opposing himself to the obligations of truth and righteousness.

But nothing is fitted to give us a deeper sense of the dreadful nature of vice, than to consider what would be its consequences, were it to become prevalent through the creation.—Into how dreadful a state of anarchy would this convert a fair and happy universe? How soon would it blast the whole beauty of God's works, and involve all nature in desolation and ruin?—*Every instance* of moral evil is a *tendency* to this. It is that *begun* which carried farther would issue in it.—We cannot, therefore, indulge an irregular desire or wrong thought, without taking a step towards all that is terrible, and contributing towards defacing the creation, and overturning all law, order, and bliss.

What we thus, from the idea of vice, may see would be the effects of it, if universally prevalent, we find in some measure verified by fact. Into this world we know it has entered—and what havock has it made? How has it spread its malignant effects through all nations and lands? 'Tis not easy for a benevolent mind to bear this prospect, or to take a particular view of that flood of disaster and woe, which vice has let in upon the human race.—From hence proceed unnumbered calamities and evils which are continually infesting us, and mingling disappointment, vexation, and bitterness with our enjoyments and comforts. This is the cruel enemy which renders men destructive to men; which racks the body with pain, and the mind with remorse; which produces strife, faction, revenge, oppression, and sedition; which embroils society, kindles the flames of war, and erects inquisitions; which takes away peace from life, and hope from death; which brought forth death at first, and has ever since cloathed it with all its terrors; which arms nature and the God of nature against us; and against which it has been the business of all ages to find out provisions and securities, by various institutions, laws, and forms of government.

But the effects of vice in the *present* world, however shocking, may be nothing compared with those which may take place *hereafter*, when the evil and the good shall continue no longer blended; when the natural tendencies of things will be no more interrupted in their operation; when the moral constitution of the universe will be perfected, and every one receive according to what he deserves. What the punishment will be which will then overtake vice, it may not be possible for us to imagine. When we seriously consider what it is in its nature and tendency, we can hardly entertain too dreadful apprehensions of the loss we may suffer by it; or, be too anxious about removing all the remains of it from our tempers, and escaping to as great a distance as possible from the danger with which it threatens us.

CONCLUSION.

HAVING completed my design in this work, I will close the whole with offering the following argument for the *practice* of virtue, which, I think deserves to be considered by all, and, particularly, by persons who are disposed to scepticism and infidelity.

In the last chapter I have given an account of some proofs of the principal facts of natural religion, particularly, of a perfect moral government in nature, and a future state of rewards and punishments. A great deal of other evidence there is, which it was out of my way to mention. Above all; the Christian revelation confirms to us whatever we can gather from reason on these subjects, and promises to the virtuous ETERNAL LIFE—A HAPPY IMMORTALITY.

I will, however, suppose the whole of this evidence to be so insufficient as to leave only a chance, overbalanced by contrary chances, for *such* a reward to virtue; and I assert that *still* our obligations will be the same, and that it will be the most foolish conduct not to practise virtue, and even to sacrifice to it all present advantages and gratifications.— For, let it be considered what any given chance for such a good must be worth.

An even chance for any given stake is worth one half of that stake; and a chance for it, unfavourable in any proportion, is worth as much of it as is equivalent to that proportion. That is; if the chance is only a *third* or a *tenth* of all the chances, its value will be a *third* or a *tenth* of the whole stake. If, therefore, the good staked is supposed to be the *future* reward of virtue, and its value is reckoned only equal to the value of all *present* good, it will be right to give up for it a *half*, a *third*, or a *tenth* of all present good, according as the chances *for* obtaining it are a *half*, *third* or *tenth* of all the chances *for* and *against* obtaining it.

If the value of the future reward of virtue is supposed *greater* than the value of all present good, it will be right to give up for it a proportionably greater part of present good; and the future good may be so great as to render *any* chance for it worth more than all that can be enjoyed in this life.— The same is true of the value of any means of avoiding a future evil. Though we suppose it improbable in any given degree, yet what saves us from the still remaining danger of it may be worth, on account of its nature and magnitude, more than any thing that we can resign or endure.

In other words. Any given chance for a given good is worth somewhat. The same chance for a greater good is worth more; and consequently when the good is infinite the value of any chance for it must be likewise infinite. The future good then promised to virtue being infinite, and the loss of it with which vice threatens us being an infinite evil, it follows that *any apprehension* that religion *may* be true, or the *bare possibility* of such consequences to follow virtue and vice as Christianity has taught us to expect, lays us under the same obligation, with respect to practice, as if we were *assured* of its truth.

I must add, that though it should be imagined that (through some strange confusion in the affairs of the world, or an extravagant mercy in God) by *vice* as well as by *virtue* we may stand a chance for happiness hereafter; yet, if we will but allow that the one is in any respect more *likely* to obtain it than the other, it will still be the greatest madness not, at all adventures and the risque of every thing, to adhere to the one, and avoid the other. For it is evident, that the smallest *improvement* of a chance to obtain a good, increases in value as the good increases, and becomes infinite when the good itself is infinite.

CONCLUSION

It is not, I think, possible for any one to avoid conviction in this instance, who will not assert that it is *certain* that Christianity is false, and that there is *no* future state; or that, if there is, virtue gives no better chance for happiness in it than vice. It would be inconsistent in a sceptic to assert this, and it may be presumed that no man in his wits will assert it. Let it however be asserted; it would, even in this case, be no very great matter for a man to be so far diffident of himself, as to use the precaution of living in such a manner that if at last the worst should happen, and his confidence prove vain, he may have nothing to *fear*. But no degree of unbelief, short of what rises so high as this, can acquit a man from the imputation of folly unspeakable, if he is loose and careless in his life, or consents at any time to any wrong action or omission to save any thing he can enjoy, or to obtain any thing that can be offered to him in this world.

Indeed, whoever will fairly examine the evidences of religion, must see that they deserve great regard.—He that will think how reasonable it is to presume, that *infinite goodness* will communicate *infinite happiness*, and that the Creator of all designs his creatures for such a happiness, by continuing those of them who are qualified for it in being for ever to improve under his eye and care, and that virtuous men, if any, have most reason to expect such an effect of his favour: He that will reflect on the various determinations which have been given our minds in favour of virtue; the accountableness of our natures; our unavoidable presaging fears and hopes; the malignant and detestable nature of vice as before represented; the general sentiments of mankind on the subjects of a future state and reckoning; and that *spotless holiness* of the Deity, which the sacred writings in the most striking manner assert and display, and some conviction of which naturally forces itself upon every one; he, I say, who will attend to all this, cannot well avoid entertaining uneasy apprehensions as to what may hereafter happen, and be led to consider, with deep concern, how awful the future displays of divine justice *may* possibly prove, how greatly we may be concerned in the incomprehensible scheme of providence, how much may depend on what we now are, and how very necessary it is that *by all means* we endeavour to secure ourselves.—That some time or other present inequalities will be set right, and a greater difference made between the lots of the virtuous and vicious than is now visible, we have a great deal to lead us to believe. And what kind or degree of difference the counsels and ends of the divine government may require, who can be sure? We see enough in the present state of things, and sufficiently experience what the government of the world admits of, to alarm our fears, and to set us upon considering seriously and anxiously, what greater distinctions between human beings than we now observe are likely in another state to take place, and what greater happiness or misery than we now feel, or can have any ideas of, may await us in that future, *endless* duration, through which it is at least credible that we are to exist.

But with however little regard some may be ready to treat such considerations, it must be past dispute among inquisitive and impartial persons, that all the arguments taken together, which have been used to prove natural and revealed religion, produce *some degree* of *real* evidence; and that, consequently, they lay a sufficient foundation for the preceding reasoning.

To this reasoning it becomes us the more to attend, because it is that which we are continually using in the common course of life; and because it explains to us the principles and grounds upon which we act in almost all our temporal concerns. 'It* ought to be forced upon the reflexion of sceptical persons, that such is our nature and condition, that they necessarily require us in the daily course of life to act upon evidence much lower than what is commonly called probable;

* See *Butler's Analogy, Introduction,* page 4, and chap. vi. part II. page 343, the 4th edition.

and, that there are numberless instances respecting the common pursuits of life, where a man would be thought in a literal sense distracted, who would not act, and with great application too, not only on an even chance, but on much less, and where the probability was greatly against his succeeding.'

What precautions will men often use against the most distant and imaginary dangers?—Why will they neglect using an easy and reasonable precaution against the *worst* and *greatest* of all dangers?—What eager and restless adventurers will they become, what pains will they take, and what risques will they run, where there is any prospect of acquiring money, power, or fame, objects in themselves of little value, and which to despise would be our greatest dignity and happiness? Why then are they so unwilling to take any pains, or to run any risques, in order to obtain blessings of *inestimable worth*, and to secure a chance for *eternal* bliss? How strange is it that they should so little care to put themselves in the way to win *this Prize*, and to become adventurers here, where even to fail would be glorious? When will the following truths, so interesting and indisputable, sink deep enough into our hearts; 'that by such a course as virtue and piety require, we can in general lose *nothing*, but *may* gain *infinitely*; and that, on the contrary, by a careless ill-spent life we can *get nothing*, or at best (happen what will) *next to nothing*, but may *lose infinitely*?'

This brings me to what cannot be omitted in the present argument without doing it great injustice. The reader has observed, that it has gone upon the supposition, that there is a very great probability against religion and a future retribution, and that virtue requires us to sacrifice to it *all our* present enjoyments. The reverse of both these suppositions appears in reality to be the truth. There is not only an *equal chance*, but a *great probability* for the truth of religion. There is nothing to be *got* by vice, but the best part of present good is commonly *lost* by it. 'Tis not the *happiness of life* that virtue requires us to give up; but our *follies, our diseases,* and *miseries.* What, according to this state of the case, must we think of the folly of a vicious choice! How shocking is the infatuation which makes us capable of it!

APPENDIX,

ADDITIONAL NOTES,

AND A

DISSERTATION

ON THE

BEING AND ATTRIBUTES OF THE DEITY.

APPENDIX.

NOTE A.

P. 34. 'In every idea is implied the *possibility* of the existence of its object, nothing being clearer than that there can be no idea of an *impossibility*, or conception of what *cannot* exist.'

Dr. REID, in his very valuable work on the intellectual powers of man, contests this assertion. Essay 4th. Chap. iii. And his principal reasons seem to be, that we can understand a *proposition* which expresses what is impossible; and that we are often, in mathematical demonstrations, directed to *suppose* what is impossible. But *supposing* and *conceiving* are not the same. There is no absurdity which I may not be directed to *suppose*; but it does not follow from hence, that there is no absurdity which I may not *conceive*. A believer in transubstantiation may *suppose* that Christ held his body in his hand and gave it to his disciples; but if he was to say that he had a clear and distinct conception of it, he would make himself as ridiculous as if he was to say he *saw* it.

A man may also understand what is meant by a proposition which expresses an impossibility, as when it is said that the whole is less than a part. But, certainly, he can have no real conception of this. He may also *think* that he has a clear *idea* of an object when he has it not, just as he may *think*, that he has a clear *perception* of an object when he does not perceive it. But as, in the latter case, he must believe the existence of what he thinks he *perceives*; so, in the former case, he must believe the possibility of what he thinks he *conceives*. It should be particularly considered here, that it is the *conception of objects* I have in view, and not the *understanding of propositions*; and that impossibilities, not being realities, conceptions of them would be conceptions of nothing.

NOTE B.

P. 34. 'Matter is infinitely divisible.'

This is a property of matter which convinces me that I do not know what it is, and that the common ideas of it are extremely inadequate. The maxim of the schools, *omne ens est unum*, seems to me indisputable. What can that be which is neither *one* thing, nor any *number* of things?

Is it absurd to say, that one thing has moved another, and that another *in infinitum,* without any *first* mover? And is it not equally absurd to say, that a particle of matter may be divided into other particles, and these into others *in infinitum* without ever coming to a particle that is properly *one?*

It is no solution of this difficulty to say that there are atoms which, having no pores, cannot be divided except by the power of the Creator. For such an atom, consisting of parts, and there being a possibility that one part should exist in one place, and another in another, it is, in reality, as much a multitude of atoms, as if they were actually separated. Whatever is really *one* cannot be divided without being annihilated. This is true of that being which every one calls *himself.* Half *himself* no one can conceive of.

Such are the difficulties which press my mind with respect to the nature of matter. They have, however, no effect on my belief of the existence of a material world. In this case, as in numberless other cases, I feel my own ignorance, without being led to reject convictions which I am forced to receive though not able to explain. I know my will moves my limbs. There is not any thing more familiar to me; nor, at the same time, is there any thing which I understand less.

NOTE C.

P. 39. 'It should be observed, that I have all along endeavoured to avoid speaking of an *idea* as an *image* in the mind of the object we think of. A writer of deep reflexion has charged this language with laying the foundation of all modern scepticism. *See* Dr. REID's *Enquiry into the human mind on the principles of common Sense.*'

I am always mortified when I find, that my sentiments are different from those of the writer to whom I have now referred. Mr. HUME makes the immediate object of the mind in perception to be the same with perception itself, and thus annihilates all *external existence.* Dr. REID, if I understand him, asserts (in his Enquiry, &c. and also in his *Essays on the intellectual powers of man*) that there is no such object, and thus seems to me to annihilate all *perception.* When we investigate the properties of triangles or circles, are there not objects, independent of our minds, then *present* to them? We call these objects, *ideas.* This word generally signifying the apprehension or conception of an object, it is improperly used to signify the object itself of conception; but the poverty of language obliging us to this, it must be excused; and care must be taken not to be misled by it, as I think Mr. HUME and some other writers have been.

In such instances we call, I have said, the objects present to our minds, *ideas.* If ideas have no existence, and *nothing* is present to our minds when we contemplate these objects, does it not follow that we then contemplate *nothing*? The same enquiry may be made with respect to our perception of *external* objects. These objects themselves not being present, if perceived, they must be perceived by *ideas* of them. Nor will it follow from hence, that we can have no assurance of the existence of external objects. All ideas imply the *possibility* of the existence of correspondent objects; and our belief of the *actual* existence of the objects of sense, we may resolve (as Dr. REID does) into impressions on our senses *forcing* belief at the moment of the impression, in a manner we cannot explain. And this may be done to more advantage on the supposition of ideas than without it. For scepticism seems to be less favoured by supposing that, in perception by our senses, there is *something* distinct from the mind and independent of it really perceived, than by supposing that there is nothing then perceived. It is unavoidable to enquire what this is. The Dissertation that follows these notes will shew how I am inclined to think on this subject. The truth is (if I mistake not) that the just answer to this enquiry would carry us higher than we are willing to go, and imply a presence of the Deity with us and dependence upon him more close and constant and necessary, than we are apt to suspect or can easily believe.

NOTE D.

The point which I have endeavoured to prove in the 3d section of the 1st chapter, appears to me, on reviewing it, to be so evident, that I am afraid I shall be thought by many persons to have *trifled* in this section, and *wasted* my time and attention. It is, indeed, in my opinion, a reproach to human reason that there should be any occasion for saying any thing to shew, that we express truth, and not merely an impression of pleasure or pain, when we say of certain actions that they are *right*, and of others that they are *wrong*.

After the publication of the former editions of this Treatise, Dr. SMITH (the author of the valuable work on the *wealth of nations*, and a writer above any praise from me) published his treatise, entitled, *The Theory of moral Sentiments*; the chief intention of which is to prove, that our perceptions of moral distinctions are derived from the same principle in our natures with that of *sympathy*; or that moral approbation and disapprobation are a species of fellow-feeling with moral agents, by which we are made to enter into their views and emotions and to participate in their pleasures and pains. But that our primary notions of moral good and evil are derived from sensation and not from reason, or that they are *feelings* of some kind or other, and not perceptions of the intellectual

APPENDIX

faculty, he represents as in his opinion so abundantly proved by Dr. HUTCHESON, as to make it a matter of wonder, that any controversy should be kept up about it. See *The Theory of moral Sentiments*, Part VI. Sect. 3. p. 399.

This opinion, thus delivered by so able a writer, would influence me more than it does, were it not for the contrary opinion of another writer no less able, and whose concurrence with me in all that is most important on this subject, gives me particular satisfaction. *See* Dr. REID's Essays on the intellectual powers of man, p. 728. At the conclusion of these Essays, Dr. REID intimates an intention to make the active and moral powers of man the subject of a future publication; and all enquirers after truth must wish, that nothing may prevent him from executing his purpose.

NOTE E.

P. 103, &c. I am forced to acknowledge that the observations here made on the grounds of our belief of the existence of material objects, do not entirely satisfy me: I have, however, chosen to leave them as they were in the former editions of this Treatise, imagining that possibly they may give some aid to future enquirers. Those who would be entertained as well as instructed by a particular discussion of this subject, and a full account of all the different theories and opinions concerning it, should read the two first of Dr. REID's Essays on the intellectual powers of man. —Dr *Reid*'s own opinion seems to be, that the perception of external objects by our senses, is 'a *conception* of them, and a belief of their present existence made by our constitution to accompany the impressions on our organs of sense; and of which no farther explanation can be given.' It seems to me, that, in perception by our senses, there is more than is here expressed. A conception of objects is often produced by impressions on the senses, and accompanied with a belief of their present existence, without any thing like an actual perception of them. But, whatever difficulties may attend this subject, it is certain, that the evidence of *sense*, (like that of *memory*) will always maintain its authority; and it may be best, in these instances, to content ourselves with feeling this, and to take our natures as they are, lest by refining too much, and attempting to explain what is so clear as to be inexplicable, we should only darken and perplex.

NOTE F.

On Mr. PALEY's Lectures on the principles of moral and political Philosophy.

P. 235, &c. According to this writer, our notions of moral distinctions are derived, neither from a *moral sense*, nor from *instinct* of any kind, nor from intellectual discernment and the natures of things. On the contrary; he makes them, if I understand him, to be a kind of habits of thinking (or prejudices) which we derive from education and the circumstances in which we grow up to mature life. To be *obliged* to an action, he says, is 'to be urged to it by a violent motive resulting from the command of another.' P. 49. At the same time he asserts, that this motive can be only self-love; and that we can be obliged to nothing that will not in some way contribute to our interest; (P. 51, 52.) so that (were there no future state) an action by which we could *get* nothing would be perfectly indifferent to us; and, if it puts us to the smallest degree of pain, we should be under an obligation to avoid it, tho' we could save by it a kingdom, or make a world happy. What makes the difference, he says, between *prudence* and *duty* is, that in the one case we consider what we shall get or lose in *this* world, and in the other what we shall get or lose in a *future* world. A man, therefore, who either does not believe in a future world, or who does not carry his views to it, can have no perception of duty? Mr. PALEY's definition of RIGHT is, 'the being consistent with the will of God.' P. 72. RECTITUDE, therefore, can be no guide to God's will itself; and to say that his will is a *righteous* will, is the same with saying that his will is his will, all that he wills to do being for that very reason right and fit. In short, Mr. PALEY's theory of morals seems to be resolvable into these two propositions; 'that God's command is the measure and standard of all duty,' and, 'that the duty itself of obeying his command is the necessity of obeying it in order to avoid punishment.'

Never indeed have I met with a theory of morals which has appeared to me more exceptionable; and when I think of it, I cannot wonder much at an assertion of Mr. *Paley*'s, which would, were it true, overthrow all public securities depending on tests and subscriptions. I mean the assertion, that the declaration made by a clergyman on entering his office, that he unfeignedly assents to articles of faith framed on purpose to prevent a diversity of opinions, (and containing the doctrines of the Trinity, predestination, original sin, justification by faith alone, &c.) means no more than that he is neither a *papist*, a *baptist*, nor an *antiepiscopalian*.

I will take this opportunity to add, that of the same kind with this account of morals is the account which Mr. *Paley* gives of the principles of politics. 'Civil liberty (he says, p. 441.) is the not being restrained by any laws except such as do more good than harm, or have a beneficial tendency;' and should it be enquired, where is the power lodged of making laws and of judging of their tendency? he would answer, not in the people, for the right of legislation, according to him, is not founded on the consent of the people, nor do civil rulers derive their authority from any compact between them and their people. He denies the existence of any such compact, whether *tacit* or *express*; and, in opposition to Mr. Locke's sentiments on this subject, maintains that civil authority derives it from the *Patriarchal* authority, and is the donation of the Deity collected (undoubtedly by civil governors themselves) from public expediency. Page 423.

There is likewise in these lectures a defence of standing armies, and of the inadequateness of our parliamentary representation. But what is most of all remarkable is, that, whereas Sir WILLIAM BLACKSTONE, Mr. LOCKE, MONTESQUIEU, &c. have made the essence of the British monarchical constitution to consist in the independency of the three states which compose it of one another: Mr. PALEY, on the contrary, asserts that since the retrenchment of prerogative at the revolution, the influence of the crown is become a necessary part of the constitution; and he concludes a chapter on this subject with saying, 'that an independent parliament is incompatible with our monarchy.'

I am very sensible of the merit of many parts of this work. But *these* parts of it I have read with surprize, and also with a concern, the pain of which has been much increased by the reflexion, that they contain principles which have been inculcated for many years at CAMBRIDGE, and which therefore probably have been imbibed by many young persons when under preparation for public life.

DISSERTATION

BEING AND ATTRIBUTES OF THE DEITY.

IT is happy for us, that our conviction of all that is most interesting to us is made to be the effect of immediate and irresistible perception, and not left to depend on abstruse reasonings and deductions. This is true, particularly, of our conviction of the existence of a MAKER of the world. The doubts on this subject to which some have pretended, are derived from a sophistry which is incapable of being seriously regarded, without contradicting those principles of common sense, which are our first and surest and best guides, and which *will*, and always *must*, maintain their authority in opposition to all sceptical refinements and subtleties. It is impossible to survey the world without being assured, that the contrivance in it has proceeded from some contriver, the design in it from some *designing* cause, and the art it displays from some artist. To say the contrary, or to assert, that it was produced by the accidental falling together of its component parts, must appear to every man whose understanding is not perverted, a folly as gross as it would be to assert the same of any other work of art that could be presented to him; of a commodious house, of a fine picture, or an exquisite machine.

In short; this visible universe, of which we are a part, is, *self-evidently*, an exhibition of the power and wisdom of a powerful and wise cause. It is also an exhibition of a *degree* of power and wisdom which shews the cause to be powerful and wise beyond all we can conceive. This is the same to us with an *infinity* of these qualities in the Maker of the universe; and it obliges us to conclude, that the same wisdom exists where we *cannot* see it as where we *can*, and to reckon with confidence that all appearances of irregularity are *appearances* only, rendered unavoidable by our ignorance and partial views; and which, were not this true, would imply a difficulty greater than any that now puzzles us, and not possible to be accounted for without supposing, that the world was framed by a wisdom and foresight not superior to our own.

I will add, that the apprehensions most natural to us, lead us to believe farther, that the first cause is ONE being; or at least, that the district of nature which falls under our notice, is directed and governed by ONE COUNSEL; distracted counsels being always the effect of *imperfect* wisdom, and incompatible with that consummate and incomprehensible wisdom which the order of nature displays.

These conclusions are sufficient for all practical purposes. It is not, therefore, necessary to have recourse to such reasonings as those I am going to propose. The belief of one supreme superintending cause and governor of all things, infinitely powerful wise and good, may be safely trusted to such arguments *a posteriori*, as those to which I have now referred; and which have been often and excellently stated by many of the best writers. It cannot, however, be improper to shew how they are aided and confirmed by a reasoning of another kind which appears to me very important.

The argument I have in view is the same with Dr. CLARKE's; but it will be a little differently represented, and pursued farther. Intimations of it have been given in several parts of the preceding work. I will here state it more *distinctly*, but at the same time with as much brevity as possible, hoping that such of my readers as may chuse to follow me with their attention, will supply, from their own thoughts, what the particular imperfection of language in this instance may render me incapable of stating with sufficient correctness and clearness.

The whole is an appeal to calm and patient reflexion, offered under a sense of the high and abstruse and incomprehensible nature of the subject of it.

PROPOSITIONS *and* OBSERVATIONS *for explaining the* NECESSARY EXISTENCE *of the first Cause, and for demonstrating by it his* PERFECTIONS.

THE existence of all beings is either *contingent* or *necessary*.

All beings exist *contingently* whose non-existence is *possible*; and the non-existence of all beings is *possible*, whose non-existence implies no contradiction.

Our own existence and the existence of the whole visible world is *contingent*.

All that exists contingently; and which, therefore, might or might not have existed, requires a reason or cause of its existence.

There must, therefore, be a cause of our own existence and of the existence of the world.

The cause of all that exists *contingently* must exist *necessarily*.

Thus far all the writers on the being and attributes of the Deity have agreed; but they have not, in my opinion, properly explained that *necessity* of existence which belongs to the first cause. It is the attribute which forms the grand and fundamental distinction between him and all other beings; and which, when rightly understood, will be seen to imply all his other attributes.—I will, therefore, in the following observations, give as clear an account as I can of my ideas of it.

First. The *necessity* of God's existence is different from that *relative* and *consequential* necessity which is expressed when we say, 'that there must be a cause of every effect,' and which, therefore, is only an *inference* from the existence of effects.—In other words, the impossibility of not existing implied in the *necessity* of God's existence is not an impossibility grounded upon or deduced from any facts or arguments, but an impossibility appearing *immediately*, and carrying its own evidence with it; an impossibility in the *nature of the thing itself*.—It is common to say, that it is *impossible* for God not to exist, and that he *cannot but* exist. But till this observation is attended to, it is saying nothing of particular importance on this subject. It is language that may be used without having the least notion of the true nature of the necessity of the Divine existence. From hence it follows, therefore,

Secondly, That the necessity of God's existence implies that his non-existence cannot be *conceived* without a contradiction. For were not this true, his non-existence would be *possible*, every thing being so that is really conceivable, and which does not imply a contradiction.

Thirdly, The *necessity* of God's existence implies that it is necessary, not merely as an efficient cause of other existence, but to the very *conception* of all other existence.—Were there any beings to the *conception* of whose existence this being is not necessary, such beings might be conceived to exist *alone*; that is, they might be conceived to exist *without* him, which is the same with conceiving him not to exist, and consequently, with the *possibility* of his non-existence. The conception of the *separate* and *independent existence* of any beings, is the same with the *conception* of the non-existence of all *other* beings. Could we conceive this visible world to exist by itself; were there no conception of the necessary being required to the conception of its existence; it would follow that there is no such being. This itself would be conceiving his non-existence. We can, for instance, very well conceive of *space* and *time* without presupposing, in that conception, the existence of a *material world*; and this is conceiving it not to exist; and therefore, proves it to be contingent. And could we, in the same manner, conceive of the *material world* without *space* and *time*, these themselves likewise would appear to be contingent.*

* 'What exists necessarily not only must so exist alone as to be *independent* of any thing else; but (being *self-sufficient*) may also so exist *alone* as that every thing else may *possibly* (or without any contradiction in the natures of things) be supposed not to exist at all; and consequently (since that which may possibly be supposed not to exist at all is not necessarily existent) no other thing can be necessarily existent. Whatever is necessarily existing there is need of its existence in order to the *supposal* of the existence of any other thing; so that nothing can possibly be supposed to exist without presupposing and including antecedently the existence of that which is necessary, &c. &c. These sort of things are very difficult to *express*, and not easy to be *conceived* but by very attentive minds. But to such as can and will attend, nothing (I think) is more demonstrably convictive.' See the Answer to the first letter from a Gentleman in

APPENDIX

There can, therefore, be no difficulty in finding out the Deity. If we are at a loss here the reason must be some great mistake and prejudice. We have him continually in our thoughts. We see him every where and in every thing. He is the *power* by which we act, the *intelligence* by which we understand, and the *time* and *place* in which we live and move and have our beings. In order to obtain an actual sense of his existence, we have nothing to do but to consider what there is that answers to the account now given of the *necessity* of his existence. Do we not find it particularly in *abstract duration* and *space*? These are necessary to the conception of all existence. They cannot in thought be destroyed. Annihilation being a removal from them, their own annihilation is a contradiction. See p. 24.—The like is true of *abstract truth* and *possibles*. To annihilate *truth* is the same with making truth to be a falshood; and, therefore, a contradiction in terms. To annihilate *possibility* is to make it the same with *impossibility*; and, therefore, also a contradiction.—But there remains to be mentioned other characters of necessary existence no less important and evident.

Fourthly, Necessity of existence admits of no *limitation* or *imperfection*. It can have no more relation to any one time or place or degree of any quality than to another. All degrees of all perfections being *in themselves* equally conceivable and possible, a reason is to be always given why a being who possesses a perfection in *one* degree does not possess more or less of it. We can, for instance, conceive any given portion of matter to be larger or smaller, and to exist in an infinity of places different from that in which it does exist. Its size and place are, therefore, contingent; and must have been determined by some cause.

This observation is applicable to all beings that are limited in respect of time, place, or degree of any quality; and therefore, no such beings can exist *necessarily*.

Fifthly, A necessary being can possess no perfection in the manner of inferior beings; that is, by a *participation* of it as something distinct from itself and independent of it. In this way he can no more possess a quality in its *highest* than in its *lowest* degree;

Gloucestershire, inserted at the end of Dr. Clarke's *Evidences of natural and revealed Religion.*

or *infinitely*, rather than *finitely*. For an account or cause would, on this supposition, be as much wanted of his possessing it *infinitely* rather than *finitely*, as of his possessing it in any *one* degree of finiteness rather than another.—For instance. A being existing necessarily cannot be *omnipresent* by existing *in* space as all contingent beings do; because, on this supposition, we might conceive of immensity *without* him, and there would be the same reason for requiring a cause of his existing in *all* rather than in any *part* of it, that there would be, were he limited in this respect, to require a cause of that limitation. In short; a being whose existence does not constitute infinite space can no more exist *every where* without a cause, than he can *any where*. And the like is true of his eternity, and of every attribute and perfection that we can apply to him. A being, who is intelligent by the *perception* of truth as somewhat independent of him, can no more be *perfectly* intelligent without a cause, than he can be so *imperfectly*. It must be just as proper to ask a reason or cause of his knowing *all* truth rather than a *part* of truth, as of his knowing any one part of truth rather than another. —The like is true of *power*; and the result is, that the being who exists *necessarily* must possess these attributes in a manner peculiar to himself. He is intelligent, not by the *apprehension* of truth, but by *being* truth; and *wise*, not by knowing all that is knowable, but by being that intellectual light which enlightens all other beings, and which makes them wise and knowing. He is therefore, WISDOM, rather than *wise*; and REASON, rather than *reasonable*. In like manner; he is ETERNITY, rather than *eternal*; IMMENSITY, rather than *immense*, and POWER, rather than *powerful*. In a word; he is not *benevolent* only, but *benevolence*; not absolutely *perfect* only, but absolute *perfection* itself; the root, the original (or to speak after Dr. *Clarke*, and perhaps still less improperly) the *substratum** of all that is great and wise and good and excellent.

The Deity, Sir *Isaac Newton* says, 'by existing *always and every where* CONSTITUTES infinite space and duration.'† This, in my

---

* Dr. Clarke has applied this language only to the *eternity* and *immensity* of the Deity; but none of the modes of expression here used are strictly just, nor perhaps is it possible to find any that are so.

† *Deus durat semper et adest ubique, et existendo semper et ubique durationem et spatium, aeternitatem et infinitatem* CONSTITUIT. Cum unaquaeque spatii particula sit *semper*, et unumquodque durationis indivisibile momentum *ubique*, certe

opinion, expresses a most important sentiment. The argument grounded upon it and derived from it which I have endeavoured to represent, is, I doubt not, the argument which Sir ISAAC NEWTON had in view when, at the end of his first letter to Dr. BENTLEY, he intimated that there was an argument for the belief of a Deity, different from that taken from the appearance of design in the constitution of the world, which he thought a very strong one; but which it would be most adviseable to suffer to sleep, till the principles on which it was grounded were better received.*

The following inferences are suggested by this reasoning.

First, It shews an incorrectness in Dr. CLARKE's language when he speaks of *necessity* as the *reason* and *ground* of God's existence. The meaning of this language is obvious; but it has been mistaken, and given occasion to the rejection of an argument† which leads to a juster manner of conceiving of the Deity than can be possible without it.

---

rerum omnium fabricator et dominus non erit *nunquam nusquam*. Omnipresens est non per *virtutem* solam, sed etiam per *substantiam*, nam virtus sine substantia subsistere non potest. In ipso continentur et moventur universa, &c. Deum summum necessario existere in confesso est: et eadem necessitate *semper* est et *ubique*. General *Scholium* at the end of Sir *Isaac Newton's Principia*. [Substantially the same passage from Newton is quoted as a footnote in Clarke's final reply to Butler.]

* See the 4th volume of Sir Isaac Newton's works, P. 433. 'There is yet another argument for a Deity, which I take to be a very strong one; but till the principles on which it is grounded are better received, I think it more adviseable to let it sleep.' The letter which concludes with these words, is dated in 1692. The principles referred to in them were afterwards *intimated* by Sir Isaac Newton in the general *Scholium* at the end of his *Principia*, and *explained* at large by his friend Dr. Clarke in his book on the evidences of natural and revealed religion; and particularly, in the letters to a gentleman in *Gloucestershire*, (well known to have been Dr. BUTLER then a student in a dissenting college at *Tewksbury*,) and two other letters inserted at the end of the last editions of Dr. Clarke's *Evidences*, &c. The first letter to Dr. BUTLER is dated in Nov. 1713; and the last, in April 1714.—The first edition of *Newton's Principia* was published in 1686; and the second edition, with the addition of the *Scholium* just mentioned, in 1713.

I have given these dates to shew with which of the names now mentioned (three of the greatest this world has ever known) the mode of reasoning adopted in these pages has originated.

† See a tract lately published (and entitled, *A demonstration of the being and*

APPENDIX

Dr. CLARKE has sometimes even called *necessity* the *cause* of God's existence. This in so able a writer is a wonderful inaccuracy. It might however have been excused, for it is evident, that he meant no more than that (as some account is to be given of the existence of all that exists) the *account* of the existence of the first cause must be, that it is *necessary*, or that *necessity* is an attribute of his existence. In reality; such is its nature that it *admits* of no reason, and *wants* no reason to be given for it. Does any one want to be informed, why a thing cannot remain after it is taken away, or be and not be at the same time; why the whole is greater than a part; two different from twenty, &c?—The NECESSITY (or SELF-EXISTENCE) of the Deity is an attribute of the same kind with the SELF-EVIDENCE of those primary truths on which all science depends, and which, did they not prove themselves (or require a reason to be given for them) it would follow, that there are reasons of reasons *in infinitum*, and consequently that there can be no such thing as truth or reason at all. In like manner; were there no existence which required no reason to be given for it; that is, were there no being whose non-existence can no more be conceived than contradictions can be conceived to be true; it would follow, that nothing could ever have existed.

Secondly, This argument furnishes a proper answer to the enquiry, why the first cause does not himself need a cause as well as all inferior causes. Nature, as atheistical writers have said, 'has in itself a principle of order and regularity, and here we should rest. If we enquire farther, and suppose a cause of the order of nature, there will be equal reason for requiring a cause of that cause, and intelligence in the Divine mind will want as much to be accounted for as that which we see displayed in the creation.'—This is an objection which, tho' it may puzzle, cannot possibly have any effect on the belief produced by common sense in the existence of an efficient cause of this world. It is (as I have observed in the introduction to these observations) as incapable of influencing conviction in this case as it would be were it applied,

attributes of God) by Dr. HAMILTON. I have read this tract with pleasure and improvement; but, at the same time, not without being discouraged by finding that a writer of such discernment should reject an argument which appears to me so important as Dr. CLARKE's.

with the like view, to any other obvious effect of contrivance and skill. It suggests, however, an enquiry which occurs naturally to every one who attends to this subject; and the preceding reasoning gives a full answer to it. Certain it is, that there is a manner of existence *peculiar* to the first cause; and we have seen what that is.—Of the world and all that exists in it; and, in general, of all limited beings, we know by intuitive perception that their existence is *contingent*; and that, consequently, there must be a *cause* which has determined their existence: But of this cause himself we know that, existing *necessarily* in the sense I have explained, he can want no cause, and that the very idea of *causality* when applied to him is a contradiction.

Thirdly, We are led by this argument to reflect on the nature of God's presence with us, and the absurdity of some of the doubts which have been entertained with respect to his existence and attributes. It appears, that he is always present with all beings, not merely by his *notice* and *influence*,* but by his *essence*; and that the belief of his existence is unavoidable, and implied in the very act of endeavouring to suppose its annihilation. So *real* is it as to be the ground of all reality, and of the *conception* of all reality. There is nothing so intimately united to us; nothing of which we have so constant and irresistible a consciousness. We meet him in every truth we contemplate, in every idea that passes through our minds, and every instant that measures our existence: And for this very reason we overlook him. We cannot believe that he is so near us as he is; and because *every thing*, he becomes *nothing* to us. Wonderful, indeed, are the conceptions of some learned men on this subject. Rather than recognize his nature in what they know to be necessarily existent, eternal, and infinite; they run into contradictions, and will not allow existence to any thing except what exists after the manner of *contingent* beings and *second* causes. They speak of his *immensity*, but immensity (that is, infinite space) is *nothing*; and, therefore, his existing *every where* must be the same with his existing *no-where*.—In like manner; they speak of his existing through all *duration*, and of his knowledge as extending to all *knowables*, and his power to all *possibles*; but *duration*,

* Non per *virtutem* solam sed per *substantiam*. See the quotation from *Newton*, in p. 291.

knowables, and *possibles* (however presupposed in every notion of intelligence, efficacy, and existence) are nothing; and the belief of the contrary is, according to them, derived from analogies and prejudices which have misled us.

Fourthly, The necessity of God's existence, as it has been now explained, affords us an intuitive perception of the INFINITY of all his attributes.—To suppose that any perfections, as they exist in him, are limited (or that he possesses only a given share of them leaving an infinity behind belonging to no being, and having no nature for its *substratum*) is a monstrous absurdity. It is reducing him to the rank of contingent beings; and the same with supposing these perfections not to be *themselves*.

Fifthly, The preceding reasoning evidently implies the UNITY of the Deity. It is contingent existence alone that admits of diversity and multiplicity. Simplicity and unity are included in the idea of necessity. Every necessary truth (the equality, for instance, of an angle in a semicircle to a right angle) is one, a division of it into *two* truths being self-contradictory, because either the same with dividing it into itself and *another* truth, and, consequently, *no* division of it; or the same with dividing it into two *other* truths, and consequently its *annihilation*, that is, its *falshood*.* The like is to be observed of that infinity of abstract truth and intelligibles, the necessary existence of which forces itself into our thoughts, and is the foundation of every idea of reason and intelligence.—Particular truths are only partial views of the self-existent and parent mind, as the divisions we make of *time* and *place* are only partial conceptions of that eternity and immensity which we know to be incapable of division; and which, however apparently *different*, are yet so perfectly *one*, that neither of them can be conceived without the other, every point of *immensity* being necessarily *eternal*, and every moment of eternity being necessarily *immense*.†

In short; there are numberless beings who *occupy* duration and

---

* In the same manner precisely the division of *ones-self* into *two selfs* is contradictory, because either the same with a division of ones-self into ones-self and *another*, which is *no* division; or the same with a division of ones-self into two *others*, which is *annihilation*.

† *Unaquaeque spatii particula est* SEMPER, *et unumquodque durationis indivisibile momentum* UBIQUE. NEWTON's general scholium.

space; but there can be only *one* being whose existence *constitutes* duration and space.—There are numberless beings who participate of perfection in an infinite variety of degrees; but there can be but one being who is absolute perfection *itself*. There are numberless beings who are powerful, wise and benevolent; but there can be but *one* being of whose nature, power, wisdom and benevolence in necessary union and forming one idea, are the essential attributes.

Sixthly, From the preceding reasoning may, I think, be inferred the particular importance of the question discussed in this treatise. My principal design has been to shew that right and wrong are distinctions in the natures of things; and that moral obligations constitute a part of eternal truth and reason. If then the natures of things and eternal truth and reason are the same with the nature of the Deity, it follows that he must be a being of complete moral excellence. The following observation may help to illustrate this.

An argument for the goodness of God has been taken from that part of the constitution of the world which makes pain, when it exceeds certain limits, to terminate either in *its own* destruction or in the destruction of the *sufferer*. This, if derived from arbitrary appointment, is a merciful appointment, shewing pain not to be the end of the maker of the world. But, if derived necessarily from the nature of pain as such, it is a circumstance in the natures of things which indicates more decidedly the will of the first cause. The truth is; that pain and disorder imply weakness and self-destructiveness; and that, on the contrary, happiness and order, implying strength and stability, tend necessarily to preserve, augment, and perpetuate themselves.

This shews us what the final issue of events must be. But that *preference* of happiness; that *repugnance* to pain; that discernment of moral obligation, and *approbation* of beneficence, which (if I have argued rightly) are unavoidable to all beings who perceive *truth*, shews this more plainly, by proving beyond a doubt, the holy disposition and benevolence of that nature which is the sacred root of all that is true, and right, and good.

Lastly, This argument is, in the highest degree, encouraging to our hopes. It shews, that it is even a contradiction to suppose a single circumstance in the administration of the universe, which ought to have been otherwise than it is; or any events to happen of which it may be truly said, that nature would have been *better* constituted and the course of events *better* directed, had they been excluded. This, according to the preceding reasoning, is the same with supposing truth to be falshood, and possibility *im*possibility; or, in other words, the same with supposing the *annihilation* of *necessary* truth and reason—of that eternal and almighty and omnipresent intelligence and goodness, which are by their natures indestructible, and must be all controuling.—We have, then, the fullest assurance, that all is well under God's government, and that every thing may be expected to take place in the creation which can be a just object of desire. This throws a reviving light over the creation, and should teach us to welcome all that happens, trusting implicitly in that wisdom which, because perfect, we cannot fathom; ascribing confidently whatever looks dark to our own blindness; and studying diligently to exhibit in our own conduct that benevolence and rectitude which govern all things, under a conviction that, if we do this, we cannot fail of being infinitely happy.

F I N I S.

INDEX

Index

Index

Index

Index